LIVING LEFT-HANDED

LIVING LEFT-HANDED

DIANE PAUL

BLOOMSBURY

First published 1990
by Bloomsbury Publishing Plc, 38 Soho Square, London W1V 5DF

This paperback edition published 1997

Copyright © 1990 by Diane Paul

The moral right of the author has been exerted

British Library Cataloguing in Publication Data
A CIP record for this book is available from the British Library

ISBN 0 7475 3253 2

Printed by Cox & Wyman Ltd, Reading, Berks.

ACKNOWLEDGEMENTS

Fitting a study of the nature of handedness into an already overflowing work schedule has been no mean task. The more I researched, the deeper I seemed to sink into a legacy of conflict and contradiction, left behind by bustling researchers.

For guiding me out of the labyrinth and boosting my own humble layman's research and theories with the support of intelligible offerings, I am indebted to all the people who wrote to me giving first-hand case histories, who are unfortunately too numerous to mention individually, to those who have deliberately requested anonymity in the interests of their children and to teachers and schools who have helped by answering questionnaires.

My thanks also to everyone who responded so magnificently to my request for background information or interviews, also too numerous to mention here.

Special thanks must go to Dr Jean Alston for reading my chapter on handwriting and making some helpful suggestions and for the latest research in orthoptics; Ruth Barrie for details of her selective report on dentistry; Dr Dorothy Bishop and Dr Marian Annett for providing me with details of their most recent research; Albert M. Galaburda, MD for the details of his research in the USA; Dr Maung, Colne Health Centre for his survey; the *Ministère des affaires sociales et de l'emploi*, Paris, for the French report on left-handers in industry; Doreen Plenty for details of her birth theories; Olive Shapley, for allowing me to print her delightful childhood memory; Kate Sladden, for allowing me to quote from her excellent dissertation and Charles Wood for his theses on architecture and fast-ball sports.

Above all, I owe a debt of gratitude to my former teachers at

Whitefield Stand Grammar School for Girls (1951–1956) and my
family, whose attitude to my right-brained left-handed peculiarities
resulted in my writing this book.

CONTENTS

LIVING LEFT-HANDED

PREFACE

Anaxagorus indeed asserts that it is his possession of hands that makes man the most intelligent of the animals; but surely the reasonable point of view is that it is because he is the most intelligent animal that he has got hands. Aristotle, *De partibus animalium* IV X.

My research into the phenomenon of why some people are left-handed and the effects of left-handedness in a right-handed world has been something of a personal adventure. The idea came as one of those twilight flashes of inspiration that arrive, quite unexpectedly, when in a half-awake, half-asleep state. I have no idea what provoked it as I had never been consciously aware of my left-handedness, other than when people had noticed me writing.

It was my research which sparked off a host of long-forgotten memories – of discrimination at school and at home, the significance of which had passed unnoticed at the time – and which served, therapeutically, to dispense with several time-worn complexes, the origins of which had never faced their roots until I began to dig them up.

The project produced an extra bonus for, while carrying out the necessary research, the feedback from left-handers complaining about the way they had been treated at school, at home and in the workplace included several pleas for left-handed utensils. Letters came in from all over the country from left-handers or parents of left-handed children who were crying out for left-handed scissors, can openers and other items. Having found where to obtain them, I launched a mail-order service called Lefties in October 1988, which is now a flourishing business. 'I was amazed and delighted to hear that someone has at last recognised our plight. No more struggling

1

with awkward tin openers or potato peelers! Thank you, on behalf of left-handed people everywhere … remember – all the best people are left-handed!' wrote one grateful customer. 'My uncle used to say: "Left-handed folk are no good, or they would have made tools to suit them". If only he could come back and see how well we are now provided for,' wrote another.

At the same time, I embarked on the gargantuan task of unearthing and interpreting the masses of often conflicting research material relating to laterality and hemispherical dominance, and translating it into plain English. It was a challenge no stubborn left-hander could resist.

Many contributors opened up their hearts to a fellow left-hander who could empathise with their experiences. Some of the stories were horrifying, others made me aware, suddenly, that my own failure to achieve in certain areas – notably on the domestic front – has not been due to stupidity or incompetence, as I was led to believe by teachers and family, but is a direct result of being left-handed.

To discover, in one's forties, that the reason one has never been able to cut paper or material is because the cutting blade is on the wrong side of the scissors comes as something of a revelation. And all those years, I had been labelled 'clumsy', never realising that the reason I cannot cut bread, meat or anything else in the kitchen is because the cutting edge is always on the wrong side for a left-hander.

I had been labelled stupid and clumsy and thrown out of the kitchen at an early age, then castigated for not helping with the chores. Now I was discovering that the complexes my handicap had brought me were due to society's blinkered attitude to the plight of the left-hander, an attitude that persists even in these enlightened times.

Commercial obstacles

The major hurdle came in acquiring goods for my catalogue from several household-name domestic appliance manufacturers, from whom wresting information and trading terms was only achieved by appealing, in desperation, to the managing directors. One sales rep admitted that general company policy is to get goods onto the market as fast as possible, whether or not they are adequate, resulting in customer complaints and product withdrawal. This is how I discovered that greed comes first, the user being the final consideration. So what chance do left-handers have? Paradoxically, one firm refuses to supply us with a product on the extraordinary assumption that it can sell as many dictating machines as it makes and doesn't need our business. Several other firms produced guffaws of laughter, accompanied by discriminatory remarks of the 'Why don't you try standing on your head?' variety. West German and American firms, predictably, replied by return of post, and were eager to do business with us.

What are all these implements that confuse the left-hander? The list of complaints include: irons with the cord on the right; milk pans and ladles with the lip on the left; electric kettles, water and measuring jugs with the measure on the back; safety switches of DIY power tools which the left hand covers, locking them in the 'on' position; combination planes which discharge sawdust directly at the user; pins on brooches affixed the wrong way round; playing cards with pips only on the left; corkscrews; screws; scissors; steak knives; potato peelers; pastry forks and servers; fish knives; can openers; cheque-book stubs; function buttons on computerised equipment; telephone kiosks with no space for left-hand writing; door handles; musical instruments; cooker knobs and many, many more inconvenient items which a little more design forethought and consideration could eliminate.

Other irritations include dressing children, lacing shoes and tying ties (bows tied left-handed tend to stand vertically), zipping trousers (little boys look like Quasimodo pulling up zips), fastening flaps and wrap-overs on anoraks and hooks and eyes on bras. Even boomerangs present their problems – they drop to the ground, unless the aerofoil is on the opposite side for a left-hander.

Seals out of water?

Then, my research began to open new horizons and the complications of cross-laterality entered into the enquiry. Why are some people left-handed, others right-handed? There are varying degrees of handedness – some people are left- or right-footed, some left- or right-eyed – and there are confusing combinations.

Some find their handedness a problem, others – a significant majority of brisk, no-nonsense schoolteachers – are aghast that anyone should find it a disability and claim it has never affected them. Like the intolerance of former smokers to those who indulge, they are highly scathing of left-handers who claim difficulties, putting it down to their laziness and lack of industriousness.

Which? magazine, quoting a 1930s psychologist in their 1979 Left-Handed Report, had this to say about us: '... they squint, they stammer, they shuffle and shamble, they flounder about like seals out of water. Awkward in the house, and clumsy in their games, they are fumblers and bunglers at whatever they do.'

Educational provision

Two significant factors emerged which I wanted to pursue. Although researchers claim no significant increase, observation appears to indicate more left-handers in the community. But still no provision is being made by the majority of education authorities to deal with learning difficulties. It is in the formative years that left-handedness presents itself as a 'handicap' – indeed, the Design Council's information on suppliers of left-handed utensils appears on a list labelled 'handicapped'.

Educational obstacles

The hardest time of life for a left-hander is during the early school years when a child is learning to read and write. Taking instruction in handicrafts and sport can be confusing and can be the arbiter of future complexes if a sensitive, self-conscious child feels he or she is being singled out for special tuition or is unable to perform those tasks as easily as other children.

The fact that the child is left-handed escapes the one important person who needs to be aware of it – the child itself. It assumes that its inability stems from its own ineptitude. Complexes, nervousness, stammering and self-consciousness can all be the by-products of a left-handed person's embarrassing childhood experiences.

'... I can quite clearly see myself at five years old starting school, and the teacher towering over me, and grabbing the pencil from my left hand and pushing it into my right and saying: "Never do that again", which gave me an inferiority complex which has been with me the rest of my life,' commented one 71-year-old.

Some blame has to be laid at the door of the teachers themselves. Some are not even aware of the left-handers in their classes. There are those who recognise the problem but have neither tact nor patience to deal with it sympathetically. Others do not recognise it at all, judging from the amount of distraught parents who told me of their child's assessment as 'backward' or 'slow'. Several had been placed in remedial classes until some sharp-eyed person had spotted the source of the real learning difficulty or until the frustrated parents had finally touched the soul of some sympathetic official.

'Educationally there has been no disadvantage to being left-handed. I train teachers – with an interest in special educational needs – and our research programmes and search of the literature indicates people who claim difficulties with learning because they are left-handed may have reasons based in fantasy rather than reality. Defence mechanisms may be involved to excuse shortcomings in several areas. There is no substantial and scientifically accurate empirical work to indicate left-handed people do worse across the board of attainment. However, this has not stopped business/ financially-minded people selling remediation programmes to left-handed people or trainers who want to make a livelihood from treating left-handed people ... if you do discover any research findings which contradict my claims please let me know so they can be subjected to acceptable statistical analysis and interpretation,' was the attitude of a teacher trainer.

Manual dexterity

The second interesting point stemmed from the fact that some people had been originally right-handed but had had to adapt for medical reasons. After some initial difficulties, they had done so with no problem. This had led me to ponder on the degrees of left-handedness, for most left-handers can do many things with their right hands but right-handers are generally useless with their left hands.

Sometimes left-handers are forced to carry out tasks with their right hands because of design considerations.

Many bat with the right hand yet throw with the left. We are taught how to bat, usually by right-handers. But picking up a ball and heaving it is a natural function which needs no tuition. If both left- and right-handers can learn to adapt then we must all carry the innate ability to be ambidextrous. But why do we not all use both hands?

When a human being is deprived of a sense, the remaining senses take over. Their efficiency is increased and their awareness is heightened. Blind people 'see' with their fingers. Their sense of hearing is heightened. All our senses working simultaneously rob us of the ability to highlight one area of sensation – we take in an entire landscape, rather than concentrating on one detail. If people listen but they do not hear, it is because so many other impressions are crowding in from other senses.

Can it be that ambidexterity would rob us of our manual dexterity? Must we concentrate on attaining efficiency with one hand, because spreading the tasks between two hands simultaneously would be less effective? Could we even overload our brain? Do we have some in-built mechanism which prevents us from developing our total potential? Is that the line between genius and madness?

Or is this not a natural phenomenon at all? Could our single-handedness be self-inflicted, rather than genetic or pathologically based? Has the advance of culture, at some point in our evolution led us to favour the use of one hand over the other, the one that feels most natural, because social advances have no longer necessitated the full use of both hands for survival? Are we just too lazy to develop our full potential?

The left-handed phenomenon has never been completely solved, but over the centuries dozens of wide-ranging theories have been postulated. The trouble is that there is no way of knowing which one is correct.

Meanwhile, research continues unabated in universities all over the world. Leading authorities have published hundreds of research papers, medical articles and books, many of them far too technical for the average left-hander's comprehension. Sadly, after all these years of painstaking research, no one has thought of suggesting more practical solutions to the physical discomfort of the left-hander, or implemented any teaching or learning methods that could be instituted in our schools. We are at the mercy of well-meaning

6

researchers who see us only as statistics. We have to remind ourselves that dyslexia has only recently been officially recognised and that some of our problems are common ones. And even now, some people still refuse to accept that dyslexia exists.

Even the side we sleep on has come under scrutiny. According to advice columnist, Claire Rayner, most men sleep on the right side of the bed unless they are left-handed.

'They sleep on the side that leaves their caressing hand free. Left-handed men sleep on the left for the same reason,' she said. According to psychologist, Dr David Lewis, right-handed men sleep on the right for primitive protection, not sexual reasons. 'They lie on their left side leaving their right hand free to protect their genitals. This is instinct. For a left-handed man, it will be the opposite,' he said. Switching sides may lead to marital conflict.

Longevity arguments

Researchers in Canada are doing their best to kill us off quickly, at least before we reach the average age of 63.97. Psychologists Dr Stanley Coren, of the University of British Columbia, and Dr Diane Halpern of the California State University, San Bernadino, recently found that at the age of 33 southpaws start to drop off, that a mere five per cent make it to 50, and by 80 the game is over. One explanation was that low-weight babies, who are often left-handed, might have a reduced survival chance, while another concerned a greater chance of accidents and stress in a right-handed world. I would prefer to believe that many of the surviving righties were lefties who preferred to use their right hands. As we shall see from my research into sport, they could not have chosen a worse criterion on which to base their investigation.

Their figures were derived from births, deaths, throwing and batting hands of players listed in the US Baseball Encyclopaedia and the sample, warned Harvard Medical School's Dr Albert Galaburda, was too small to be taken seriously – 236 southpaws as against 1,472 right-handers (whose average age of death was 64.64 years).

Left-handers take heart, for anyone over 50 is likely to have been forced into changing hands, which may well account for the dearth of older lefties. Holbein, who died aged 46, was a plague victim,

Leonardo da Vinci died at 67 (not bad for the 16th century) and Michelangelo kept going until he was 89, which is not bad for any century. Picasso died aged 91, Sir Rex Harrison, 82, Sir Charles Chaplin, 78 and Greta Garbo, 85.

'... the world is a sinister place for them; the world is very definitely set up for right-handers,' commented Professor Coren, who received death threats from outraged left-handers after his research was published in the American Journal of Public Health in 1989.

Hot on Coren's heels came the expected reversal of such an alarming prognosis. Max G. Anderson of the Canadian Statistical Analysis Service, Vancouver, writing in *Nature* magazine, claimed that Coren had used unadjusted birth dates. Using criteria based on throwing hands of baseball players, he regrouped the data and concluded that possibly stress or discrimination against left-handers accounted for a decrease in the sinistral population.

'Our lifespan has presumably been genetically selected for good reproductive fitness. There would, therefore, have been selective pressure to evolve a linkage between left-handedness and a factor for increased longevity, partially offsetting the lower longevity otherwise associated with left-handedness,' he said.

If this were so, removal of handedness-related stresses in modern times would have created an about-turn for sinistrals.

'The advantage of being left-handed parallels the advantage of being female in affluent societies, and I suggest these have a similar evolutionary explanation.' According to Anderson's hypothesis, it appears that left-handers should live longer than right-handers among Americans but die earlier in countries with 'low and approximately equal male and female longevities still prevailing.'

But according to Coren, in addition to reports on the effects of stress on left-handers in industry and education, left-handers, by their very nature, appear to handle stress less well than right-handers. Not only do they have the normal everyday stresses experienced by right-handers to contend with but they experience the additional stresses of living in a world designed for right-handers (in many cases unconsciously so) and attempting to hold their own in a world where brain organisation works differently from their own. Stress, in any event, is not necessarily a bad thing, nor is there any proof that it is accountable for the demise of the left-handed population. I remain unconvinced by either argument.

Learning to cope

By the time they reach their teen and adult years, left-handers have learned to cope and have adapted to right-handed implements and tools. They have taken their 'handicap' for granted and forgotten it even exists. Most would find it hard to relearn their tasks with their left hands. It is only when someone introduces them to a pair of left-handed scissors or hands them a pack of playing cards with the pips on all four corners that they suddenly realise how much easier they can cut paper – and in a straight line – or that they aren't faced with a sea of blank spaces when they fan their cards from right to left.

How dangerous is it for a left-handed worker to stretch across with his left hand to switches or tools placed on the right? And how dangerous is it for a left-hander to use tools and implements honed for right-handed use or with controls on the right? These were some of the questions I set out to answer.

The average right-hander does not relate to left-handers at all. Unless there is a left-handed member of their own immediate family, there is no reason why they should be aware that left-handed people exist or that they experience discomfort or awkwardness performing certain tasks or carrying out certain functions.

Right-handed children of left-handed parents will also suffer some confusion. They will inevitably be taught some tasks the left-handed way. Not only can this be confusing for them but they will then find themselves at odds in a right-handed world. This is one reason why a Census survey would show inaccurate statistics. Mixed-handers in families are frequently victims of laterality, arguing over the direction in which the phone should lie, or the kettle. If the cook is left-handed, no one else will be able to use peelers, knives and other utensils. Left-handedness therefore does not just pose problems for the left-hander.

'Our daughter was married a few weeks ago and I decided to write a poem for her about the different aspects of life concerning her home life with us and I mentioned in the poem her left-handedness', said one right-handed mother.

Your being left-handed didn't leave us much doubt
As to what had happened when we looked about,
To see the chaos after using the iron,
The hoover, the shower, thought you had the strength of a
    lion,
You could bend objects that weren't meant to be bent,
And send objects home broke that had only been lent.

Living Left-Handed is not intended to be an academic work, although it has been necessary to review an enormous amount of research material on the various aspects of laterality. As a lay person of limited educational achievement, I humbly apologise if I have misinterpreted any of the data or omitted to mention any relevant research.

The Bible, the culture, traditions and legends of the majority of civilisations have damned the left and favoured the right, throughout history. Despite society's efforts to subjugate, convert and inconvenience us, we continue to exist in ever-increasing numbers.

An anthropological study would probably form the subject of another book. What I really wanted to know was: Am I thick and clumsy or do other left-handers have similar problems to my own? How do they cope with certain situations? Were there some interesting case histories which we could all share? What have manufacturers done to ease our discomfort? Do children need any special support? Personal interviews and correspondence revealed some useful information and also gave me an insight into the character and feelings of those concerned. Helped by personal experience and existing research, I was able to follow the ongoing campaign waged by researchers bent on discovering the secret of sinistrality.

By the end of my journey, I had passed some fascinating landmarks and chalked up innumerable milestones before reaching my destination. But I am still a statistic, one of a number between two and thirty per cent. The real research is yet to be done; how to overcome its drawbacks, how to exploit its advantages and how to pave a more comfortable way for tomorrow's left-handed children.

Diane Paul, Manchester, 1990.

1
HOW THE LEFT WAS LOST

World trends

There are estimated to be one to two hundred million left-handers in the world: nine million in the United Kingdom, over seven million in Italy, five million in Japan, thirty million in the United States of America, and forty-eight million throughout Europe. Figures vary from ten to twenty per cent of the population and are difficult to obtain because an official census of sinistral people has never been carried out in any country.

In 1886, left-handers made up 70 per cent of the Punjabi population, in 1932, nearly 8 per cent in Switzerland, only 3.8 per cent in Stuttgart and 4.6 per cent in Berlin. (By 1974, the overall German statistics had strangely reduced to 0.44 per cent.) In 1933 there were 10 per cent in Palestine, and in 1953, 5.5 per cent in Scotland. In France in 1962, 11 per cent of men were left-handed and 9 per cent of women. In 1983, there were 11 per cent in Japan, and in the UK in 1985, one survey among 15- to 65-year-olds produced 30.7 per cent left-handers. In 1921, 11.9 per cent were found in special schools and 18.2 per cent among mental defectives.

American surveys range from 2 per cent in New York in 1911 to 4 per cent in Ohio in 1930 and 6.4 per cent in Detroit in 1941. Nationwide, figures varied from 1 to 29 per cent in 1927 to 11 per cent in 1960. In 1952, the United States Army revealed that left-handers made up 8.6 per cent of recruits. Of them, 7.8 per cent were passes and 9.7 per cent were failures.

Even though these figures are so disparate, to include them in future population censuses, as has been suggested, would probably create even more confusion. Most statistics are gathered by researchers from their work with schoolchildren. They do not always take into account the adult population but are thought to be a fair indication of statistical trends.

But because of the various degrees of laterality, and the fact that some people may be more right- or left-handed than they think, a question on an official Census form to determine laterality percentages would probably produce totally misleading results and is not to be recommended. The only true record would be produced by laterality testing, which ideally should be done at various stages of a child's development.

The famous and the infamous

Despite their 'sinister' origins, a high percentage of left-handers have hit the headlines over the years. The first noted left-hander was Mucius Scaevola, a hero of Roman legend, who was ordered to be burnt alive after an assassination attempt on Porsenna, the King of Etruria. But he won the King's favour and pardon by fearlessly holding his right hand in the fire. Thereafter, he was known as 'left-handed Mucius'.

Since then, the line of left-handers has passed down through Alexander the Great, Charlemange, the Emperor Tiberius, Lord Nelson (for whom there was no alternative) and Joan of Arc (whose portrait in the copy of her trial, now in the National Archives in Paris, reveals her holding her sword in her left hand), to one-third of all United States' Presidents since 1945, including Truman, Ford, Reagan (who was changed), Bush and Clinton.

Statesman and philosopher, Benjamin Franklin, was a left-hander who, in addition to helping frame the American Constitution, found a moment to pen an appeal for the left in the form of 'A Petition to Those Who Have the Superintendency of Education':

'There are twin sisters of us; and the eyes of man do not more resemble, nor are capable of being on better terms with each other than my sister and myself, were it not for the partiality of our parents, who made the most injurious distinction between us.

'From my infancy I have been led to consider my sister as a being of more educated rank. I was suffered to grow up without the least instruction, while nothing was spared in her education. She had masters to teach her writing, drawing, music and other accomplishments, but if by chance I touched a pencil, a pen or a needle I was bitterly rebuked; and more than once I have been beaten for being awkward, and wanting a graceful manner ...

'Must not the regret of our parents be excessive, at having placed so great a difference between sisters who are so perfectly equal? Alas! We must perish from distress; for it would not be in my power even to scrawl a suppliant petition for relief ...

'Condescend, sir, to make my parents sensible of the injustice of an exclusive tenderness, and of the necessity of distributing their care and affection among all their children equally. I am, with profound respect, Sirs,

'Your obedient servant,
'THE LEFT HAND'

In the UK, Prince William is left-handed, King George VI was changed over and Queen Victoria was ambidextrous.

Prince Charles experienced an enforced change to the left when he broke the humerus in his upper right arm after a fall on the polo field in June, 1990. Much concern was shown for the heir to the British throne when complications set in after the two breaks, above his elbow, were set in plaster at a cottage hospital in Cirencester.

A month later, HRH was still in pain, there was little sign of healing and a holiday in Majorca did not help. The Queen's Medical Centre, Nottingham, recommended a three-hour operation involving a hip bone graft, which took place at the end of August.

Although his sporting life was at stake, he was expected to resume the use of his right hand eventually. In the meantime, the Prince switched sides and was reported as having '... perfected a scratchy signature ...' and the ability to paint, sketch and shake hands with his South Paw. 'Life on the left will never be good enough for Prince Charles,' proclaimed the *Daily Mail*, whose main concern was whether he would ever be able to play polo again.

Of present-day politicians, only the Shadow Foreign Secretary, the Rt Hon Gerald Kaufman and the Rt Hon Lord Jenkins of Hillhead have admitted to being 'of the left', while the right wing keep their left-handed leanings to themselves.

In the world of entertainment, creative left-handers abound. Among them are George Burns, Charles Chaplin, Bernie Clifton, Michael Crawford, Leslie Crowther, Robert De Niro, Richard Dreyfuss, W. C. Fields, Uri Geller, Rex Harrison, Rock Hudson,

Derek Jameson, Danny Kaye, Michael Landon, Marcel Marceau, Harpo Marx, Anthony Newley, Ryan O'Neal, Robert Redford, Paul Shane, Telly Savalas, Rod Steiger, Dick Van Dyke. Female left-handers in the entertainment business include Carol Barnes, Jean Boht, Carol Burnett, Greta Garbo, Judy Garland, Betty Grable, Olivia de Havilland, Goldie Hawn, Hope Lange, Shirley Maclaine, Marilyn Monroe, Kim Novak, Su Pollard, Esther Rantzen and Eva Marie Saint.

Composers and musicians include C. P. E. Bach, Benjamin Britten, Bob Geldof, Jimi Hendrix, Paul McCartney, Cole Porter, Prokofiev and Ringo Starr. Fashion designer Zandra Rhodes is left-handed, as are cartoonists Calman and Ronald Searle, and artists Albrecht Dürer, Hans Holbein, Paul Klee, Edwin Landseer and Pablo Picasso. Both Michelangelo and Leonardo da Vinci were ambidextrous.

They are prolific, too, in the world of sport, boasting such famous names as Babe Ruth, John Barnes, Bjorn Borg, Bob Charles (golf only), Brian Close, 'Little Mo' Connolly, Jimmy Connors, Mark Cox, Jaroslav Drobny, Guy Forget, Neale Fraser, Sara Gomer, David Gower, Herol Graham, Marvin Hagler, Ben Hogan (golf right), Ann Jones, Bill Knight, Rod Laver, Henri Leconte, John McEnroe, Martina Navratilova, Manuel Orantes, Tony Roche, Gary Sobers, Mark Spitz, Roscoe Tanner, Roger Taylor, Guillermo Vilas and Mark Woodforde.

Other prominent left-handers include Albert Einstein, Herbert Hoover, Nelson Rockefeller, Billy the Kid, the Boston Strangler, the Black Panther and Jack the Ripper.

Today's famous left-handers might well have joined fellow sinistral Joan at the stake had they been born in earlier centuries, for the left-handed minority have endured a traditionally bad press throughout the ages. To discover why, we must delve back into history.

Animal connections

Experiments with animals have revealed little in relation to the origins of handedness for animals have paws, not hands, which have superior values and uses for humans, in particular dexterity. And animals appear to have no particular preference for either paw. Some researchers have noted such peculiarities as the elephant digging roots more with the right tusk, dogs being consistent in which hind leg they raise when urinating, saddle horses trained to canter off on the right foot, which seems to create problems for some, the discovery of variable hand preferences in some monkeys, the predominant right-sidedness in rats and a divided preference in squirrels and cows.

The results indicate that there are no special leanings to any one side over the other. Animals, on the whole, tend to be ambilateral, although they can be trained to the specific use of one particular side and a minority are one-sided, by chance.

Prehistoric evidence

'Every man did what was right in his own eyes. Some handled their tools and drew with the left hand. A larger number used the right hand, but as yet no rule prevailed. In this, as in certain other respects, the arts and habits of that period belonged to a chapter in the infancy of the race, when the law of dexterity, as well as other laws, begot by habit, convenience or more prescriptive conventionality, had not yet found their place in that unwritten code to which a prompter obedience is rendered than to the most absolute of royal or imperial decrees.' Sir Daniel Wilson, *The Prehistoric Man*, 1876.

Archaeologists, unearthing Stone Age relics from between 100,000 years ago and 4,000 BC, have found that aboriginal man had no particular hand preferences. Neolithic man's flint tools were honed for left and right use in equal measure. In the Paleolithic era, humans used whichever hand suited them best. Some used tools and drew with their left hand and an equal number seem to have used their right hand.

In 1890, hand-held stonescrapers unearthed in France and Switzerland had double edges. Around 56 per cent of them were honed for left-handed use. In north Surrey, Neolithic flint pounders, awls and borers were found to be made equally for right and left-handed use, indicating ambidexterity. Stone implements, arrow blades and spearheads left by North American Indian aborigines in the USA clearly revealed a higher left-handed bias than in later eras. Thirty-three per cent of the rock drawings were made by left-handers.

Other anthropological findings at the turn of the century revealed a higher percentage of left-handed artists than we find in today's society and a more equal distribution of hand preference. Primitive Australians, Africans, Hottentots, Bushmen, Bantus and Pygmies were all found to favour the left hand.

Anthropologist, Paul Sarasin (1856–1929), found some wedge-shaped stones and hatchets in Moustier, France, sharpened on the left and others on the right side, indicating an equal number of left- and right-handers in the Stone Age and this was echoed in other areas. It seems to have been during the Bronze Age that the preference for right-handedness occurred, revealed by the cutting edges of tools and the sickle, made for right-handers only, a preference which has persisted down the ages.

Cultural significance and social pressure

As man's implements became progressively more sophisticated, from stone to bronze to iron, society's cultural habits advanced from basic hunting, fishing and farming. Stone Age tools were sufficiently simple and primitive to afford use by either hand with no problem. Bronze Age tools, however, were more advanced and could not be switched to either hand. The maker decided on its sidedness, not the user, who also had to pass it down through generations of descendants who were obliged to use that hand. But it meant that the user could develop special strengths on one side of his body, making for more speed and efficiency on that side.

Children have their skills passed on to them by the adults in society, who have already formed their own hand preference and the tradition is passed on, by social pressure. Right-handedness, or dextrality, became adopted as part of man's culture and passed into the social code, taking on religious, moral and magical significance. Left-handedness became inconvenient and eventually virtually taboo, ostensibly so as not to hinder the advancement of civilisation. As the right gained ground on all fronts, inevitably, the left began to decline in acceptability, becoming associated with the more negative aspects of abnormality, darkness and wickedness.

Some cultures reacted in quite extreme ways. In Albania, left-handedness is said to be banned. The Indonesians bind their children's left arms to their sides to prevent use. The Kaffirs scald and bury their sinistrals' left hands in the hot sand. Zulu children are also banned from using their left hands. In Arab countries, the left, or 'unclean hand', has traditionally been used for personal hygiene (likewise among Hindus), while the right hand is used for eating. The origin of the phrase, 'to give one's right hand' for something, relates to the custom of cutting off a thief's right hand, thereby rendering him useless, for the left is not socially acceptable. Today's more educated Arabs have a more relaxed attitude towards left-handedness, although in India the taboo still persists. Rural Japanese women are likely to be divorced if caught using their left hands. African women from certain tribes of the Niger river are not allowed to cook with their left hand. In the Maori language, the right side denotes the male (strong, virile and good) side, while the left side denotes the female and everything bad. Ironically, although there are more left-handed men than women in the world, the left side in most cultures is always correlated with women – in Buddhism, Yin, the weak side and the weaker sex – and the right, strong, Yang, with men. Only the American Zuni Indians and the Chinese come out in favour of the left. When I lived in Paris, the French constantly noted my left-handedness, with loud exclamations, as though I was some kind of phenomenon. It does not appear to be encouraged there, nor in Germany, although left-handed shops in both countries do exist. A shop has been in existence in London for over 20 years and each American state has at least one left-handed store. In Juniata College, Darby, Pennsylvania, a special scholarship is exclusively reserved for left-handers.

Language of left and right

'The stranger greets thy hand with proffered left? Accept not: 'tis of loyalty bereft. Left-handed friends are underhanded foes; True openness a swordless right hand shows.' Harvey, *Sheep in Wolves' Clothing*, 1.98.

To reinforce the negative concept of left-handedness and the left side, the language of the left reflects the cultural background, its progress and advancement among the different societies. Abram Blau in *The Master Hand* lists the right as 'permanence, force, power, strength, grace, dexterity, dispatch, godliness, rectitude, truth, goodness, and sanctity.' In direct contrast, the left represents, 'the opposite, the reverse, the lack, the negation of all the traits and characteristics attributed to the right hand.'

The word 'right' comes from the Latin *rectus* meaning straight, erect and just, a position of honour. The word for left, *sinister*, from the Latin for left, denotes 'a bad omen, inauspicious, evil, awkward, wrong, perverse, improper, unlucky, unfavourable, and bad.' In Latin and Greek, the left hand was the shield hand or *laeva*, or the pocket hand, *sinister* deriving from the word *sinus* or pocket of the toga. Even the Anglo-Saxon word for left, *lyft*, means weak or broken, the left arm being the weak arm, while *riht* means straight, erect or just. In Germany, left is *licht* or *leicht*, meaning light or fragile.

We have even invented phrases to reinforce these emotions, such as 'right-hand man' (coined during the Middle Ages when the King's favourite was seated on his right), 'left-handed friend', 'two left feet', 'left behind' but 'right behind one' and 'right on'. We talk of left-handed marriages, compliments and oaths. The bar sinister was reluctantly bestowed on the bastard son, an unlucky state of affairs for any noble family. In politics, we inherited the French custom of labelling 'right wingers' (nobles) and the 'left wing' (pre-revolutionary capitalists). The propaganda machine has worked well over the centuries in most countries to indoctrinate the people with an abhorrence of the left.

Today, we have inherited a host of derogatory nicknames, most of them indigenous to individual areas. These range from 'Mollydooker' (woman-handed) in Australia to 'cack-handed' (from the French 'caca' for excrement) in England.

'... it definitely influenced my personality – I was aggressive – I *hated* being called "cack-handed Clara" ', commented one woman on her left-handedness. In Scotland, we are 'Corrie-pawed', in Cornwall 'Clicky-handed', in the West Midlands 'Keggy-handed', in Lancashire 'Kay-fisted', in the North of England 'Cuddy-wifters' and in the South, 'Skivvy-handed'. The list goes on.

Biblical discrimination

'Evil and Good are God's Right Hand and Left.' Philip James Bailey, *Festus, Proem.*

In general terms, the Bible does little for the left, offering at least

100 references in favour of the right and around 25 references unfavourable to the left. These are not all aimed at the left hand but the left side. 'Then he will say to those on his left, "Away from me, you that are under God's curse! Away to the eternal fire which has been prepared for the Devil and his angels!" ' (Matthew, 25: 41). This does not necessarily denote that all left-handers are cursed.

Left-handed Ehud, of the tribe of Benjamin (which seems to have boasted quite a few left-handers), fared better than most when he stabbed King Eglon of Moab with a dagger he had secreted on his right thigh, in order to help save the children of Israel. But Biblical allusions to the good right and the bad left abound, throughout the Old and New Testaments. The Talmud tells us: 'Let your left hand turn away what your right hand attracts.' Sotua, 47.

But it was the goat (or scapegoat) which was chosen to represent the dark and evil left-hand path, in contrast to the lovable and useful sheep which took the right (in both senses of the word) road. The cloven-hooved goat's links with the great god Pan probably gave it the push over the edge needed for it to be associated with the Devil. But it was St Matthew who, in the Parable of the Sheep and the Goats, finally split the left and right in the name of Jesus. In the Vision of Judgement all nations will be divided before the Son of Man when he appeared, as the sheep on his right and the goats on his left. Those on his right will inherit the Kingdom and those on the left hand will be cast into Hell.

It seems out of character for the Great Man to be prejudiced against such a minority group. Although Jesus was obviously not referring to left-handers in particular, the allusion was enough to damn the left side forever and, with it, those who favoured the use of their left hands. It would be a blasphemy not to carry out Church rituals with the right hand: the sign of the cross, the blessing, the taking and offering of the wafer and chalice of wine. In the marriage ceremony, right hands are joined together, while the metal wedding ring, to ward off evil, is placed on the left hand's third, or 'charm' finger.

'Let not thy left hand know what thy right hand doeth,' Matthew, 6:3 (King James version), said Christ in his Sermon on the Mount. Overmuch has been made by previous writers on the subject of these Biblical quotations, and they were obviously not intended to be taken literally. The more commonsense translation in the Good News Bible states: 'But when you help a needy person, do it in such a way that even your closest friend will not know about it.'

Biblical art comes down firmly on the side of the right. Depictions of Christ and God always show them blessing with their right hands, while, in direct contrast, the Devil is always seen hurling curses with the left. Even Michelangelo, a presumed ambidexter, depicted Eve holding the apple in her left hand four times, and we all know what the outcome of that was.

It has been theorised that man's obsession with sun worship and sun gods created a bias to the right or east in countless early civilisations, with the exception of the Chinese. The Buddhists favoured the symbolic Red Bird, Yin (south) and tortoise, Yang (north). The left road of life was perilous, while the right eightfold path was propitious. In India, left and right castes dominated the Hindu religion.

The Greek stance

Aristophanes subscribed to the theory that we were all created round and that there were no back, front, left, right, wrong or right sides to us at all. In anger at man's arrogance, Zeus split us in half and tossed us to Apollo who made us face forwards. If we didn't behave, we could be split again and made to hop on one leg – the right one presumably. Classical Greek literature is riddled with bias to the right and disdain of the left, even according to Parmenides' belief that the male foetus was carried on the right and the female on the left.

Plato described the wonderful place in which the soul rested after it left the body so that it could receive its sentence. The Judges sit between two openings, sending the righteous down the right-hand road leading to Heaven and the criminals down the left-hand road leading downwards. Parables must have travelled far in those days.

In Plato's *The Laws*, the Athenian blames laterality prejudices on 'the stupidity of nurses and mothers ... Indeed, the natural aptitude of the two arms is the same, and it is ourselves who have made them unequal and who do not use them as we should,' he says, thereby creating another prejudice towards woman's irresponsibility.

In Greek mythology, Uranus (Heaven) united with Gaea (Earth), creating seven children, the Titans. The youngest, Cronus, attacked Uranus while he slept, with a flint sickle, castrating him with the left hand and throwing the genitals and sickle into the sea. The severed organ gave birth to Aphrodite but the event did not do much in the way of public relations for the left hand.

The Roman stance

The left fell from favour after the Roman augurs, a religious body of prophets, changed sides. The Roman augurs originally faced the south, so that the east or left side was favourable. The Greek augurs faced the north, rendering the left side unfavourable. Although the Romans overran the Greeks, they unfortunately adopted the Greek custom.

Originally, a lightning flash from left to right was lucky, upon which the Assembly had the day off. The flight of birds from left to right was also propitious. But the Romans by tradition favoured the right, adopting the right-handed handshake, entering a friend's home right foot first and inventing the left-to-right alphabet (not to mention the Fascist salute).

Witchcraft and the left

'Michel Udon and Pierre Burgot confessed that they rubbed their left arms and hands with a certain powdered ash, and that when they touched an animal, they caused it to die.' Boguet, *Examen of Witches.*

No wonder then that superstition of the left became correlated with all things evil, and in particular, the Devil and witchcraft. The evil eye is on the left and the Devil's rituals and spells are carried out traditionally with the left hand. The Grand Cabbala, some kind of a man-goat, is said to shake hands with his left. The 'Devil's mark' was usually found on the left side of the body.

Satan's followers make the circle widdershins, or anti-clockwise, the antithesis of all good sun worshippers. The word is of German derivation – *widersin* means against the direction. Doing things the opposite way to the norm is the cult's way of ridiculing traditional religion. The name Satan is taken from the Talmud's Samael, the Chief of Satans and Prince of Demons, *Se'mol* meaning left.

During the Middle Ages, it was, of course, natural to persecute anyone who deviated from the norm, be they red-headed, threenippled or left-handed. Superstition was based on fear and those who did not conform to the herd's cognisance of what was acknowledged to be the norm, by virtue of its majority, could be condemned, to eradicate that fear and absolve one's conscience. Fear of witchcraft had its origin in the guilt experienced by the less charitable members of society who slammed the door in the faces of poverty-stricken old ladies who begged for a crust. It was easier to assuage one's guilt by blaming them when the milk turned sour. The cult of Black Magic with its left-orientated Black Mass was something else.

Superstitions

'If left-hand fortune give thee left-hand chance, be wisely patient'. Quarles, *Emblems*, iv, 1.4.

Judas Iscariot was unlucky enough to spill the salt on the table in da Vinci's painting of *The Last Supper*. My mother always threw a pinch of fallen salt over her left shoulder, this superstition stemming from the belief that this is where the Devil stands, the right being the spot where your Guardian Angel hovers. The righteous, of course, always stood on God's right.

The left having been negated to a subsidiary and socially unacceptable role, it was no wonder that hopes and desires could be dashed in simple minds by its intrusion in the most mundane happenings. The Scots were wary of which foot went first into their breeches and of putting their 'skir' or left foot down first when entering a house. Another unlucky omen was to put one's left shoe on the right foot by mistake.

An itching left palm can signify financial loss, it is bad luck to pass the wine with the left hand, or pass the wine bottle anti-clockwise round the table. A feud raged for nearly 20 years between the households of William Hargill and Lord Stourton in the 16th century after Lord Stourton proffered the left-handed toast to the Hargill family, with whom he was out of sorts.

Left-handed cultures

It has been queried whether the Hebrews represented a left-handed culture owing to the fact that they write and read from right to left, but so do the Arabs. In the Old Testament (Judges, 20:16), the tribe of Benjamin in Gibeah boasted 700 specially-chosen left-handed men … 'and every one could sling stones at a hair breadth and not miss', a little ironical when you consider that the word 'Benjamin' stems from *Ben Yamin*, or Son of the Right Hand. They were, eventually severely trounced by the Israelites, being no match for their 400,000 soldiers.

In Chronicles I, 12:2, a company of left-handed soldiers from the tribe of Benjamin who met David 'were armed with bows and could use both the right and the left hand in hurling stones and shooting arrows out of a bow'. A famous left-handed Inca in pre-Spanish Peru was named Lloque Yuponqui, or 'one who is left-handed and renowned for pious acts'. Sardinians have been pictured with shields on the right arm holding swords in their left hands, as have many Knoters of the 5th century BC pictured at the Metropolitan Museum of Art in New York. There are many depictions of Egyptians carrying out their daily tasks with the left hand and even a legend that Alexander the Great discovered a left-handed country whose inhabitants tried to convince him that the left hand was more honourable because it was closer to the heart.

In 1990, the British press reported the discovery by Russian scientists of 75 per cent left-handed Taimyr natives living in Russia's Artic north. It was thought that right-handers aged quicker in extreme cold, but they could find no other satisfactory explanation for this phenomenon.

Today's left-handers are more liberally treated, compared to previous generations. So how do they fare in contemporary society, and how are they perceived by the dextral majority?

* * * *

2
FIRST DAY AT SCHOOL

I got into trouble for the state of my schoolwork and was made to do it again. Inky shirtcuffs meant the cane, lines and extra homework ... apart from being a complete non-academic, it contributed to a lot of my unhappiness at school. All the weaknesses I had grown up with left me when I went into show business. Bernie Clifton.

Linda Morrison, five-and-a-half years old and naturally an obedient and polite little girl, had no presentiment of trouble when her mother took her to see the headmistress of the infants' department of the local council school.

It wasn't until the headmistress said in a kind voice, 'Of course, she mustn't be separated from Evie Edwards,' that Linda's heart sank.

Evie was a year older than her and they had lived next door to each other for as long as she could remember. Their parents and the neighbours had always liked to see them as devoted little friends and probably only Linda and Evie knew the depths of their mutual dislike.

But Linda could hardly explain all this to the headmistress at their first meeting and so it happened that, on her first day at school, she was put, not into the babies' class but into an older children's class and shared a desk with Evie.

'Fold your arms,' said Miss Knight, the teacher.

Linda had never seen anyone like her before. She had a very red face, a tight black satin dress, a lot of jangly beads and a frizzy bird's-nest of hair.

'Come along, Linda Morrison,' she said, 'didn't you hear me tell you to fold your arms?'

24

Linda went very red, and looking round at the other children copied what they were doing, but it seemed most unnatural.

'And sit up … sit up,' said Miss Knight. 'We don't want round-shouldered little girls in this class.'

Then she opened a thin book and began to call out their names.

At first, Linda couldn't understand what was happening and when Evie's name was called, she said a strange word and unfolded her arms and sat back. Linda wanted to ask her what the word was but Evie wouldn't take any notice of her.

'Linda Morrison,' said Miss Knight; 'Linda Morrison.' Linda wanted to say 'Yes' but she was swallowing so hard that it wouldn't come out.

'We don't want little girls in this class who can't answer to their names properly,' said Miss Knight but, luckily, she went on to the next one and Linda cautiously unfolded her arms and sat back.

And then came Scripture. No one bothered Linda, and for the first time she breathed more easily and even ventured to look about her at the unfamiliar surroundings.

Her eye took in the wooden floor and the sharp little desks; the tall locked cupboards and the dark red hot-water pipes; the picture – high up on the wall – of a boy, a cat and a dead fish.

But always her eyes came back to the alarming Miss Knight; somehow more alarming because Linda, too young then for the intricacies of English spelling, didn't know about the 'K' at the beginning of her name. 'Miss Night – Night – Night', she thought and the world seemed dark indeed.

Time to write

'Come here, Linda Morrison,' said Miss Knight, busily cleaning the blackboard, 'and sit at my desk. I want to see how advanced you are.'

Linda picked up her new pencil box with the draught-board lid and slowly went out to the front of the class.

She climbed on to Miss Knight's chair, slid back the lid of the box a little, and peeped inside. She saw rows of shining pencils of all colours – all sharpened to meticulously fine points by her father.

He had done them the night before while her mother was laying out clean white socks and small black button boots, a new handkerchief with 'L' embroidered in one corner and a green and white gingham frock with French knots, in which it had been decided she should make her first appearance at school.

She was horrified to feel a lump coming in her throat. She began to wonder what her mother was doing on this long, long morning. And as she thought of the familiar routine of the housework, Linda knew for the first time the pain of separation.

'Now, Linda,' said Miss Knight briskly, 'no daydreaming. I want you to write your full name on this label, and then we'll stick it on your pencil box.' And she put a sheet of pink blotting paper and a shiny label with a gummed back on the desk.

'Get out a pencil, Linda,' she said, 'and don't waste any more time.'

She turned back to the class who were beginning to get restive and Linda selected her red pencil with a soft lead. She grasped it firmly and bent over the desk.

'Oh no-no-no-no-no,' said a voice at her elbow and Linda was so frightened that she almost fell off the chair. 'Oh no-no-no-no. We don't hold our pencils in our left hand. We hold our pencils in our right hand, don't we, children?'

'Yes, Miss Knight,' chorused the class, glad of any diversion.

'Here's a little girl who thinks we hold our pencils in our *left* hands,' said Miss Knight, pleased with her success.

The class giggled and Linda blushed but said, 'I always hold things in my left hand; for everything. And I can't write at all with my other hand.'

'Now, Linda,' said Miss Knight. 'We never say "can't" in this class, do we, children?'

'No, Miss Knight,' chanted the class.

'Say that after me, Linda,' said Miss Knight. 'We never say "can't" in this class.'

'We never say "can't" in this class,' said Linda, filled with rage and shame.

'Because it's your first day,' said Miss Knight, 'you may use your left hand. But you must tell your father and mother that they will have to break you of the habit immediately.'

She turned away to the blackboard and Linda, her hopes of doing something to please this terrifying teacher now sadly damped, bent again over the desk.

Breathing hard, her tongue out, legs twisted round the chair rail, slowly and with infinite pains she traced it out: LINDA MARY MORRISON. She remembered everything her father had told her and she did it beautifully.

'Hurry up, Linda,' said Miss Knight, 'haven't you finished yet?'

'Yes,' said Linda.

'Well bring it over here then,' said Miss Knight.

Linda went across the room with the label but as Miss Knight took it from her, a frown creased her face and the little girl's knees began to shake.

'I don't think you're a very truthful little girl,' said Miss Knight.

Linda went very red and then pale.

'When your mother brought you in here this morning,' went on Miss Knight, 'you told me you could write.'

'Yes,' said Linda, lost and bewildered.

'This ...' said Miss Knight, 'is not writing. This is ... what is it, Evie Edwards?'

'Printing,' said Evie, with a self-satisfied smirk.

'Printing,' said Miss Knight. 'Now go and *write* your name and be quick about it.' She crumpled up the label and threw it into the wastepaper basket. 'The LCC,' she said, 'does not provide us with labels for us to waste them.'

But Linda stood rooted to the spot. She knew instinctively that this wasn't her shame only. She realised that she had disgraced her mother and father as well.

Panic sets in

With despair she thought of last night's excitement and of her mother getting her clothes ready. She thought of her father carefully sharpening points on her pencils. She remembered how, only that morning, he had cleared the breakfast things out of the way and once more, slowly and patiently and lovingly, had helped her trace LINDA MARY MORRISON on the back of one of his letters, so that she should surprise them all at school with her lovely printing.

She felt as though *he* had been crumpled up along with the sticky label and flung into the wastepaper basket.

'Come along,' said Miss Knight, 'I can't have little girls who sulk in my class ...'

At last, Linda's brother was fetched from the big boys' department and told to take her home.

'And tell your mother I don't want her back until she's learnt not to be a cry baby,' said Miss Knight. 'I can't have cry babies in my class.'

'Old cat,' said Bill, when they were in the playground. He found the clean new handkerchief, with the 'L' in the corner, in the pocket of Linda's green and white gingham frock, and tried to wipe away his little sister's tears.

But the knife had gone too deep and not even the security of *home* and *mother* and the special dinner in honour of her first day at school could console the little girl. It wasn't until late that evening that the whole story came out, and then they had to promise her that she need never go back to Miss Knight.

Next morning, her mother took her over to the school and left her in the playground while she talked to the headmistress. Linda prayed that Miss Knight wouldn't look out of the window and see her.

The headmistress soon came out and, taking Linda into her warm room with the coal fire, kissed her and gave her a peppermint humbug. Then she took Linda and her mother along to the babies' class where they were playing 'Nuts in May'. Linda saw that the room was bright and sunny and had nice pictures – low down so that you could see them – and no desks at all, only little chairs and tables.

There was a teacher in a green smock who was young and pretty and who took Linda's hand and showed her the vases of flowers on the window ledges, and the bowls that would be planted with bulbs, and the jam jars with tiddlers in them, and the green wire cages with stick insects inside, and the boot boxes full of silk worms.

And then she sat down and took Linda on her knee and said: 'A little bird told me that you do lovely printing. Do you think if I gave you a big sheet of paper you could print LINDA MARY MORRISON for me right across the top?'

A true story

The above is a true story. I have reproduced it in its entirety to convey the feelings of the five-year-old child, separated from her

28

parents with whom she obviously enjoyed a warm relationship, thrown into an unfamiliar environment with more advanced children, one of whom she disliked intensely, and a totally intolerant teacher.

The first day of school, for any infant, is a gateway to the world, and one to which the vast majority of children adapt eventually, if not immediately. But Linda Morrison suffered additional humiliation. She was held up to ridicule because she was left-handed and this was not acceptable to her teacher or the rest of the class. It is interesting to note that she was the only left-hander in that class, so her sense of isolation on that first day of school must have been more acute than the average child's first day experience.

Indeed, we learn that the true story didn't come out until late that evening. What horrors she must have suffered until she could pluck up her courage to tell her parents.

Happily for Linda Morrison, her parents and the headmistress were intelligent enough to transfer her to the class she should have entered in the first place, but not all left-handers are that lucky. For some suffer similar humiliation at the hands of their own parents.

Nowadays, there is less emphasis on changing lefties, which may account for the increase in statistics, but no one has felt it sufficiently important to gather any official data.

The year of our tale was 1915 and the school came under the aegis of London County Council. Linda Mary Morrison is now in her eighties. Her real name is Olive Shapley and she lived in Didsbury, south Manchester for most of her life.

The real Linda Morrison

Olive was a BBC radio producer and presenter for many years, beginning in 1934 when she joined the staff of *Children's Hour* in Manchester. She had read History at the University of Oxford and took an education diploma before moving into broadcasting.

In New York, she produced documentaries and interviewed such luminaries as Eleanor Roosevelt and Paul Robeson. In London, she presented *Woman's Hour*, and had her own radio series called *The Shapley Files*, before moving on to televison.

After her retirement in 1970, she turned her home into a trust for unsupported mothers and babies for fifteen years. Then she opened it up for the Vietnamese refugees – no mean achievements for a left-hander who couldn't do joined-up writing at the age of five!

She wrote the story of Linda Mary Morrison's first day at school for the Swedish Broadcasting Service on 14 September, 1960, forty-five years after the event. She hadn't forgotten the pain of the incident even then.

'My father had to battle for the right for me to write left-handed. He taught me to print with my left hand. I trained myself to use my right hand but I can't write a letter with it,' she said.

She also taught herself to eat with her right hand. 'I was going to London on a train. Someone opposite was eating left-handedly and doing it so clumsily. He kept spilling things and everyone was looking at him, eating with one hand. I thought I was not going to do that,' she said.

Most left-handers eat with the knife and fork held the same way as right-handers – that is the way the table is laid and the way they are taught by right-handers. But give them a spoon or a single fork and they automatically revert to their left hand.

Sometimes hand-eye co-ordination is a problem for left-handers and it can reveal itself when eating. Often, the table settings can impede left-handed movements.

'I was very clumsy and bad at opening things and clumsy with my hands. I have never been good at needlework and sew with my right hand. I played hockey but I was awful at games.

'I taught for a short time, but thought that standing on the left of the board and moving across with my writing was awkward,' she commented.

Teaching left-handed

Chris Moore, a former headteacher from Stockport, Cheshire, and a left-hander, was luckier in that she started school with a left-handed teacher. Like most teachers, she has experienced little difficulty herself, other than a few minor irritations.

But she agrees that left-handers can display poor table manners. 'They can be awkward. You have to learn to eat the correct way. I remember my mother saying, "If you ever go out to dinner with anyone, you would feel very bad if you couldn't eat properly."

'Father always took us for a special meal at Christmas time in

Manchester. He took us out to a restaurant and I remember this woman coming across and saying, "Congratulations".

'I didn't know what she was talking about. "I can tell that your little girl is left-handed and you have my compliments in having taught her how to eat correctly."

'I remember thinking what was so different about that. I didn't think anything about it, didn't realise how much work my mother had put in and it must have been obvious to somebody else who was left-handed.

'She said she always felt ashamed when she went out for a meal with friends that she couldn't use the cutlery in the correct way. At school, I always had to put the left-handed children on the left side of the table, otherwise they nudged people,' said Chris Moore.

'The proportion of left-handers is certainly growing. I never found the teachers a problem but the parents often apologised for their children.'

* * * *

3

SPARE THE ROD

Yes I am left-handed and no – I don't have any problems being so. Esther Rantzen.

If the parents often apologised for their children, some children must have felt that there was an ongoing conspiracy between parents and teachers to confuse and harass them.

Remember that at the tender age of five, a left-handed child doesn't comprehend the urgency parents and teachers feel to change their handedness. What do they know of 'the unclean hand', goats and sheep and Roman augurs?

If some kind of communication could have been embarked upon between parents/teachers and child, it is perhaps possible that many left-handed children could have been prevented from experiencing those subconscious reactions attributable to being singled out for punishments or special tuition, many of which have followed them through life.

'I get very angry about attitudes to left-handedness but then I wasted ten years of my life being made to feel utterly useless and stupid and very miserable. Only to find I was not silly, just left-handed and possibly slightly dyslexic. I now have a degree but still feel I am not as clever as other people because my spelling is odd, and my writing poor,' said one left-hander.

Too often, children are regarded as 'them' or 'they'. Adults know what is best for 'them'. No need to explain the 'whys' and 'wherefores' to the child or even to ask how 'it' feels. 'Children should be seen and not heard,' goes the old maxim, resulting in a nation known for its inability to express itself.

At five years of age, I was the only pupil forced to stay behind after school in an empty classroom where I was urged to write line after line of 'p's, 'b's and 'd's until I had learned to write them the right way round.

In common with dyslexic children, left-handers often reverse their characters. Some also indulge in mirror writing, writing from right to left and producing words back to front. I also have the ability to read fluently upside down which has stood me in good stead during job interviews.

My after-school writing therapy produced the following reaction: I felt isolated from my companions. I couldn't comprehend why I, alone, had been singled out for 'punishment'. No one told me why I had to undergo this humiliation or what was so wrong with the letters I produced naturally. And it was boring.

I felt self-conscious under the hawk-eyed teacher's watchful gaze. Like most five-year-olds, I was becoming an independent little person, wanting to do things my own way, no longer reliant on nappy changes or bottle feeds.

I was strong-willed. Consequently, my handwriting has always been appalling (nobody was going to tell *me* how to write). And I still reverse symbols like ticks and pound signs, which slipped through the net of those watchful hawk-eyes. Only if a child does not stop reversing is there a sign that something may be pathologically wrong.

Disruptive behaviour

I developed a rebellious nature and balked at authority for the rest of my life. There are not many children of six who are hauled up before the headmistress and threatened with expulsion from kindergarten if they do not curb their unruly behaviour.

It is said that there is a high proportion of left-handers among criminals and the psychologically disturbed. I have been unable to substantiate this theory but research has revealed a high percentage of left-handers among maladjusted children.

If some left-handers are disruptive, it may be some form of rebellion relating back to the authority which tried to alter their natural handedness in early life, or to the frustration of trying to cope in a right-handed world.

Nowadays, there is little emphasis on changing lefties, which possibly accounts for their highter visibility – lefties are coming out of the closet. But until ten or twenty years ago, a pretty horrific fate awaited any child who showed signs of picking up a pen with the left hand.

Olive Shapley was not in isolation as a child. The majority of left-handers over fifty who wrote to me had suffered similar indignities, the main offence being the ubiquitous ruler poised over tiny knuckles. Mainly, left hands were tied behind the back and arms were slapped, but some children were caned, relentlessly, and books were tied inside the elbows of others to prevent mobility altogether.

Punishments

One poor child had to wear a red ribbon on her right wrist to remind her it was *wrong* to use the left hand, others were placed at the back of the class, and those who found it difficult to use their right hand were punished for not trying. They simply couldn't win.

A sixty-two-year-old woman wrote that she had suffered in her formative years from 'the jibes and humiliations heaped upon my innocent head by right-handed and assumedly right-minded persons. Actually, my very first tormentor was my highly intelligent teacher who not only declared that left-handedness was unseemly, but positively outrageous.'

The poor child looked around the kindergarten class in amazement, wondering who could be the culprit and, to her horror, discovered it was she, herself.

'I will not have a left-handed child in my class,' proclaimed her teacher, then promptly refused to allow the ashamed child to gather up her belongings and leave.

'I was told to keep my hand in my pocket – or behind me – anywhere that would keep it out of trouble. Within a month I was unable to speak without stuttering and I also took to bed-wetting.'

Fortunately, the child had a left-handed mother who had been 'changed' and who appreciated her daughter's dilemma. She instantly flew to her rescue and 'went up the school' where her 'devastating attack' upon the teachers was likened to a rhinoceros charge.

The teachers cowered before her, although it appears that no

34

blows were exchanged. And it did the trick, for the youngster was never again told to hold pens, pencils, scissors or anything in her right hand.

'However, the memory lingers on and is perhaps the cause of my constantly anxious state,' she wrote.

The comment is an interesting one and one that ought to have been explored in depth by child psychologists of the time. Certainly, similar comments have been made to me by many 'lefties' who attribute their anxiety states or nervous disorders to such infantile experiences.

Speech defects

Stuttering occurs when the speaker gets stuck on the same syllable. Stammering differs in that it appears as a verbal block followed by a sudden rush of words. The speaker knows what he or she wishes to say but the brain does not co-ordinate with the mouth.

Stammering can also be experienced by right-handed children on starting school and can sometimes be attributed to natural nervousness. It often clears up quite quickly when the child settles down to its new surroundings, but if a child is particularly anxious, it can persist, necessitating speech therapy.

For many years, it was thought that if a child was forced to change hands, a stammer developed because of confusion caused to the dominant hemisphere in the changeover. It must be stressed, however, that not all changed left-handers develop a stammer. Educational psychologist Cyril Burt, in *The Backward Child*, noted that, of children who stammered, 6.5 per cent were left-handed and 1.7 per cent right-handed. He also discovered that 11.9 per cent of left-handers had stammered in the past, as opposed to only 3.2 per cent of right-handers. He noted that twice as many mixed-dominant children stammered as those who were left-sided. Stammering among left-handers, 6.1 per cent. Among 'backward' left-handers, however, the ratio was larger – stammering being more than twice as common. (Squinting among left-handers was also high on his observation list.) A significant increase appeared in schools where rigid rules against left-handedness were enforced and where, not surprisingly, even the statistics for right-handed stammerers rose, which seems to indicate a nervous origin. For those of a sensitive disposition, the risk must surely have been greater. Burt described it as 'a symptom of the general impairment of muscular delicacy'.

Stammerers are thought to have less well-defined dominance for language in the left hemisphere. If mixed-dominants have speech in both hemispheres, one can see how the two halves of the brain could be battling it out for domination and that the confusion creates the speech defect.

One changed seven-year-old, who was told he made the class look untidy because he leaned the other way to the rest, soon developed a stammer. Throughout his school life, he found people did not have enough patience to hear him out and his resultant self-consciousness snowballed as he thought people were laughing at him. On receiving speech therapy at St Thomas's Hospital, London, he found singing the words or shouting them relieved the stammer. Subsequently, he became a Lance Corporal, shouted to his heart's content, and gained confidence, whereupon his impediment improved.

Findings on this subject are too vast to consider in depth here. It is generally thought that around ten per cent of children stammer during the lateralisation process, particularly if speech is delayed, usually between the ages of three and five and that boys are more likely to stammer than girls. It can also be familial, with links in families with high incidences of twinning and left-handedness. It also varies in different countries (it seems to be completely absent in China and low in the USA).

Stammering and research

Some researchers refute the connections between changed handedness and speech defects; yet others have linked them directly to lack of lateralisation. Wendell Johnson, a former stammerer who eventually became Professor of speech pathology and psychology at the University of Iowa, believed there was no connection between handedness and stammering. His own childhood experiences led him to try everything from pebbles in the mouth, like Demosthenes, to alternative therapies and chanting 'Have more backbone and less wishbone' while swinging dumb-bells on a therapy course for stammerers. He even tried to become left-handed to fall in line with the generally held view that stammering and sinistrality were linked, to no avail. He was quite relieved to discover that later research proclaimed no links between the two and wrote a book about it.

The most recent study, by Dorothy Bishop at the University of Manchester, looked at handedness, clumsiness and developmental language disorders. It proved little in relation to weak cerebral lateralisation and found no significant differences in left- and mixed-handed children than in the control group used. Bishop concluded that pathological left-handedness was not unusually common in language disorders and that delayed brain maturation, rather than brain injury, was the root cause of such persistent disorders.

Leaving statistics aside and looking at practicalities, if the left-handed child is singled out because he or she is different to others, or is forced into performing in the opposite way to his or her brain's dictates, it is no surprise if a stammer or bed-wetting develops. Whatever the findings of researchers, the evidence clearly shows that these children were not born with stammers and speech defects. These disabilities appeared *after* they were forced to change hands. Some observers believe the nervousness to be the result of the stammer, whereas those afflicted, have actually *experienced* the initial nervousness which precedes the stammer, which then sets up a cycle. Some left-handers, depending on their psychological make-up, will be more prone to emotional disturbance than others, so not *all* will stammer; other children stammer from the time they are able to speak, whether or not they are left-handed, so the two issues should not be confused.

Poor King George VI – a changed left-hander – is the usual specimen trotted out to illustrate the point, but judging from the harsh upbringing and, from all reports, the lack of affection showed to him by his parents, he would probably have developed a stammer had he been born right-handed.

More discrimination

In Scotland, one mother refused to allow the teacher to change her child but '... at the age of eleven years I suffered a great deal of hassle from a teacher – she taught art subjects, which I hated – and she used to hold me to ridicule as I smudged the page.

'It really gave me an inferiority complex and I suffered the punishment of the leather strap on my hand many times. When I put out my right hand she would demand the left one – it's useless anyway, she would say!!'

'... the teachers were relentless. I hated school. Had I been allowed to use my left hand, I think I would have enjoyed school and been a better scholar. So much of my time and effort was spent struggling to use my right hand,' came a heartfelt letter in mirror writing from a 70-year-old woman.

But teachers alone are not to be blamed for these indignities. Some parents also went to extraordinary lengths to prevent their left-handed offspring from following their natural bent, often forcing them to change hands even before the teachers had a chance to go to work.

Some left-handed parents who had suffered themselves at school tried to make sure their children would not go through the same educational traumas by changing them over before they even started school.

And it wasn't always parents who had the say. One left-handed lady was under considerable pressure as a child to use her right hand for writing. 'This was traumatic in that I dreaded certain well-meaning uncles who would make me use my right hand. All figure "2"s were backwards as were "b" and "d" and "z"s to me. The pen and pencil were often taken out of my left hand and placed in the right ...'

'Traumatic' might be a strong way of putting it but it is a word that crops up again and again and parents sometimes had a lot to answer for:

'I had an older sister who was left-handed, but as a child I remember the trauma of our Dad when she attempted to use the left hand. This "trait" was literally knocked out of her and some sixty years on, I have a very neurotic sister. It was as if she had the plague ...'

'... let's hope parents these days accept this "fault". It was literally knocked out of my sister – she achieved "right-handedness" at what price? She is and has been very mixed-up and when she left school she went to London to an aunt – rarely coming home after that. Her one achievement – she became a lovely pianist. (No opposition regarding which hand?)'

One woman attended nine primary schools and in nearly all was reprimanded for being left-handed, suffering a variety of indignities. She was relieved to find, on becoming a college lecturer in later life, that left-handed students were on the increase each year. 'It seemed obvious to me that teachers (and parents?) are not nearly as concerned about this as they were when I was a school pupil, and I'm relieved to note this.'

Maybe not, but by 1935 things hadn't changed all that much for they were still tying left hands behind backs at a school in Bath, Avon, and one woman, now in her early thirties, complained of a feeling of 'failure and uselessness' as the result of being changed.

In 1948 a left-hander then aged eight, came under the jurisdiction of a teacher who 'seemed convinced she had some divine message condemning left-handedness as something akin to witchcraft.

'For the next year, until I moved on to someone more enlightened, I learned nothing and was terrified of going to school.'

Over the years, she has never forgotten her tormentor and still sees her quite clearly, judging from the graphic description she gives. 'The flat chest in the tight hand-knitted jumpers, the eucalyptus soaked hankie, the long bony fingers and the jade ring always ready to strike at the forbidden left hand.'

One 72-year-old 'leftie', changed in childhood by her granny and by her teacher when she was seven years old, sought an assurance from the headmaster when her second son started school that 'history would not repeat itself in the same sinister(!) way that it affected me. He assured me that this would not be the case, as pressure was no longer exerted on left-handed pupils.'

Educational attitudes

In general terms this is probably true. Enlightenment brought with it the theory that left-handers should be left to their own devices and the abolition of corporal punishment.

So what are the education authorities doing to help left-handers regain acceptance into society and throw off the mantle of 'anti-social perversion', as one infant teacher put it? In most cases, nothing at all for most educationalists claim that left-handed children have no problems.

Those who do recognise the problems take pains to seat left-handers on the left of double desks so there will be no nudging of elbows, to provide left-handed scissors, to advise on correct postures and pencil holds for writing and drawing.

Guides on how to teach left-handed children to write correctly are freely available, but most education authorities do not provide them. This is left to the conscience of individual teachers who may, or may not, feel strongly that their left-handed pupils need a helping hand. Certainly no provision is made at teacher training colleges on how to counsel left-handed children.

The very fact that no statistics have been gathered on left-handed people by any official body indicates that their importance is considered negligible. Few of the educational organisations I contacted were able to provide any information on left-handed children, and many did not even bother to acknowledge my enquiries.

The UK Department of Education and Science frankly admits that it has no information or statistics on left-handed children, while its Assessment of Performance Unit does not include left-handedness as a variable. It does admit, however, that left-handedness is an important dimension of learning and possible learning difficulties.

Statistics for children with other special educational needs are freely available and amounted to 138,067 in 1988.

Maladjusted children

Maladjusted children are provided for under the 1981 Education Act. As many as one in six are left-handed, according to Alan Rimmer who runs a school for disturbed boys. As a remedial teacher, one of his main tasks has been to teach left-handers.

Kellmer Pringle, in a study on the incidence of some supposedly adverse family conditions and of left-handedness in schools for maladjusted children carried out at the Department of Child Study, University of Birmingham, investigated left-handedness as one of six adverse conditions thought to be associated with 'broken homes'. She found twice as many left-handers among the maladjusted children as should have been expected, in proportion to the incidence of left-handedness within the child population.

The main four adverse conditions studied were divorced parents,

40

the presence of a step-parent, the death of one parent and illegitimacy which affected around 60 per cent of the sample tested. Left-handedness and adoption were two extra issues.

The question arises whether left-handed children subjected to emotional stress react less well than right-handed children in a similar environment, or whether their left-handedness has been highlighted or held to ridicule in an already stressful environment.

Various teachers working with maladjusted children have observed high incidences of left-handedness in their ranks, in one school as high as 75 per cent, and noted their problems as behavioural rather than educational.

R.S. Illingsworth claimed that 12 per cent of children in special schools were left-handed compared to 5 per cent in ordinary schools. Today, special needs teachers report around 30 per cent of left-handed pupils, but education authorities do not accept it as an issue. At the Institute of Education, University of London, Audrey Curtis, UK National President (OMEP), and a left-hander to boot, informed me that, based on her experiences as a senior academic at the Institute, she had never encountered any difficulties personally.

As a former school teacher, she claimed that few children, in her own experience, had learning problems specifically as a result of using the left hand. She attributed this to the more relaxed approach now adopted by schools.

'... to most educationalists it is not considered as a cause for learning difficulties,' she added.

One researcher, working in conjunction with the University of Loughborough and looking into the teaching of left-handed children in the secondary age range in Craft Design and Technology and Special Needs, complained to me about the lack of knowledge among advisers in CDT and Special Needs, the difficulties encountered in researching and also about the equipment available.

Incidence of left-handedness

In 1860, people who wrote left-handed were said to represent only 2 per cent of the population. In 1957, they were put at around 7 per cent. In *The Right Brain*, Blakeslee claims the figure has been 10 per cent since the Stone Age but that their incidence has been suppressed. In *The Ambidextrous Universe*, Gardner, in 1967 reported 25 per cent, many of whom, he admitted, had been changed to right-handers.

The *Daily Telegraph* in 1988 gave the figures as 13 per cent for Italy, 10 per cent for Europe and 13 per cent for America. *The Ace Bulletin* reports 13 per cent boys and 10 per cent girls. Mensa left-handers account for 20 per cent of their membership.

But recent American surveys claim that left-handers constitute from 15 to 20 per cent of the population.

There is no doubt that left-handers are increasing and that far from experiencing no particular educational problems, there will always be those who find that adapting to a right-handed world, represents a stress which they are ill-equipped emotionally and psychologically to handle. Others will not

But those who do need to be helped, not ignored. A lot will depend on the sympathy of teachers but more will depend on how prepared teachers are to cope with this bizarre educational problem. Claiming that the situation does not exist simply because one has never experienced it oneself is inexcusable.

Teacher Janet Withersby has a particular interest in cross laterality. A right-hander, she herself has a dominant left eye and she understands the anomalies. She has more cross laterals in her class than pure left-handers.

'It is a problem. Some children have linguistic articulation difficulties, movement difficulties and reversal. Some left-handers are non-starters and they really don't develop for a long time.

'I see those with particular abilities now who really lagged behind in the thirds. Numeracy is a problem but their spatial awareness is amazing. They are good on shape and direction but not numeracy.'

Because she studied the problems of left-handed pupils, she became increasingly aware of the function of the two halves of the brain and the different roles they play. It is this that education authorities should be looking at and not whether or not a child writes with its left hand.

These investigations could throw light on learning difficulties experienced by right-handers also. First, the reasons for a child's hand preference need to be officially defined. Second, the significant role played by hemispherical dominance in a child's behavioural pattern needs to be studied so that solutions can be reached which can contribute towards ameliorating the educational system for the benefit of children with learning or behavioural problems.

Need for investigation

Innumerable tests have been made by psychologists over the years. Many of them have disagreed with one another. The relationship between laterality and educational abilities has been studied, including the testing of ears, eyes, hands and feet. Reading and writing have been covered. At least eighteen tests for eye dominance exist but to what effect?

The educational problems remain, because the main study has been overlooked. Anxious parents are far more interested to know what measures the education authorities are prepared to take, beginning at teacher training level, to help their left-handed children overcome their difficulties.

One of Janet's pupils had particular problems with writing. 'His brain dominance was wrong for writing. It is a special need but no education authority would classify these children as "special need",' she said.

Today all special need children are entitled to special educational backing. In a mainstream school they have to produce a statement outlining their special needs and the recommended provision to accommodate them. The statement outlines the problem and suggests a solution. It is then supposed to be signed by the education authority and the parents. But the education authorities are unable to sign many of these statements because they cannot afford to meet the needs, consequently statements are said to be piling up in education offices around the country.

'Left-handers don't stand a chance. Their problems are so much less acute than other children's. It is something we need to be aware of from the start. Left-handed children lay a different emphasis in their early years and it really does need airing,' said Janet.

'No question is put by the teachers to the school psychiatrists more frequently than "How should I deal with a left-handed pupil?" ' (Burt, 1958). In 1970, the British Births Cohort study revealed that at least 1 in 50 of all ten-year-old children could be described as dyslexic, with normal cognitive ability but difficulty in sequencing, poor writing and frequently left- or mixed-handedness.

Thirty per cent of ten-year-olds used their left and right hand inconsistently and were poorer than average at maths as well as reading. So how do we fare today?

Modern attitudes

The mother of a five-year-old, left-handed, Birmingham girl wrote to tell me about the day she collected her daughter from a playgroup she attended two mornings a week when she was three years old.

'She seemed rather upset about something. I asked the person in charge of the playgroup if Sophie had been all right because of her seeming upset. This is the reply I got: "Well, we have been trying to get her to use her right hand in painting and drawing activities because she is caggy-handed".

'I must admit I was furious and didn't realise until then that something like that could upset Sophie so much. I was then told that people who were left-handed weren't supposed to be all there, a bit thick, rather dense.

'Needless to say I never took Sophie back to the playgroup again. After that I started to take more notice of the way she drew pictures, the way she held a paintbrush and even the way she held her knife and fork, where it had never bothered me or Sophie before.

'And yet now it really seemed to be playing on my mind. My eldest daughter Meena is right-handed and she did seem to pick things up a lot faster than Sophie and I started to wonder whether what the playgroup leader had said was right. And yet Sophie was so bright, cheerful and happy.

'When Meena started nursery at three, she could write her own name, tie her shoe-laces, etc. and yet I sat for hours and hours with Sophie trying to teach her the same but she just didn't seem to be able to pick it up as well as Meena had done.

'I did get her to start to write her name one day but she wrote it backwards and wrote it down the page rather than across it ... then came the day for her to start nursery. I can remember going to the open afternoon, to show Sophie her classroom and to meet her new teacher, Miss Smith.

'I mentioned to her that Sophie was left-handed at which she looked at me puzzled as to why I should have mentioned it at all. I did not tell her about what the playgroup leader had said to me and thought I would just see how Sophie got on first at the nursery.

'Well one day, not long after, Sophie came out of nursery with a beautiful picture of some faces and flowers and in the top left-hand corner was her name, "Sophie". "Look Mummy," she said, so proud of what she had done, "and I done my own name," she said.

'Well, I could have cried. I went to see Sophie's teacher and then decided to explain to her what had been said to me some several months before and how I had been very anxious over those words from the playgroup leader.

'Sophie's teacher said to me: "There is no doubt that Sophie is definitely left-handed and there is no way that we would force her to use her right hand in any way. She is getting on marvellously," and she told me to stop worrying.

'Sophie soon began to learn to tie her shoe-laces and do everything that Meena had been doing at that age. The teacher even supplied her with a pair of left-handed scissors, which is something that I didn't even think about or know you could get.

'I came to the conclusion that she was just a bit slower than Meena had been at picking things up and that her being left-handed had got nothing to do with it whatsoever.

'Sophie is now in the second year of the infants. At school, and on parents evenings, I get glowing reports. In fact, she does just as well, if not better, than someone who is right-handed.

'I apologise if I have gone on and on but I would just like other mums and dads to know that if their child turns out to be left-handed, so what. Let them get on with it. Their child is just as bright as the next.'

So much depends on the attitudes of the teachers but it would appear that some – and this is by no means an isolated tale – have not progressed since 1915 when Olive Shapley was a child.

If I labour the point it is because we must not forget. Right-handers are generally unaware of the problems experienced by their left-handed counterparts and such stories may come as a surprise to them. And it must not be overlooked that the stigma continues into the 1980s, albeit in a diluted form.

Despite all the protestations, those who did learn to use their right hand without any psychological side effects were at an advantage in life in that they had developed the ability to use both hands, which would stand them in good stead in a right-handed world. But at what cost?

* * * *

4
THE RIGHT BRAIN

My left-handedness has only caused occasional aggro to others, never myself!! ... in cricket I bowl left-handed and bat right-handed!! The only plea I would make is for left-handed cheque books. Filling in those bunched up stubs is a real bind! Leslie Crowther.

Before determining what can be done to help ease a left-handed child into a relaxed educational environment, we need to ask ourselves what is so different about the left-hander? It is usual to assume that they just do things the opposite way round to right-handers. We don't know exactly why, because no one takes the trouble to explain it to us.

We take left-handers, therefore, for granted. They exist, it may be a bit inconvenient for them sometimes; they certainly look awkward and clumsy when they write but that's tough. This is a right-handed world and they just have to get on with it.

The popular theory, if left-handedness is thought about at all, is that it runs in families and has something to do with more brain development on the opposite side. Most people are unsure which side dominates which hand anyway. Side preference – eyes, feet, ears – is rarely given much consideration, probably because the hand is the feature most open to observation.

But handedness cannot be considered in isolation. For taken all together, co-ordination of hand, foot, ear and eye represent a totality that will undoubtedly place a person at a singular disadvantage if any of these faculties become mixed up and cross over.

Cross-laterality

It is generally acknowledged that it is the mixed laterals who have the worst problems in a right-handed world.

Sometimes referred to as cross-laterals, they carry out some tasks with one hand and some with the other. They may kick a ball with the left foot, throw with the right hand and have a right dominant eye. There are a variety of combinations.

Right of the road

This can be useful in certain right-world situations, such as driving a car — here, right-handers like to score over left-handers by pointing out politely that the gears are on the left so we shouldn't complain, and in Great Britain, at least, we drive on the left-hand side of the road.

They don't add that the controls and the ignition are on the right, that the doors all open the wrong way, that seat belts have to be pulled over from the right by contortive means, and that the foot controls are designed for right-handers.

Many left-handers, including myself, complain that they suffered total confusion on learning to drive because they kept putting their left foot across onto the brake or the accelerator. Only the instructor's dual controls saved them from crashing the car.

But the wing mirror is the most dangerous of all. For years, I suffered near misses pulling out to overtake at the same time as cars overtaking me appeared from nowhere. I ought to have been able to see an overtaking vehicle in the wing mirror.

It was only when researching this book that I discovered why I can't. I am left-eyed and when I glance into the right wing mirror, I am unable to get a complete picture with my right eye.

It is only when I incline my head so that I can use my dominant left eye, too, that I actually can see a car pulling out to overtake. This constitutes an additional danger as my attention is removed from the road. Had I been right-eye dominant, there would be no such problem.

The stress factor

Dr Stanley Coren attributes the main cause of death for left-handers under 55 to accidents, particularly while driving. He claims they are likely to suffer 89 per cent more serious accidents than right-handers and are 85 per cent more likely to have car crashes related to gearshifts and traffic patterns.

Although more left-handed women appear to have driving licences than right-handed ones, it is the left-handed men who are most at risk: 'A left-handed male is 135 per cent more likely to have an accident than a right-handed male when they're driving a car,' he said. This he attributed to their tendency to raise the right hand and lower the left if startled, which could make them swerve into oncoming traffic. As his studies were carried out in Canada, we must assume that in countries where driving on the left is the norm, left-handed drivers are more likely to drive onto the pavement or crash into pedestrians.

Ian McKinlay and Neil Gordon, consultant paediatric neurologists from Manchester, state, in their *Helping Clumsy Children*, that cross-laterals have the greater learning disorders, although, they add, this occurs only with a minority of children.

They define cross-laterals as people who have taken longer than normal to show hand preference and who, they claim, are the victims of 'forced left-handedness'. In other words, cross-laterals are really right-handers who, due to possible left hemisphere cerebral damage before or at birth, have gone through a reorganisation of brain functioning so that some of the roles which would normally be carried out by the left hemisphere have been taken over by the right.

Hereditary left-handers are dismissed summarily as having merely bothersome problems like needing left-handed scissors. Those of us who are left-handed and who have experienced problems of reversal, reading and writing difficulties, and discalculia (learning disability in maths), quite apart from the problems posed by right-handed utensils and equipment, are not so dismissive.

One of the biggest problems through decades of handedness research has been that well-meaning, right-handed researchers do not fully comprehend the workings of a left-hander's mind.

Left-handed people in this human guinea pig situation find themselves in a parent-child relationship. The person being tested will try so hard to please and to come up with 'right' answers, that they do not always carry out the tasks set naturally or accurately. Apart from that, the sample groups tested are not always large enough to be representative of the true life situation.

Furthermore, some of these tests have been conducted on such obscure aspects of handedness that one wonders why so much time and money has been expended on them. They generally result in the publication of learned scientific papers which seem to have no further application.

Subsequent investigations then set out to disprove the previous research and new theories are expounded which remain in equal obscurity, until a new wave of psychological thinkers challenges them.

Meanwhile the unfortunate plight of left-handers seems neither to benefit nor change over the decades of research. And, unfortunately for some, the statistics and theories of many of these pontiffs do not seem to correspond with the practical findings of parents, teachers and children in the real world.

The problems of cross-laterality are too complex to explore here. We must find out first what, if any, differences there are between left- and right-handers. Do they simply do things the opposite way round or is it more complex than that?

It is generally assumed that the two sides of the brain are mirror images of one another; that if one side is more developed than the other, it determines handedness; and that's the whole story.

How the brain works

Nothing could be further from the truth. The brain is a complex and brilliant computer. Its two sides carry out entirely different functions but work in conjunction with one another to represent a whole person. Only about one-tenth of the brain's potential is utilised. What would be interesting to know is which tenth left-handers use, and which tenth the right-handers use.

In the 1930s, the eminent physiologist, Ivan P. Pavlov, who is renowned for causing dogs to salivate at the sound of a bell, claimed that people are *either* artists *or* thinkers. Decades later, brain experiments conducted to research epilepsy reveal that Pavlov's theories may not be unfounded.

If everyone used the identical facilities that the brain offers to the same extent, everyone would think alike, would have the same abilities and level of abilities, the same awareness, and habits. There might even be peace on earth, but probably we would bore one another to death. And we might behave like robots or clones. What makes the human race so interesting is the fact that we are all individuals.

Marcel Kinsbourne, in his foreword to *Helping Clumsy Children*, points out that medical practice takes more notice now of individual differences which can hamper performance and ability and impede success in society. Unfortunately, these considerations are not sufficiently widespread yet to be of sufficient benefit.

To gain an understanding of why left and right-handers are not just carrying out functions in reverse but are functioning, thinking, feeling and working out problems differently, we need to know something about the brain and how it works. Only then can we appreciate why left-handers are disadvantaged in a world designed for right-handed people.

I am neither able nor qualified to outline scientifically the complex functioning of the human brain, but I am able to simplify the issue somewhat, to further this discussion of left-handedness.

Brain halves, or cerebral hemispheres, look identical, and, to put it crudely, the overall structure resembles a walnut. The hemispheres are joined together at the base by a bundle of over 200 million nerve fibres, called the corpus callosum, and these nerve fibres pass messages to the hemispheres. Although they look identical, they carry out different functions, passing some messages to the right hemisphere and some to the left.

The familiar curves and furrows that pinpoint our brain lobes control specific functions, such as language, memory, knowledge, decision-making, sensory input, and motor responses.

The left hemisphere, dominant in right-handedness, controls speech, writing and abstract thinking, while the right hemisphere, dominant in left-handedness, controls non-verbal memory, emotions and concrete thinking.

Because different functions are controlled by each hemisphere, individual personality and modes of perception will differ, depending on which hemisphere is more developed. And right or left dominance, as we now know through studies undertaken with stroke and accident victims who have changed 'sides', can be either inherited or developed.

If, then, we all consciously developed our weaker hemispheres so that their propensities equalled our dominant hemispheres would we form a superior race?

Leonardo da Vinci

The most outstanding example of someone who is thought to have been a dual-brain genius is Leonardo da Vinci (1452–1519). Michael Barsley in his *Left-Handed Book* referred to him as the Patron Saint of the Sinistrals and it is generally accepted that da Vinci was left-handed. Nevertheless, some authorities have suggested that he was ambidextrous originally, but that later on he began to use his left hand following an injury to his right.

Barsley acknowledges that five hundred years after Leonardo's birth, Norman Capener, FRCS, emphasised, in a letter to the *Lancet*, that Leonardo does not appear to have been clearly right-hemisphere dominant, from a neurological viewpoint. And that a mirror drawing, assumed to be the artist's left hand, reveals a middle finger deformity on what may in fact be the reflection of his right hand.

Certainly no mention is made of Leonardo's outstanding abilities early on in his career. If Capener's theory is correct it would in turn back up the theory that hemispherical development can be achieved.

It is in his later years that Leonardo seems to have acquired his multiplicity of talents, and to have become painter, sculptor, architect, engineer, stage designer, musician, writer, student of physical sciences, mathematician, geologist, anatomist and natural historian.

In his various forms of expression, Leonardo emerges as a scientist-cum-artist, rather than as scientist versus artist. Fact and intuition, concrete and abstract thought, logic and emotion fuse together, generating a legacy of what seems to be whole brain co-ordination.

It is an aspect of the artist that is open to exploration. The late art historian, Lord Kenneth Clark, published *Leonardo da Vinci* in 1939, an acknowledged classic work, which he subsequently revised and reprinted. But even Clark admitted that pieces of the puzzle are difficult to put together. He wrote that: 'In particular, very little effort has been made to gauge how far Leonardo's knowledge increased and scientific method improved as his life went on. Some idea of Leonardo as a mind developing by contact with other minds is necessary if we are to form a true picture of him, and compare his scientific activity with his development as an artist.'

Elsewhere he records: 'There is no doubt that the nerves of his eye and brain, like those of certain famous athletes, were really supernormal, and in consequence he was able to draw and describe movements of a bird which were not seen again until the invention of the slow-motion cinema.'

Dualistic nature

On a personal level, Clark credits the artist with a two-sided nature that linked up virility and effeminacy, for the artist was a known homosexual. This dualism seems significant in the light of Leonardo's supposed co-ordination.

Sigmund Freud, in his book, *Leonardo da Vinci – A Memory of His Childhood*, a study of Leonardo's youth and the supposed connection between his genius and his sexual leanings, also notes the duality of the man. On the one hand, Leonardo was quiet and gentle, refusing to eat meat on the grounds of animal cruelty, freeing caged birds in the marketplace, opposing war, describing man as 'the worst of the wild beasts'.

On the other hand he followed condemned criminals to the execution block, studying and sketching their distorted features, designed advanced offensive weaponry, and became chief military engineer to Cesare Borgia, whom he accompanied uncritically on campaigns.

Leonardo made assiduous investigations into the scientific background of natural phenomena so that the workings of the cosmos are reflected in his art forms.

In his later book, *Landscape Into Art*, published in 1949, Clark wrote that 'Leonardo's scientific knowledge of nature, and his even more extraordinary intuitions as to the hidden potentialities of matter, have enabled him to pass into a different world from the old Mediaeval apocalypse with its confused oriental symbolism; and to arrive at a vision of destruction in which symbol and reality seem to be at one.'

Much of Leonardo's acquired knowledge was recorded in notes and illustrations, rather than in works of art. He finished little of what he began, for his obsession with science gradually overwhelmed him. Perhaps his left brain won.

Scientist v artist

In Leonardo, the analytical scientist combined with the intuitive artist, the left brain with the right. At all times he wanted to know why things worked in addition to how. He was assiduous in his pursuit of the kind of knowledge that might explain the workings of the universe to him, and his vast storehouse of knowledge grew out of his natural curiosity. He was basically self-educated, having received only the limited training of a poor Florentine apprentice, albeit in the studio of the famous sculptor and artist, Andrea del Verrocchio (1435–88).

He read widely and taught himself Latin at the age of forty-two in order to pursue insights set down in the writings and philosophy of the Ancients, gradually developing his brain beyond its natural propensity and using it to the full.

In 1989, the Hayward Gallery in London, on the South Bank, mounted a magnificent Leonardo da Vinci exhibition wherein fifteenth-century designs and doodles combined with twentieth-century technology to realise some of his visions.

A new generation was treated to a display of specially constructed models based on his drawings for engineering, military and architectural projects. The models included da Vinci's famous and magnificent pedal-operated flying machine, with its thirty-six foot wingspan, computer graphics analysing his perspectives and symmetry, and a priceless collection of six hundred of his drawings housed in the Royal Library at Windsor Castle.

Da Vinci's amazing Notebooks, which have been parcelled out to a number of museums, contain a wealth of observation, written in minute left-handed mirror writing from right to left of the page in reversed letters, and dozens of doodles of identifiable objects, which only surfaced as viable projects many centuries later, including ball-bearings, aeroplanes, bicycles, tanks and advanced military weapons.

The Notebooks date back to da Vinci's early years in Milan in

1482 when, at the age of thirty, he worked as sculptor, painter, engineer and designer of pageants to the Sforza court. Sir Cyril Burt claims in *The Backward Child* (1957), that the artist did not write backwards until the age of twenty.

Mirror writing

The reasons for Leonardo's mirror-writing obsession have never been satisfactorily explained, but everything from secretiveness to deliberate mystification have been propounded. The widely held view that he wished his heretical writing to be hidden from the Church does not preclude the possibility that the clergy were able to read backwards or see through mirrors.

Clark dismisses this view too and points out that the Church made allowances for even more heretical ideas than da Vinci's at that time, and that his scientific researches were conducted with the approval of the Church. Even his dissections were permitted and carried out in the ecclesiastical hospitals of Florence.

But Clark's theory that da Vinci's mirror writing stems directly from left-handedness is too simple. Had he been left-handed in his youth, the habit would surely have been corrected. Some of his manuscripts moreover are written normally, from left to right.

Mirror writing can occur in certain mental states, including abstraction or daydreaming; or during a changeover from one hand to the other. Either circumstance could have been applied to da Vinci, if the theory of a damaged right hand is upheld, and in fact Cardinal Louis of Aragon observes that by October 1517 when da Vinci was in his sixties, he had a paralysed right hand. Here again, mirror writing can be symptomatic of several disorders, among them hemiplegia, or paralysis of one side of the body.

It is interesting to note that most children who reverse letters eventually do learn to adapt to the socially accepted norm. Those who are unable to convert, because they cannot distinguish the difference between left- and right-formed letters, are usually mentally defective.

Doubtless Leonardo had his own reasons for maintaining his eccentricity, but thin lines have often been drawn between genius and lunacy. Clark describes him as 'abnormal'. According to Sir E. H. Gombrich, in *The Story of Art*, his contemporaries thought him strange and uncanny.

An example of mirror writing

My own view, based on the evidence, is that it was his private shorthand. It was easy enough for him, became a habit, and gave him a measure of privacy. No one who keeps a diary likes to feel that the personal outpourings therein may be read or scoffed at by others. A lot of da Vinci's observations were revolutionary and he may well have felt that his haven of jottings wherein he immersed his thoughts was not for the eyes of other men.

Researchers have observed that right-handers who change to their left tend to mirror write more easily than write from left to right, indicative that the dominant hemisphere is still trying to maintain control.

Jack Fincher, in *Lefties*, points out that the famous American laywer Louis Nizer, a right-hander, continually doodles faces of the jurors with his left hand while listening to testimony in court. This, he claims, gives him a deeper insight into their characters and personalities.

And Californian art teacher, Ann O'Hanlon, tried the experiment of making her class of nuns, whose artwork was proving too rigid for her taste, switch to their left hands. This apparently did the trick, relaxing them and producing more imaginative work. It is a technique she continues to pursue in emulation of the Renaissance masters who encouraged their pupils to use both hands, including almost certainly Leonardo's teacher, Verrocchio.

In 1928, Dmitry Sergeyevich Merezhkovsky published a historical novel on the artist's 'secret' life, entitled *The Romance of Leonardo da Vinci*. In it he portrayed da Vinci as one who had awakened too early, alone in the darkness while others still slept. And he claimed that da Vinci drew with his left hand and painted with his right hand.

Drawing left-handed

Certainly, the artist's cross-hatching was done with the left hand, moving from left to right on the page. Left-handers draw faces in right profile while right-handers draw them in left profile, and many of da Vinci's works are right profile depictions: for example, the *Portrait of Isabella d'Este* (1500) and *Madonna and Child with a Yarn Winder* (1501), but this is not true of all his work. One has only to look at his studies of figures digging, carrying, etc. (c. 1503) to note that he was equally competent drawing either left- or right-orientated subjects.

Barsley points out that in at least two drawings for the *Mona Lisa*, her left hand was positioned over her right — a natural pose for a left-hander — but that this was altered in the final painting. He suggests that the artist thought it would look odd and therefore changed the positioning.

If we are to indulge Merezhkovsky's hypothesis da Vinci's right hand took over the final painting after his left-hand drawings, or even more controversially, the final painting could have been painted by one of da Vinci's right-handed students.

A recent controversy, in the national press, hypothesised about whether or not the work is a self-portrait and a mirror image — all of which merely veils the enigmatic subject more mysteriously. Freud certainly saw evidence of Leonardo's narcissism in *La Gioconda*'s mysterious smile — traces of this same smile are perceptible in several of his other portraits.

Sinistral or dextral, the fact remains that this extraordinary man, in his ongoing search for knowledge and truth, employed regions of his brain that would normally have been left undeveloped and which remain so to most of us throughout our lives.

The split brain

Our split brain makes us unique in the animal kingdom. The symmetrical brains of animals carry out identical functions, but the human brain's halves are home to different functions.

Biased research and thinking (on the part of presumably right-handed scientists) in the past had attributed higher intellectual functioning to the left hemisphere. It was, therefore, always known as the major hemisphere, while the right hemisphere received only minor credit.

It wasn't until the early 1950s that each hemisphere received valid analysis when an American neurologist, Dr Roger Sperry, and a team of researchers from the University of Chicago and the California Institute of Technology working on a treatment for epileptic patients, proved that the human brain functions asymmetrically.

Advances in brain surgery enabled neurosurgeons to observe individual workings of the two hemispheres by a process of freezing one half of the brain or by administering mild electric shocks during surgery, enabling the patients under local anaesthetic to describe the resultant effects. In another operation the nerve fibres that link the hemispheres were cut to halt the spread of disease from one hemisphere to the other (commisurotomy). The hemispheres were able to function independently of one another, sometimes competing for dominance. Patients opened a door with one hand and closed it with the other due to lack of communication between the brain halves. These advances, however, only enabled surgeons to monitor a patient's reaction when one hemisphere was 'frozen'. Russian neurophysiologist, Vadim Lvovich Deglin, researched this area extensively at the I.M. Sechenov Insititute of Evolutionary Physiology and Biochemistry of the USSR Academy of Sciences in Leningrad. During the 1960s and 1970s, the brain was observed during electro-shock treatment, as part of a treatment programme for mental illnesses.

Delivering a paper at an international meeting of experts, organised by UNESCO in Varna, Bulgaria in 1975, he described how one hemisphere can be paralysed by electro-shock treatment while the other hemisphere remains active.

By administering shock first to one hemisphere and then to the other, it is possible to observe the same individual's reactions as each hemisphere is immobilised in turn and to compare these reactions with normal behaviour.

The left hemisphere

When only the left hemisphere remained active, patients became more talkative and articulate, responding to speech sounds easily, but they spoke in monotones and their perception of tone was impaired. They did not, for example, recognise the extent of vocal emotional changes, (i.e. anger, concern), differentiate between male and female voices, or recognise tunes.

In visual tests, they could not select pairs of identical geometrical figures or pinpoint missing details in diagrams of familiar objects. Memory of verbal, but not visual material, was considerably improved. They knew where they were and the date but were unable to recognise specific hospital areas and seasons. Emotionally, they became happier and more optimistic. In other words, their abstract, conceptual thinking improved, while their imaginal thinking deteriorated.

When the right hemisphere was active, patients seemed reluctant to speak and their vocabulary was considerably reduced. While they could recognise familiar objects they could not remember names. In brief, verbal memory was impaired, visual memory was improved. Emotionally, a negative outlook developed.

All the opposite characteristics of 'left hemisphere' dominance were revealed. Namely there was a falling off of verbal perception and abstract, conceptual thought and an improvement of imaginal perception.

From this, researchers deduced that the left hemisphere governs logical, abstract thought, while the right hemisphere governs concrete, imaginal thought, and each hemisphere contains its own speech, memory and emotional tone.

Although the left hemisphere has always been associated with speech functions, it is obvious that there is more to speech than just a verbal concept. Intonation and vocal characteristics are equally important contributory elements.

Deglin theorised that the characteristics of speech, memory and emotions displayed by the right hemisphere are more 'ancient' than those displayed by the left verbal hemisphere, mainly because speech and abstract thought developed late in mankind's evolution. He suggests that these functions began simultaneously with the use of the right hand in work activities – dominated by the left hemisphere – and that the left hemisphere's natural imaginal functions were accordingly suppressed to allow verbal communication.

The right hemisphere

The right hemisphere then evolved further, fine-tuning its functions so that two individual brains fully emerged. Deglin theorises further that babies may be born with two right hemispheres. He bases this on the fact that they do not acquire the power of speech initially. Since the right hemisphere dominates the left hand, what finally determines hand preference – heredity or environmental factors? Nature versus nurture?

Pavlov's theoretical artists and thinkers can now be realised. Right-hemisphere dominant people are the imaginative artists while left-hemisphere dominant people are the abstract thinkers. But, although one hemisphere may be more powerful, both hemispheres must work together to produce a total concept and to strike a balance.

In my preface, I hypothesised that if one sensory organ was inactivated, the remaining senses might increase their efficacy. By studying individual hemispheres in isolation it is clear that a hemisphere working independently does improve its abilities, indicating that an inhibitory factor is at work when the sides function together. This is possibly to keep either side from becoming too powerful.

Further advances in human brain surgery over the past few decades have enabled surgeons to remove a complete hemisphere (hemispherectomy). The results have proved that the remaining hemisphere can carry on all brain functions and, eventually, work perfectly well alone.

Stan Gooch, formerly senior research psychologist at the National Children's Bureau, describes a hemispherectomy, in his book *The Double Helix of the Mind* (1980), which was conducted on a right-handed 47-year-old male patient by Aaron Smith of the Nebraska College of Medicine.

After attacks of speechlessness and seizures in his right arm and on the right side of his face, the patient was given a full left hemispherectomy. For ten weeks after the operation, he was unable to converse or comprehend speech. Then he began to repeat single words and to answer questions. Five months later, he suddenly recalled old, familiar tunes and a month later, he started forming sentences.

The first hemispherectomy, in 1928, was performed on the right side but surgeons then started to take such drastic action on the 'major' left hemisphere. In 1966 a man from Omaha who undertook this surgery, regained his speech immediately (albeit only curses for a while) and later his mobility. Since then many such operations have been performed successfully on adults and children.

Gooch insists emphatically that no actual transfer of function from one hemisphere to another takes place. He states that both hemispheres always contain both sets of functions. His belief is that some kind of liberating process takes place, enabling the remaining hemisphere to spring fully into operation.

Speech and handedness

Speech is not a natural phenomenon but an invention of mankind. Deglin's theory of brain evolution implies that the left hemisphere develops an ability to cope with human speech and abstract thinking.

If we accept this theory, that babies are born with symmetrical hemispheres capable of carrying out the same functions, then handedness is something that develops along with speech, as one hemisphere gains dominance over another. Can it be that the creation of speech itself has created a preponderance of right-handed people, who are dominated by their left hemispheres?

To add further confusion, about 70 per cent of left-handers have speech in their left hemisphere, while some have speech in both hemispheres.

Doreen Kimura conducted extensive research at the University of Western Ontario, Canada, in the early 1970s on free and self-touching movements of hands in relation to speech and cerebral dominance.

She found that speech and handedness were connected and that the hand used most by people to express themselves while speaking corresponded to the hemisphere which controlled their speech.

Left-handers, although gesturing mainly with their left hands, were found to use their right hands as well, whereas right-handers only used their right hands, indicating that the speech of left-handers is more bilaterally organised.

Gooch's theory, however, does not explain why right-handed left hemispherectomy patients eventually begin to write with their left hands, and vice versa. If the remaining hemisphere contains all the propensities of both brains, why don't they remain right-handed or become ambidextrous?

It has been conjectured that one hemisphere is a spare, ready to take over in case the other becomes damaged. Dr Julian Jaynes, an American psychologist, writing in *The Origin of Consciousness in the Breakdown of the Bicameral Mind* (1976), theorises that our prehistoric ancestors were not able to think because they had no language and no self-awareness.

Intuition

He claims that the tribal chief could communicate his wishes to his followers and that these messages were received in the right − the intuitive − brain. Because the messages related only to an external world, prehistoric man heard voices in his head constantly.

Colin Wilson, investigating life after death in his book *Afterlife*, believes that we have subjugated our telepathic and intuitive ability in order to cope rationally with the immediacy of modern dangers and survival. When intuition occurs in the subjective intuitive right brain, he believes it is now passed to and interpreted by the objective rational left brain.

Left-handers often display a high degree of creativity, excelling in music and the arts. Can it be that they are more in touch than the average right-hander with their prehistoric intuitive right brain, because of its dominance over the left?

If Wilson's theory that our analytical left brain has taken over and our powers of creative perception have been subdued is correct, there is no reason why they cannot be reactivated. Indeed, this awakening can take place through meditation, where the mind achieves successively higher levels of consciousness and awareness.

An immense storehouse of untapped power lies in the mind. Most people walk around in a state of sleeping wakefulness a majority of the time but if everyone made a conscious effort, like Leonardo, to awaken the brain's latent abilities, genius might become commonplace.

More important is the fact that most of us do not make full use of the abilities we possess already. Thought is cloned from the schoolroom into the workplace – we are fitted into available niches. How many people are unhappy in their work? How many children are punished for their inability to master certain skills, while other talents are disregarded?

It would make better sense to pinpoint the particular talents and abilities of each individual child during the educational process and to nurture those talents at the expense of arbitrary skills, instead of putting children through the awful stress of having to master subjects which they can't or don't want to master.

Similarly, if more attention was paid to left- and right-brain characteristics by career advisers and personnel officers, a more productive, happier workforce might emerge.

'I have over the years suffered comments by R-Handers on how clumsy left-handers appear. My answer to that is something I was told years ago – that left-handedness is a sign of genius. Da Vinci and Einstein were left-handed and so was Jack the Ripper and they never caught him,' comments a left-hander.

* * * *

5
THE LEFT CONNECTION

It is only the certain knowledge that left-handedness is a sign of superior intelligence that makes me persevere in an unfair world. C. J. K., Glos.

When I was a very little boy I had a great-uncle who played cricket for England (F. G. J. Ford) who was a left-handed bat. He told my mother: 'Never force him to use his right hand. If he is left-handed he will get into teams as a left-armed bowler that he would never get into otherwise.' This also proved a great benefit as I found myself playing in the Rugby Eleven in 1940 and 1941 and the Oxford University Eleven in 1942 ... when I was wounded at Anzio in 1944 I had a revolver in my right hand and a grenade in my left. I was shot through the right hand ... had it been the left hand no doubt the grenade would have gone off! Marmaduke Hussey, Chairman, BBC.

At birth, the corpus callosum is smaller and not as well developed as that of an adult's, indicating that human babies may be split-brained. Young children may have language in both hemispheres until the left side begins to predominate around the age of two with the onset of speech. By adulthood, the left has usually taken over as the dominant hemisphere, while the abilities of the right have diminished, leaving nonverbal communication, music, spatial ability and facial recognition as its functions.

A newborn baby can only communicate by crying. It breathes through its nose, and is unable to breathe through its mouth until around six to eight months when its larynx and jaw drop down sufficiently. The baby cries to attract attention for its major needs

– food, comfort, warmth and love. Later it begins to coo and, at around eight weeks old, to babble.

Speech begins to develop when the babbling ends, at around nine months, when the baby will begin to imitate the sounds it hears from the people around it and form actual words. By the age of four, it should have acquired the language and dialect characteristics of its surroundings. It is only *homo sapiens* who have the intellect to develop language as a means of communication and expression, whereas other species rely on babbling and other noises to attract attention and fulfil their needs.

While we can trace the development of the left brain and see that it is logical, that still doesn't explain what factor determines which of the hemispheres will gain dominance or why not everyone has a dominant left hemisphere.

Past interpretations have included prenatal damage or damage during birth, carelessness in infant handling, heredity, eye domination and just plain cussedness and attention-grabbing. Or, as Sir Cyril Burt put it: 'heredity, habit and a half unconscious perversity'.

Nursing sides

One theory was that if the mother made a habit of holding the baby on her left so that her right hand was free, the baby's right arm would be squashed against her, leaving the left hand free to grasp things. Ergo, it grew up left-handed.

Burt's studies revealed that 73 babies were carried on the left arm as opposed to 27 carried on the right. He then looked at 100 famous depictions of the Madonna and Child and found the infant Jesus on the left in 59 paintings and on the right in 41. He concluded that in addition to habit and other factors, there must be a genetic link, however slight.

Burt's theories are being revived today at the University of Liverpool where Drs John Manning and Andrew Chamberlain have been looking at the maternal habits of monkeys and apes. They have found the same phenomenon among chimps, gorillas and possibly orang-utans. Their tests reveal that four out of five women also hold their babies left of centre, whether they are left- or right-handed. Men opt for right or left in equal numbers. Dr Manning is convinced of a genetic tendency in humans and their common ancestors, the African apes, dating back six to eight million years, which predates the human bias towards right-handedness.

Dr Manning disagrees with the 1960s/70s theory that babies held on the left will be soothed by the mother's heartbeat, and believes there may be some connection with the specialisation of the right hemisphere of the brain, which deals with the emotions and dominates the left side of the body.

If nerve impulses from the left eye and ear connect with the right hemisphere, that part of the brain can interpret better the child's moods. The baby also has a better view of the left side of its mother's face which will highlight expression more than the right.

The researchers have been handing out eye patches to Liverpudlian mothers to see if they change their cuddling sides when their left eyes are covered.

Emotional negativism

In 1946, Dr Abram Blau, chief psychiatrist at the New York University Clinic, came down hard on lefties in his book, *The Master Hand*, when he referred to sinistrality as a 'deviation in the learning process' due either to 'an inherent deficiency, physical or mental, faulty education or emotional negativism'. He was one of the old school, who recommended a switch to dextrality.

Sinistrals, he proclaimed, would have to recognise early on that they were 'abnormal and a sort of misfit in this right-handed world'. Among their characteristics he listed 'obstinacy, inordinate orderliness, parsimony, rigidity, a tendency to over-intellectualisation and self-willfulness', a list from which I, personally, will admit to scoring four out of six.

Blau also noted more left-handers among men, mental defectives, juvenile delinquents and those with psychiatric abnormalities. If, at this point, left-handers are getting depressed, they should remember the many famous achievers who 'suffer' from this 'sinister trait', e.g. President Bill Clinton, Paul McCartney, John McEnroe, Michael Crawford, and a host of other high earners.

About ten per cent of the population has been left-handed since the Stone Age. In the United States, the figures ranged from two to ten per cent between 1932 and 1970. Those figures are steadily mounting, yet still no clue to the true nature of left- versus right-handedness has been accepted officially.

Most early investigations into handedness highlighted the right hand, the left hand being considered unworthy of study. One extraordinary hypothesis advanced to explain the preponderance of right-handers was credited to Thomas Carlyle (1795–1881), who believed that handedness was 'the oldest institution that exists'. Carlyle, listed in Catherine Morris Cox's *The Early Mental Traits of Three Hundred Geniuses* (1926), with an IQ of between 140 and 150, was forced to change from right- to left-handedness.

Primitive Warfare Theory

Carlyle's Primitive Warfare Theory attributed left-handedness to the fact that our ancient warrior ancestors held their shields before their hearts with their left hands, so that they could fight with their right. King Richard I apparently upheld this view, inaugurating official battle rules by making his men fight from right to left, protecting the heart with the shield. These traditional rules were overturned, eventually, by Napoleon, when primitive hand-held weapons were beginning to wane.

It was long-accepted that this original tradition was passed on to perpetuate the free use of the right hand and had continued by natural selection, virtually eliminating left-handedness.

The Mechanical Theory

Another bizarre theory in the Age of Enlightenment, when thinkers and scientists questioned everything from Genesis to Galileo, was that the visceral organs on the right side weighed more than those on the left.

Professor Alexander Buchanan (1798–1882), of the University of Glasgow, produced The Mechanical Theory, relating to the position of the body's centre of gravity. He claimed that because its position enabled people to balance more easily on the left foot, it left their right foot free for use and this right-sided bias to action was complemented by the right hand. His left-handers had a misplaced centre while ambidexters' centres favoured neither foot.

Mendel's Laws

By the beginning of the twentieth century, left-handers were beginning to be noted as a growing force and, therefore, worthy of study. H. E. Jordan and F. Ramaley looked at genetics and heredity. Both favoured the laws of heredity formulated by the Austrian biologist, Gregor Johann Mendel (1822–1884), in which the inheritance of height, colouring and other characteristics could be predicted in families.

Between 1854 and 1868, Mendel taught physics and natural history at an Augustinian monastery in Brunn (now Czechoslovakia), where he was a monk and where he explored the laws of heredity with peas in the garden. For eight years, he painstakingly nurtured and studied around 10,000 plants before publishing his findings on 8 February 1865. That is considered to be the birthdate of modern genetics, despite its late acceptance.

Mendel crossed plants which contained wrinkled peas and those which contained round peas, producing progeny which were round – the first generation. These he labelled 'dominant' and he allowed 253 of them to grow into plants which self-fertilised into 7,324 peas. Of these second-generation hybrids, 5,474 were round – almost three times as many as those which were wrinkled (1,850). The wrinkled peas, he labelled 'recessive' (from the verb to recede).

Applying the same principles to human beings, Mendel's Theory of Heredity came into being, although it was too complex to be accepted during his lifetime and was only verified in 1900 by three European botanists working independently.

In humans, each cell contains 46 chromosomes. As cells divide to form new cells, each chromosome replicates itself so that the new set of chromosomes can join the new sister cells. Mendel's 'hereditary factors', or genes, are arranged in pairs, one from the mother and one from the father. Partner genes occupy the same positions on partner chromosomes, which pair up at fertilisation and divide at the formation of the next generation's cells.

This pairing is directed by the genes, each pair of which controls a particular characteristic. But while partner genes may control shape in the pea, in some cases one may produce round peas, while its partner may produce wrinkled ones. These type of genes are called alleles (allelomorph means 'different shape') and we will see later how modern-day research applies this theory to laterality in human beings.

Ramaley's left-handers constituted about a sixth of the population and were classified as 'Mendelian recessives'. H. D. Chamberlain, in 1928, disagreed and studied left-handed writers. He accepted the hereditary viewpoint as he found that the incidence of left-handedness was higher among those with at least one left-handed parent.

Eye dominance theory

In the 1920s, B. S. Parsons was looking at eye dominance as the root of left-handedness. He felt that a baby's voluntary movements depended on sight and that speech and memory belonged to the whole body, rather than one side.

As we shall see shortly, mixed laterality would rule out his theories, which account for neither congenitally blind left-handers nor those who were forced to change handedness because of social pressures.

Animal research

During the 1930s, an inordinate amount of research was carried out on the brains of rats – the human brain at that time being impossible to monitor while functioning normally. It was only during the 1970s that later operations to sever the corpus callosum to relieve epileptic seizures heralded new opportunities for the study of left- and right-hemispherical behaviour.

Rodent laterality traits revealed that they had a preferred paw, the majority favouring the right, and a few ambidexters showing no preference for either. But many tended to use one paw for one function and another for a different function. And their preference could be altered by tampering with the opposite hemisphere to the preferred paw.

It was deduced that neither social customs nor chance could be responsible for hand preference if it showed as far down the line as the rat and that attempts at anaesthetising the relevant dominant parts of the brain resulted in a change of paw usage, indicating that brain organisation, probably localised, played a significant part.

Other researchers studied cats and primates in the 1950s and birds in the 1970s. Birdsong was found by Nottebohm to be in the left-brained speech hemisphere while Cole (1955) found cats preferred to use their left paw in the main. Monkeys and chimps, oddly enough, appear not to favour either hand. But again, researchers disagreed heartily with one another.

In any event, findings in relation to humans were squashed on the head by researchers who pointed out that speech played a significant role in determining hemispherical dominance and handedness, and that handedness displayed by humans was a different type to that of animals.

The nearest they could come to finding any correlation to the human cause was in the case of the African mountain gorilla, some of whose number have been noted beating their chest with their right hand and who are said to have asymmetrical skulls with a longer left side – characteristics which may fill the left-hander with relief and occasion a suspicious sideways glance at their right-handed colleagues.

Miscellaneous theories

Ira S. Wile of Boston, covered exhaustive ground in 1934 after obsessive and detailed research into left-handedness, even positioning himself on street corners to identify the number of people holding packages or umbrellas in their left hands. He found that seventy per cent carried them closed in the left hand but only twenty per cent did so when the umbrellas were open. Research from observation alone is always a dangerous thing but doubtless Mr Freud would have argued that left-handers are more fascinated with a rolled phallic object than with an unfurled functional one.

At the beginning of the 1950s, A. Trankell looked again at the Mendelian theories of the earlier decades, pointing out from his tests on Stockholm schoolchildren that people lacking a dominant factor could still be right-handed, but for other reasons. He challenged earlier researchers, particularly Chamberlain, whose data, he claimed, was suspect and eventually produced proof of a Mendelian domination in right-handers but no proof of what happened if it was missing.

More recently, in 1979, Doreen Plenty from Bath, who noticed that many children born third in families seemed to be left-handed, despite their parents' dextrality, decided to carry out a survey of her own, and wrote to the *Sunday Express*.

'It had got to a point that I began asking left-handed people if they were the third child in the family. This is the case with our third child, my husband's sister and one of our nieces,' she commented. She conjectured, also, whether the third child born of left-handed parents, might be right-handed.

The paper published correspondence on her observations from all over the country. Although the reactions were varied, one third-child left-handed schoolgirl from Southport assessed eight left-handed friends and found that two-thirds of them were third children. There were left-handed parents with right-handed third children, and one Suffolk woman found it curious that of her four children, the three left-handed ones were dark-haired with brown eyes and the third (right-handed) child had fair hair and blue eyes.

Elsewhere, it has been theorised that the first and last child (if the latter was born when the mother was middle-aged) were likely to be born left-handed, a phenomenon attributed to hormonal changes. This was, in fact, the pattern in my own family.

Older mothers have more left-handers

Further research into sinistrality by Professor Stanley Coren in Canada has revealed that women over 40 years of age are more likely to have left-handed babies, possibly accounted for by the more difficult pregnancies and deliveries that have a higher chance of occurring at that age.

Coren found that women aged between 30 and 35 were 25 per cent more likely to give birth to left-handers and that the chance increased by 69 per cent if the mother was between 35 and 39. In the 40-plus age group, it was 128 per cent more likely that the mother would have a left-handed child.

Among the reasons Coren gives are prolonged labour, breathing difficulty at birth, low birth weight and biological trauma experienced by multiple birth babies. 'What we find is that, overall, the left-handers run about a half-inch shorter and about three pounds lighter than the right-handed pitchers,' Coren is reported as saying in the *New Scientist* (21 July 1990).

However, what is curious is that many of the recent revelations of Coren's long-term investigations into laterality have simply replicated what other researchers into the subject have discovered long ago.

The major alternative theory to minor natal brain damage was that language development was delayed owing to slow brain maturation in some children, a theory which supported the argument for mixed laterality.

Could the cause lie in a gene? No regular pattern in families has been proven so far. Some left-handers are the only ones in their family, although most are not aware of the handedness of previous generations. If it is genetic, then there would be no such thing as one left-handed identical twin, for if both came from the same egg they would surely contain the same gene.

Twins and left-handedness

The incidence of left-handedness among twins is higher than among single-born children. Around twenty per cent of identical twins boast one left- and one right-hander. It is thought that in the case of single-egg (monozygotic) twins, the left-right pattern has been formed by the time the embryo splits, producing mirror image beings. Fifteen per cent of them are left-handed compared to eleven per cent of twins born from two separate eggs (dizygotic) which have been fertilised at the same time.

Siamese twins, born from the same egg which splits incompletely, are exact opposites and one will always be left-handed. All their characteristics are opposite, including the direction of their hair whorls. The fingerprints on the right hand of one will resemble those on the left hand of the other and even the visceral organs of one will be reversed.

The suspected causes of left-handedness among twins may range from genetic factors to prenatal intra-uterine crowding, but as with most laterality data, the theories tend to conflict. Nagylaki and Levy (1973) show that higher incidences of mental deficiency, brain damage and infant mortality occur in twins than in single-born children, and this may be related to foetal positioning. It is also interesting to note that around five times as many twins stammer as in the population at large, which may suggest a genetic link with left-handedness.

Heredity and genetics

In general, it has been suggested that left-handedness in some individuals is familial. In a handedness study of 1,094 six-year-old children born at St Mary's Hospital, Manchester, in 1971, 17.5 per cent of the children were left-handed, compared to only 6.2 per cent of their grandparents and 10.6 per cent of their parents. This probably reflects the less rigid attitude employed by parents and teachers in successive later generations. (It was also found that boys born by breech delivery and children born to women over thirty-eight years of age were more likely to be left-handed.) Left-handers not accepted as pathologically or environmentally determined, tend to be classified as hereditary left-handers.

The right shift factor

Dr Marian Annett, a prolific researcher into handedness at the University of Hull's Psychology Department during the 1970s, claimed two determining factors to lateral assymetry – the first, an accidental variation in all animals, which produced a normal distribution of differences between sides, and the second, a factor peculiar only to humans, shifting the distribution in favour of right-handedness – what she calls 'the right shift factor'.

Normal dominance was assumed to be genetic with a bias towards language in the left hemisphere, along with dextrality. Annett believed that pure left-handers were fairly rare and that mixed laterals, which she placed at one-third of the population at that time, many of whom wrote with their left hand, had, in fact, experienced a 'right shift factor'.

If the right shift factor was weak or didn't exist, so that speech developed in either or both hemispheres, left- or right-hemispherical dominance in both handers would occur. With no right shift factor, a speech delay might occur, along with 'accidental variations' of hand preference.

It is interesting to note that she also found that right-handed women had fewer speech and reading problems than right-handed men and that there were slightly more of them. Recent research has shown the opposite for left-handers, where the men appear to predominate.

Normal distribution between the hands in skill is occasioned by chance, says Annett, not inheritance. If this were the case, would there not be a more equal spread between right and left-handers, perhaps? Albert Einstein once said: 'I cannot believe that God plays dice with the Universe.' Would there not be chaos throughout nature if there were not some underlying law determining the normal distribution of differences?

A gene for speech

The right shift factor itself is inherited and causes the displacement of distribution to the right, although it does not determine handedness *per se* − some people who prefer to use their left hand may still possess a right shift factor. 'The right shift factor is due to whatever puts speech in the left hemisphere − a gene for left-hemisphere speech,' said Marian Annett. This genetic bias, by giving an advantage to the left hemisphere, simply increases the chance of right-handedness.

But she believes this gene must have costs, as well as benefits, otherwise it would be more widespread, and that one copy of the gene may be advantageous but two copies would be risky. Ability tests carried out by Annett and Margaret Manning at the University of Leicester on primary schoolchildren in 1988, revealed that strongly right-handed children fared the least well and that the decline in abilities weakened from left to right across the laterality scale.

Tests for hand preference and hand skill revealed that strong right-handers had weak left-hand skills, rather than good right-hand skills, and performed poorly on several tests for intelligence and educational attainment. Strong left- and strong right-handers were found to be more at risk from reading difficulties, which might indicate a tie-in with dyslexia.

'The costs of left hemisphere specialisation are not just to right hemisphere functions but to overall brain power, that is, general intelligence,' found the researchers. 'The present findings show for the first time that the reduced dextrality of highly talented groups is part of a trend which runs throughout the population; it applies not only to talented versus average children, but also to average versus dull.'

Dr Annett's studies show that left-handers are high in all-round intelligence, with a leaning towards genius, and that one-third of the extreme right-handers have the most learning difficulties and limited talents.

If two speech genes are inherited, one from each parent, a person is likely to be strongly right-handed. Dr Annett tested children from 10 schools in Rugby, who carried out simple tasks moving pegs between rows of holes. She found the highest IQs among the left-handers who also used their right hands and right-handers with a facility for left-hand use. These groups were thought to be maximising the use of both hemispheres.

The strongly right-handed 9- to 11-year-olds performed less well than the others in maths and English tests. 'Although left-handers are usually slower to develop speech and reading skills, once these are mastered, they have a better all-round ability than pure right-handers, who are less able to perform tasks controlled by the right side of the brain, such as solving three-dimensional problems, recognising shapes and working on more practical and creative things,' she said.

At the University of Chicago, bio-psychologist Jerre Levy, in the 1960s, proclaimed that 70 per cent of left-handers had verbal abilities in the left hemisphere while 15 per cent had speech in both hemispheres. Annett believed this to be true of only mixed laterals, her left-handers having *their* speech in the right hemisphere. And while Levy believed that their right hemisphere would have its spatial awareness diminished to allow for the extra verbal abilities, Annett held that spatial skills developed in preference to verbal ones.

Edgar Miller, also from the University of Hull's Department of Psychology, replicated some of Levy's 1969 tests in 1971, proving that there are differences in ability between right- and mixed-handers, probably due to differences in brain organisation. His expectation was that pure left-handers would show a similar level of abilities to right-handers but he had not carried out any tests on them as he claimed that they represented only 4 per cent of the population.

At that time, the generally accepted figures for consistent handedness were 60 to 70 per cent right and 4 to 12 per cent left.

Levy and Thomas Nagylaki, a University of Wisconsin geneticist, believed that two genes were responsible, one which influenced the language hemisphere and the other which influenced the hand that hemisphere would control.

It had always been understood that the connecting nerve fibres of the corpus callosum crossed over so that the dominant hemisphere controlled the opposite hand. They found that although normally 80 per cent did so, in some cases less than half did not and messages were being sent straight down the same side. This created a further enigma of two types of left-hander – one dominated by the left hemisphere and one dominated by the right.

Inverted hand postures

Levy's researches took her into the realms of the hook – the curious style adopted by many left-handed writers who hold the hand above the paper and curve the arm round, so that the pen is pulled along rather than pushed. The most logical reason for this is that the writer is not obscuring the page. But this uncomfortable-looking habit is practised also by a minority of right-handers, who have no logical reason to do so.

Levy noticed this trait first in her right-handed husband, afterwards noting it among other right-handers. Furthermore, she found that in Israel, where right-handers suffer the disadvantages of Western left-handers on account of their right to left writing, many left-handers still made the hook.

She decided that writing was not the dominant issue here but brain organisation and a possible link with the left- or right-hemisphered left-hander. She theorised that hooking left-handers had language in the left hemisphere, which fitted in nicely with the same-side neural theories she had found with Nagylaki. The same would be true for the five per cent of right-handers whose neural fibres did not cross. They would have speech in the right, instead of the left, hemisphere and would make the hook in writing.

Non-hookers, whose nerve fibres did cross, would have language in the opposite hemisphere, indicating that those left-handers would be mirror images of the right-hander.

Levy tested her theories in collaboration with psychologist Marylou Reid on 73 university students, namely 24 right-handers, 24 hooking left-handers, 24 non-hooking left-handers and one hooking right-hander. Both spatial and verbal abilities, normally resident in opposite hemispheres, were tested.

Because the eye passes information to the opposite hemisphere, right-handers would normally be expected to excel in passing verbal images flashed to the right eye to the left (language) hemisphere and in passing spatial images – in this case locating dots – flashed to the left eye, to the right (spatial awareness) hemisphere. Left-handers would perform the other way around.

The actual results revealed this to be so for the non-hooking right-handers and the hooking left-handers. Likewise, the hooking right-hand control and the non-hooking left-handers performed alike, indicating that the two sets were mirror images of one another.

She further found some extraordinary discrepancies in performances between men and women in both groups. In the right-handers/hooking left-handers group, the men outshone the women on spatial abilities and the women outshone the men on verbal abilities. In her non-hooking left-handers group, the results were reversed – men, verbal; women, spatial. In other words, handedness aside, women are dominated by whatever function is located in the left hemisphere and men are dominated by whatever function is located in the right hemisphere.

It was later found that with children, girls developed their left hemisphere first and boys their right, backing up their research. But their findings conflicted with all the accepted theories of the time. Most hooking left-handers insisted that they hooked because of the way they had to slant the paper and to see what they were writing. And it doesn't account for those, like myself, who hooked for a time, then stopped.

More challenges came from McGill University, Montreal, in the early 1970s, where Michael Corballis and Ivan Beale disagreed with the crossover neural theories and went for bilateral symmetry. They believed in some kind of memory techniques which replicated mirror images from one hemisphere, via the nerve fibres, into the opposite hemisphere. But their experiments were conducted mainly on animals.

In *The Psychology of Left and Right* (1976), they looked at the advantages of asymmetry and hand preference from an evolutionary and environmental viewpoint. Primitive man needed hands to fashion and use tools, which would also have to be used by other members of his group. Communication such as shaking hands must be done by two people using the same hand, so a tendency towards same-sidedness was perhaps developed for social reasons. That doesn't explain why the group chose the right hand.

Corballis and Beale believed that right-handedness had to do with a general biological gradient favouring a development on the left. This underlay left-cerebral dominance and the slight displacement of the heart to the left. It had nothing to do with speech, rather 'the control of complex manipulative behaviour'.

To confuse matters further, they believed that lateralisation of speech was determined by handedness and not the other way around. In the eighteenth century, the French philosopher, Etienne de Condillac, theorised that before speech was invented, man gestured with his arms and hands to make himself understood. This theory accounted for primitive man's familiar tool-wielding right hand continuing to be used for self-expression.

We have already noted Kimura's research into the significance of manual gestures accompanying speech in chapter 4. Her findings would seem to support this theory but they by no means establish which came first.

So manual manipulation and cerebral lateralisation were the key factors in defining handedness. Man makes his own asymmetry in the world, then has to conform to it.

Asymmetric tonic neck reflex

Leaving language ability and hemispherical dominance theories aside, an altogether different theory for handedness resulted from a study of infant behaviour in Boston in the 1970s when Jane F. Coryell and George F. Michel monitored newborn babies for their first twelve weeks of life.

The babies elicited a tendency to lie with their head turned towards the same side – usually the right – during this time, resulting in an asymmetric tonic neck reflex which placed an arm and leg on their face side. This meant that one hand appeared in their field of vision more frequently than the other. Accordingly, they became accustomed to recognising that hand and to using it eventually for certain tasks.

A similar investigation had already been carried out in the 1940s by A. Gesell and L. B. Ames. Their study of ten-year-olds revealed that all 90 per cent of right-handers studied showed right tonic neck responses at birth. Of the rest of the sample, all left-handers, 5 per cent turned to the right and 5 to the left. They concluded that left-handers were likely to display a left tonic neck reflex in infancy.

Hand-eye co-ordination may have provided an alternative theory for preferred handedness, but it still didn't explain why the babies chose to turn their head to one particular side in preference to the other, unless it was accepted as a reinforcement of the right shift phenomenon theory.

Liederman and Kinsbourne (1980) found that, perinatal damage aside, the newborn of two right-handers turned their heads to the right whereas those with one left-handed parent showed no preferences. Researchers Hecaen and de Ajuriagueira found only 2 per cent of left-handers had right-handed parents; 17 per cent had mixed-handed parents.

In 1982, questioning genetics v brain damage theories, Coryell and Liederman at the University of Boston claimed that babies with perinatal complications were more likely to be left-handers than those without, as they showed a head-turning bias to the left or no lateral preference at all compared to babies with no perinatal complications who exhibited a right-turning head bias.

Birth stress

It may well be that few of us are born without some actual physiological or psychological damage, however negligible, taking place during the force of delivery or shock of being hauled into an alien environment from the safe, secure warmth of the womb – after all, nine months of security to a foetus with no thought mechanisms must be equal to a lifetime in our own terms.

The French are great believers in natural childbirth and the squatting or underwater methods of easing the newborn through the trauma of their entry into their unaccustomed surroundings. Interestingly, babies born by obstetrician Frederick Leboyer's non-violent birth techniques have been said to develop as ambidextral, with no manual preference.

His Birth Without Violence delivery techniques excluded the aggressive, bright lights and belting-bottom traditions in favour of soft lights, massage and soothing baths and an altogether tranquil environment, resulting, to all developmental reports, in alert, bright, relaxed and tranquil children, neither predominantly left- or right-handed.

Could it be that the actual trauma of birth, coupled with the method of delivery in some cases, determines whether or not a child is born brain-damaged, however minor the damage, and that Annett's 'accidental factor' inhibiting the right shift phenomenon is an obstetric one? Obstetricians are particularly sensitive to allusions of brain damage caused during childbirth because of the reflection on their professional abilities. The term is used excessively and it is not always possible to determine whether or not damage was present before birth. One Washington paediatric neurologist claims that 5 to 8 per cent of the population has some suggestion of brain damage. Causes range from genetics to difficult birth, from smoke to environment.

Canadian psychologist, Paul Bakan, was firmly convinced in the 1970s that left-hemispherical perinatal damage produced left-handers and that, although this ran in families, it was not genetic. Such damage created a weakness in the right hand which made the child switch to the stronger left hand. But Liederman and Coryell found some non-perinatal damaged children who favoured the left.

Evidence supporting perinatal damage theories has been conflicting and inconsistent. Neuro-psychologist Satz at the University of Florida (1972) noted that 16 to 30 per cent of epileptics and the mentally retarded were pathologically left-handed. Why did natural left-handers with damage to the right hemisphere not become right-handers with inferior spatial abilities? he asked.

Dorothy Bishop, MRC Senior Research Fellow at the Sub-department of Speech, University of Newcastle-upon-Tyne in 1983, felt that if the association of left-handedness with such developmental disorders as dyslexia, stammering and minimal brain damage was caused by delayed cerebral lateralisation, there would surely be more left-handers in existence. She thought that only pathological left-handers had a disorder association and that the majority of left-handers developed normally.

If a right-hander had suffered a motor disability affecting the right side, they would switch to the left. If pathological factors influenced hand preference, then left-handers would show a higher rate of pathological disorders than right-handers.

Data from the National Child Development Study showed that pathological left-handers − about 5 per cent of left-handers − were clumsier with their right hands than right-handers with their left hands. They were also found to have more neurological and speech problems than right-handers.

Other researchers studied birth order and Barnes (1975) found that the length of time it took for newborn babies to establish breathing had significant bearing on their later preferred handedness, attributing left-hand dominance to infant temperament.

Eventually, it becomes clear why it is difficult to obtain any definitive statements, proofs or official statistics about left-handedness, its origins or development.

Most researchers have found a higher proportion of male left-handers than female. Mostly, this was thought to have been environmental. Margaret Clark in the 1950s, tested six thousand Scottish schoolchildren aged between five and twelve. She found that 8 per cent of the boys wrote with their left hand and 6 per cent of the girls. She thought that the explanation for the sex difference was not genetic but queried whether this was an anomaly of birth or whether girls tended to bow more to convention and boys towards stubbornness or independence.

The testosterone effect

In February 1985, left-hander Robin Brightwell produced a BBC2 documentary for *Horizon* in which he highlighted the research into left-handedness by the late Norman Geschwind, former Professor of Neurology at Harvard Medical School, Professor of Psychology at the Massachusetts Institute of Technology and Head of the Neurology Unit at Beth Israel Hospital, Boston.

Geschwind began his research in 1980 after visiting a Boston conference on dyslexia, which he had been studying. He was impressed by the pronouncement by Dr Simpson, one of the speakers, that he had found an incidence of myasthenia gravis, a muscular dysfunction, among dyslexics. Geschwind's reaction to what was obviously a motor rather than a language function was to suggest that further investigations should be made into a possible connection and into any other supposedly familial disorders.

Later, an Englishwoman, Jean Baker, told him of her family history of dyslexia, allergies and a rare type of arthritis. Similar stories were repeated by others. His attention was caught by the incidence of rare disorders, all of which, like the Baker family's arthritis, were caused by the body attacking its own immune system.

He remembered his predecessor, Stanley J. Cobb, had suffered from dyslexia, had had a pronounced stammer and could draw with both hands simultaneously. Cobb, on his own investigations into his complaint, found that dyslexics were often ambidextrous or left-handed. Now, it seemed, the immune system might be involved.

Geschwind persevered with his notion, despite the attitude of his colleagues who thought he was mad. Dr Peter Behan joined him in a massive survey and by 1982 they had discovered that 10 per cent of left-handers as opposed to 4 per cent of right-handers, suffered from some kind of immune complaint, where the white blood cells mistake parts of the body for invading bacteria and attack them.

Ten times as many left-handers as right-handers showed an inclination towards dyslexia and stammering, however strongly or weakly left-sided they happened to be. But although they had highlighted the existence of such an anomaly, they were unable to find a reason for it.

For a possible answer, Geschwind turned to the brain, whose asymmetry he had already proved in 1968. Together with colleague, Dr Albert Galaburda, he found that the brains of dyslexics contained cells that should not have been there and which they attributed to pre-birth.

Geschwind's subsequent foetal study was based on the higher proportion of boys than girls among dyslexics and left-handers, which could be significant. He found that the male hormone testosterone, which transformed the natural female embryo into a male, circulated in the bloodstream, around the male embryo, to the brain. Testosterone was produced in large quantities by the testicles and larger amounts are normally produced during puberty when the boy changes into a man.

Geschwind believed that overly high levels of the hormone could slow down the brain's development. As the left hemisphere developed more slowly than the right it would be at risk for a longer period of time, and if affected, the right hemisphere would then take over and grow larger to compensate, ultimately controlling the dominant left hand. He also found this to be an explanation for the 'rogue' brain cells in dyslexic boys, because they too coincided with the occurrence of high testosterone levels.

What about left-handed females, who do not produce testosterone? Geschwind found an answer to that too. The hormone is a by-product of female hormones which are produced by the pregnant mother who simply passes them on to her daughter's embryo, where it nurtures left-handedness or dyslexia, depending on the level made and the embryo's sensitivity to it.

Brightwell raised the thought-provoking point that one surrogate mother could give birth to a left-handed, dyslexic architect while a different one could produce a right-handed novelist from the same embyro, depending on the testosterone levels produced by the natural mother, thereby completely overriding its genetic heritage.

Immune disorders

As for the immune disorders which first attracted his attention, Geschwind discovered that the baby's immune system would be realising 'self' or those substances which should not be attacked after birth. If this realisation is not complete, the child's own auto-immune system will attack parts of its own body.

He found that high levels of testosterone adversely affected the thymus gland, which regulates this education, hence the high incidence of hayfever, allergies, rheumatoid arthritis, Crohn's disease, thyroid disorders, ulcerative colitis, migraine, myasthenia gravis and coeliac disease. But he also found that their immune system would be better at fighting infection and recognising malignancies, resulting in less incidence of cancer than right-handers.

In all, left-handers could be expected to have ten times more learning disabilities than right-handers and two and a half times more auto-immune complaints. Subsequent research has revealed high rates of left-handers with allergies, dyslexia and stammers, high levels of immune disorders among autistic children and high food allergy incidences among hyperactive children, all of which revealed a high rate of left-handedness. In addition, the incidence of left-handers among hare-lip patients was found to be two and a half times more than in the general population.

Even families of left-handed – but not right-handed – dyslexics have not been found to be immune from what Geschwind saw as some kind of interaction between the endocrine, immune and nervous systems taking place during foetal development.

Geschwind found a high incidence of sinistrality to be a common denominator in dyslexia, autism, epilepsy, speech delay, hyper-activity and stammering. Left-handedness is not the cause nor does it exist because of those conditions; it is an additional factor, existing in spite of them.

Savant Syndrome

A further fascinating condition found to be affected by foetal testo-sterone levels is Savant Syndrome, a very rare condition among the mentally handicapped, who seem to have traded off their language skills in favour of exceptional musical, artistic and mathematical abilities. Only 100 cases have been noted in the past century.

Many suffer from schizophrenia or the rare early infantile autism (9.8 per cent) and while some of their talents are amazing for people with their handicap, some would be considered incredible even in a normal person. Again, the ratio of males to females is higher – 6:1.

Some are brilliant pianists (often blind, which frequently occurred in the days when excess oxygen was given to premature babies). They can repeat music, however difficult, having heard it only once; many can improvise to a high standard or compose their own music without knowledge of composition. Some can calculate vastly complex streams of figures at incredible speeds, some are calendar calculators, some are artistically gifted, some are mechanically minded, others have extraordinary visual memories or extrasensory perception. They seem to rely almost totally on their right brains and, despite the suggestion of genius, their IQ is generally rated between 40 and 70.

Dr Darold A. Treffert, Executive Director of the Fond du Lac County Health Care Centre, Wisconsin, exploring Savant Syndrome in his book *Extraordinary People*, highlights the 1973 case of a left-handed six-year-old Savant with early infantile autism who had exceptional artistic talent, a great rarity. She could barely join words together and was either highly disruptive or withdrawn. Yet since she was three years old, she had produced exceptional drawings, usually copied from pictures she had seen once only.

Her psychologist at the University of Nottingham Child Development Research Unit, Lorna Selfe, wrote a book about her. In it, she reasoned that children use visual imagery in place of language. Language gradually takes over as a form of shorthand for the imagery, which inevitably falls into disuse. Because of her condition, the patient, Nadia, never developed language, so that her visual imagery was sustained and even developed through her drawing instead.

Logically, she reasoned that should she develop language skills, Nadia's talent would diminish or disappear. When she was seven years old, Nadia's language improved after she joined a school for autistic children and as it did so, her exceptional talent disappeared as predicted.

Perhaps this is an extreme example, but I use this case to reinforce the argument for encouraging natural talents in children at the expense of subjects for which they show little aptitude. By spreading the load of information we may be inhibiting creative forces which may never have a chance to reveal themselves fully. It also highlights the need to emphasise and encourage the assets and strengths of any child as opposed to the negatives and handicaps.

In the United States, every year around 70,000 bright 13-year-olds take a Scholastic Aptitude Test of their developed ability (not learned material) in verbal and mathematical reasoning abilities, designed for 17- to 18-year-olds. These reasoning abilities are understood to be right-brain activities, as opposed to their left-brain counterparts of verbal syntax and mathematical computational ability.

Highly precocious children

Inevitably, Geschwind's testosterone revelations are provoking a wave of controversy among researchers and Camilla Persson Benbow at the Iowa State University, Ames, has already discovered a biological correlation among students with extreme mathematical reasoning ability of left-handedness, allergies, myopia, sex (males), hormones and cognitive functions spread across both hemispheres. The same correlation, minus the high incidence of males, was found among those with extremely high verbal reasoning ability.

Left-handers accounted for 15.1 per cent of the sample of extremely precocious students tested and these included 4.9 per cent of Asian-Americans who scored highly among the extremely mathematically talented students. But the three main physiological traits occurring among 80 per cent of those with mathematical and/or verbal precocity were left- or mixed-handedness, asthma (and other allergies) and myopia.

Why were left-handers and those with immune disorders found among the extremely precocious verbal reasoners? 'The key is that we studied verbal *reasoning* ability. It is probably more strongly under the influence of the right hemisphere than language production or syntactical aspects of verbal ability, because verbal reasoning ability involves comprehension and the understanding of difficult words and their relationships,' commented Benbow. The same is true of mathematical reasoning ability.

Left-handers, mixed-handers and right-handers with left-handed relatives have different brain organisations from right-handers. Benbow felt that they were more likely to have cognitive functions in both hemispheres for mathematical or verbal reasoning abilities and spatial ability, rather than a specialisation of the right hemisphere.

The most recent research, by Dr Peter Hepper of the Queen's University, Belfast, found from ultrasound scans that thumb-sucking babies may be determining their own handedness in the womb. Only 5.4 per cent of the foetuses studied showed a preference for their left thumb. It is thought that this might indicate a prenatal explanation for handedness.

In 1990, one study by Canadian researchers into testosterone, at McMaster University, Ontario, found an unusually high percentage of left-handers among homosexuals.

It has to be admitted, our intrepid researchers are imaginative. We are all agreed that observation alone does not constitute sufficient evidence and that scientific enquiry must be accepted as proof of any theory. But how do we left-handers perceive the generations of researchers, scurrying around on our behalf, overtaking one another in some kind of manic marathon, shouting 'Eureka' as they pass, only to be overtaken by more streams of researchers opposing their 'proven' results and postulating yet more revolutionary answers?

It leaves us with the thought-provoking truth that left-handers have posed the greatest enigma to science of all time since the Creation, an enigma that has still not been completely solved.

* * * *

6
SINISTRAL DEXTERITY

The left-handed are precious; they take places which are inconvenient for the rest. Victor Hugo, *Les Misérables*.

Hand preference in infants

Many parents notice their offspring using the left hand for certain functions at an early age and wonder if the child is going to be left-handed. The use of the left hand by no means denotes that the child will be a left-hander, for most children change hands, sometimes favouring both at the same time, until preference is finally established.

The average parents do not consciously take the trouble to monitor and record their child's development in an area that is generally considered nowadays to be of minor importance, so their later recollections of infant hand dominance may not be accurate.

In reality, some indication of hand preference can be predicted by the right- or left-turning head bias and the tonic neck reflex mentioned in chapter 5, which shows itself first in the foetus at 28 weeks and finally disappears at around 20 weeks after birth. Again, it is unlikely that the average parent, unless he or she happened to be a psychologist or paediatrician, would be likely to notice or find any significance in this tendency.

It does indicate, however, that hand preference — unless established for pathological reasons or social pressure — is not influenced normally by environment. Researchers Gesell and Ames in 1947 published the findings of a major investigation into the development of manual preference in infants and found the emergence of a natural pattern.

The following chart illustrates this pattern:

12 weeks:	both hands
16–20 weeks:	left hand
24 weeks:	both hands
28 weeks:	right hand
32 weeks:	both hands
36 weeks:	left hand
40–44 weeks:	right hand
48 weeks:	left hand
52–56 weeks:	right hand
80 weeks:	both hands
2 years:	right hand
2½–3½ years:	both hands
4 years:	dominance shows
8 years:	established

Not all children take this long to lateralise, for some do so in the first six months or so, others have done so by the age of two or four. Gesell also found that boys formed their hand preference earlier than girls. Degrees of dominance prevail and those who lateralise early are usually strongly dominant in the chosen hand, which is why they should not be changed over, particularly at school. If they have established their preference long before, it will be too strong to be tampered with without causing problems for the child.

Eating habits

Most left-handed children, if left to their own devices, will use their preferred hands until a right-handed adult, parent or teacher, demonstrates some skill with the right hand which the left-hander will emulate. The majority of left-handers I have interviewed, including myself, eat with the fork in the left and the knife in the right hand, in the socially acceptable way.

At mealtimes, the table is set this way, few right-handers making allowances for, or remembering, their little leftie. Give a left-hander a spoon, a knife or a fork alone and it goes straight into the left hand. Most of us find it impossible to manipulate spoon and fork together for dessert as we want to use both in our left hand. The right-hand use of knife and fork is often commented upon – if we can use cutlery in the same way as a right-hander, why should we do anything else the 'wrong' way round?

When I was nineteen years old, I holidayed in Denmark where, pursued by a worldly and wealthy Argentinian, I coerced my girlfriend into accompanying us to dinner at an expensive restaurant, not wishing to be left alone with this hot-blooded-looking stranger. In the middle of the meal, he put down his knife and fork and stared in disbelief at my plate, screeching at the same time for all the room to hear, 'Look what she's doing?'

The room looked, to my mortification, at my plate on which lay a trail of ragged pieces of rare fillet steak in a kind of jigsaw puzzle effect, scattered all over the dish in an asymmetrical heap. His own steak had been neatly carved into strips, then bite-sized pieces which were despatched down his gullet promptly, leaving no mess on the plate. It wasn't until many years later that I gave up eating meat altogether, mainly on account of the social embarrassment that accrued from my feeble efforts at manipulating the cutlery.

The point of the story is that, although left-handers do fall into line with this socially acquired skill, watch closely the handling of the knife, particularly with children, which entails holding it on the food while making a tearing motion with the fork, so wresting the food away from it. The knife hardly cuts at all. Those left-handers who do not find this a problem have been well trained by their parents, an aspect of my upbringing which was obviously sadly lacking and which cost me a palatial home and a stableful of thoroughbreds in South America.

Right-hand training

Most left-handers bat and play racquet sports with the right hand. This skill is taught to them by right-handers, although some never quite manage to adapt, without any disastrous consequences as can be seen from the achievements of McEnroe, Connors, Navratilova et al. Give us a ball and we will throw it with the left hand, for nobody teaches ball-throwing – you just pick it up and heave it.

How well I remember (long before the mortifying Argentinian

meat-eating experience) being screamed at by a teacher while in a line-up of toddlers aged about five, at beanbag-throwing practice, because the instruction – five times on my account – had been to pick up the bag with our right hands and throw it. Not fully comprehending in those early years what a right hand could be, my natural inclination was to grab it off the floor with my left. Finally, it seeped through to the dragon that I was left-handed and had simply been doing what came naturally. Having reduced me to a state of nervous anxiety in the giggling assembly line – she retorted, 'You're left-handed. Why didn't you say so, you stupid thing?'

This is my earliest childhood recollection of sinistral discrimination and it is important for teachers and parents to note that, as mentioned earlier, the child is the last to know what is going on. I hadn't 'said so' because I didn't understand that I was left-handed or that other children were not. Suddenly, I was being told by someone in authority that I was a stupid thing. All the other children had got it right (literally), so why hadn't I? Ergo, I must be more stupid than the others. Was she sowing seeds for the future?

It can be seen from the foregoing that left-handers have the advantage, for they are far more adept with their right hand than right-handers are with their left, because of training, social conformity and necessity. If right-handers could be persuaded to follow suit, they would probably increase their overall efficiency and, therefore, that of the general population, at home, in the workplace, on the sports field and in any other area which calls for manual dexterity.

Ambidexterity

The nineteenth-century French science writer Adolphe-Jean Focillon believed that both hands had equal value and that the right should not be thought superior. Without the left 'it retires into a painful, almost sterile solitude,' he commented. His views may have inspired John Jackson to found the Society for Ambidextral Culture and Upright Writing in 1905, with the aim of promoting educational reform and two-handed training.

Jackson gathered many eminent supporters, among them the ambidextrous artist, Sir Edwin Landseer, who could draw two different pictures with both hands simultaneously and who taught Queen Victoria – also thought to be ambidextrous – and Prince Albert to draw. Another ambidextrous supporter was Major-General Baden-Powell who, in 1908, founded the Boy Scout Movement and instituted the left-handed handshake as its masonic-style greeting, a gesture which he copied from an African tribe he had encountered during the Ashanti War in 1896.

Although Jackson's campaign was adopted by some infant schools, and special copy-books produced, it never gathered momentum, and, needless to say, the government turned a deaf ear – the right one presumably. Inevitably, rumblings from the right heralded a wealth of abuse and criticism from those who thought them cranks and crackpots, in particular the eminent surgeon, Sir James Crichton-Browne. In his 1909 lecture on 'Dexterity and the Bend Sinister' he reasoned that a turn to the left was tantamount to striking a blow against evolution, now that majority right-handedness had been established.

In his book, *Ambidexterity* (1905), which Baden-Powell endorsed with an introduction and his signature, signed with both hands, Jackson makes an impassioned plea for man's return to the two-sided state favoured by animals, a Utopia he was never to witness. His argument was backed up by several eminent persons of the time, including Sir John Adcock, who was then chief physician to the ambidextrous Shah of Persia.

Baden-Powell, one of the society's three vice presidents, was firmly convinced of the importance and usefulness of ambidexterity to realise the maximum potential and efficiency of the individual, in the workplace and, more particularly, on the military front. 'I do not consider a man is a thoroughly trained soldier unless he mount equally well on either side of his horse, use the sword, pistol and lance, equally well with both hands, and shoot off the left shoulder as rapidly and accurately as from the right,' he wrote.

How left-handers managed that when the bolt was on the wrong side for them, is difficult to say, but they had to, losing valuable seconds in the act, which could have cost them their lives. His conclusions on the subject were that ambidexterity was harmless, healthful, expedient and necessary.

Baden-Powell's fellow vice presidents were W. H. Cummings, Mus.Doc. and Sir James Sawyer, MD. The president was E. Noble

Smith, FRCS Edin., and Jackson himself was honorary secretary, backed by a committee of over fifty. 'Justice and Equality for the Left Hand' became their watchword.

The Greek philosopher Plato was a great believer in ambidexterity and put preferred handedness down to faulty upbringing, laying the blame firmly on the side of the female − nurse or mother − which is almost as bad as left-handed Barsley's discrimination against women in his treatise against left-handed discrimination, which he entitled 'Left-Handed Man in a Right-Handed World'.

Plato believed that, especially in some sports or hand-to-hand combat, ambidexterity was essential and that children should be trained to use both hands equally for everything. Aristotle disagreed.

Depending on one's viewpoint, the ambidexter could be regarded as someone who has not developed laterality so has to use both hands for all tasks or as someone who has developed their potential more fully than most and has the ability to use both hands equally well. The logic applies equally to ambilaterals, who could be viewed either as people who have proved inadequate in developing a preferred side or those who have the propensity to be selective in certain tasks. Like most aspects of handedness, the glass can be either half full or half empty. Never forget Leonardo.

Some researchers thought that ambidexterity was a sign of changed left-handedness. Gesell thought that ambidexters were abnormal. Normality was to favour either left or right and delayed laterality went hand in glove with delayed speech. The term ambidextrous in itself implies two right hands − the adjective dextral meaning right-handed or the right-hand side, the words dexterous or dexterity denoting skill or cleverness. The word 'right' also means 'correct'.

Word play

The adjective sinistral, meaning left-handed or the left-hand side, is related only to the adjective sinister, denoting the unlucky side, threatening harm, evil, disaster, misfortune and dishonesty. Its origin stems from the bar or bend sinister in heraldry. The majority of crests had a diagonal bar which ran from left to right but if a member of the family was born 'out of wedlock', then the line ran from right to left, so it became a symbol of bastardy. A left-handed compliment is something with unpleasant innuendos. The same delineations are given in other European languages – *gauche*, *link*, *stanca* or *manca* and *zurdo*, all having unfortunate connotations for the left.

We have already noted that left-handers are far more able with both hands than the average right-hander. So, purely on a point of semantics, ambisinistrality as a measure of skill with both hands would not be in anyone's favour. Galen, according to S. T. Orton, produced the manual equivalent of the dance hall two left-footer with the *bon mot* 'ambilevous', his intention being to convey someone who was clumsy with both hands. It is worth noting the discrimination of the ambilevers with the left and the ambidexters with the right.

Degrees of handedness

In all, the population seems to be made up of six categories of handedness: those with a slight bias to the left, total left-handedness, those skilled with both hands or showing no preference, those unskilled with either hand, total right-handedness and those with a slight bias to the right. Margaret Clark considered that slight left-handers and ambidexters in childhood would eventually swing to the right in adulthood, bowing to social pressures, imitation and training, as would Galen's ambilevers. If some researchers are to be believed, it would appear that the only left-handers existing in the adult population are those strongly left and those slight left-handers who are too far below the average mentality to make the change to right, plus a few obstinate cusses who like to be different.

As we are looking at switches for conformity's sake, if society made life as inconvenient for the right-hander as it does for the left-hander, there is no reason to suppose that all six categories could not just as easily emerge left-handed for similar reasons.

In 1987, Joyce E. Whittington and P. N. Richards published the results of a study they carried out at the School of Education, University of Bath, into children's laterality prevalences related to performance, using a national sample of over 11,000 children from the National Child Development Study as their basis. They monitored children between the ages of 7 and 11, looking at attainment and ability at the age of 11.

Around 86 per cent were found to be consistent in their hand preference from 7 to 11. Those who changed were ambilateral at 7 years of age. At age 11, the left-handers scored less in ability and attainment than average, but the right-handers who had changed to the left at 7 were above average. Their study was important in relation to determining those left-handers who might be at risk of displaying learning difficulties.

Laterality tests

Laterality testing in relation to educational difficulties or attainments has been prolific for decades as has laterality testing in general, and researchers often tend to contradict one another's findings.

The results of these unending hand, foot, eye and ear tests have engendered more researchers bent on disproving the host of already conflicting theories. Whatever their findings, the education authorities firmly maintain their 'I-see-no-ships' stance on the educational issues and no doubt laterality testing will continue until someone designates a functional purpose for the results.

Too many appear to be composed of pompous, scientific, gobbledegook of no significance or interest to average left-handers or to parents of left-handed children, although very few have been conducted on a level that can be clearly understood and duplicated in the school or living room.

The Edinburgh Inventory

Probably the most widely accepted measurement of handedness today is the Edinburgh Inventory. Conducted by R. C. Oldfield, at the MRC Speech and Communication Unit of Edinburgh University, its results, published in 1971, suggest a simple way to assess handedness for use in future neuropsychological or clinical work, and it has been used as a yardstick by researchers universally ever since.

Before this, tests were carried out by presenting subjects with various tasks to perform with both hands and questions on their preferred handedness for certain everyday tasks. Conformity was the keynote, with normality weighted in favour of whichever way the majority went.

Oldfield felt that these manual tasks were inadequate and that their findings were different from those produced by the questions. Favouring the question system, he produced a simple inventory consisting of twenty items and proceeded to test a wide spread of first-year undergraduates in English and Scottish Universities. He stressed that his method may not be adequate for testing young children, and that observation of manual tasks in this case might be more appropriate. Out of 1,128 subjects (394 men and 734 women) ranging in age from twenty to twenty-one, 25.9 per cent of the men and 16.6 per cent of the women claimed a tendency to left-handedness. These figures reflect the same disparity usually noticed between the sexes. They also reveal that many people tend to correlate left-handedness with the obvious task of writing, drawing and using knives, regarding other tasks as incidental, rather than significant. Some subjects were found to be more left-handed than they imagined themselves to be, and Oldfield discovered that the question 'Are you at all left-handed?' is unlikely to produce an accurate answer.

1 Writing
2 Drawing
3 Throwing
4 Scissors
5 Comb
6 Toothbrush
7 Knife (without fork)
8 Spoon
9 Hammer
10 Screwdriver
11 Tennis racquet
12 Knife (with fork)
13 Cricket bat (lower hand)
14 Golf club (lower hand)
15 Broom (upper hand)
16 Rake (upper hand)
17 Striking match (match)
18 Opening box (lid)
19 Dealing cards (card being dealt)
20 Threading needle (needle or thread according to which is moved)

Having done this, Oldfield looked again at the twenty items and realised that some of them would be inappropriate if the inventory were to be used universally. The British, for example, unlike other nationalities, always eat with knife and fork, and traditionally the fork is held in the left hand, the knife in the right hand. Cricket bats and rakes are not used by everyone.

Oldfield found that right-handers deal cards with the pack in their right hands and assumed that this is because dealing begins to the left. 'One thoroughly right-handed man told me that he had acquired the habit of dealing left-handed by simply copying his father who had first taught him card games,' he wrote. The tennis racquet was manually neutral: '... having regard to the frequency of back-handed strokes generally, it is difficult to see any advantage in right-handed, as opposed to left-handed, use of the racquet. It is possible that it derives from some indiscernible, subtle features of the play tactics of (generally) right-handed opponents.'

All this and a certain chauvinistic assumption that men did not usually wield a needle, led him to the conclusion that some items should be withdrawn and he later reduced them to ten, as follows:

1 Writing
2 Drawing
3 Throwing
4 Scissors
5 Toothbrush
6 Knife (without fork)
7 Spoon
8 Broom (upper hand)
9 Striking match (match)
10 Opening box (lid)

Assessing the results

Scores achieved by groups tested on the Edinburgh Handedness Inventory range from −100 (complete left-handedness) to +100 (complete right-handedness). The laterality quotient is found by subtracting the number of left-handed actions performed from the number of right-handed actions performed. The result is divided by the number of actions and multiplied by 100. Questionnaires of this sort do not always present a true indication of preferred handedness, particularly in adults who may have, consciously or unconsciously, changed preference for certain tasks since infancy. Some left-handers carry out some tasks with their right hands because right-handers have taught them that way. The same is true of right-handers taught by left-handers. One school survey reported 16 left-handed writers out of 34. This abnormally high result was attributed to their left-handed first- and second-grade teachers. Some implements do not lend themselves to left-hand use, such as can openers, corkscrews and right-handed scissors – many lefties use their right hands for convenience.

Subjects may answer one way in a questionnaire with sincerity but perform differently if put to the test, proving a case for assessment by observation and questionnaire combined. Others simply change their minds from one time of testing to the next. In one survey, the subjects were wrong in a quarter to a half of their performed tasks compared to their previous written statements.

As we have seen, there are so many degrees of laterality that it must be nearly impossible to find a way of analysing the results of these tests to produce an accurate sample of handedness, left or right. Researchers would have to produce statistics for each type of laterality, rather than clear-cut dextral or sinistral figures. One survey produced data ranging from 2 to 35 per cent left-handers. Another researcher who tested 57 five- to thirteen-year-olds, found 16 of them were left-handed – the following year when he re-tested the same sample, all but one were right-handed. Testing children by observation is probably more efficient, for, as noted earlier, asking questions can recreate the anxiety of the exam room, resulting in the child trying too hard to produce the 'right' answers.

Is handedness really the issue? Perhaps researchers should be assessing right- and left-brain hemisphere people, for those may be the only two clear-cut categories into which human beings can be classified. There do not appear to be any population studies for them, yet this data could be highly significant in terms of human behaviour, education, industry, culture and the future progress of mankind, and might be put to good use.

Testing for torque

Theodore H. Blau, researching into laterality, tested for torque – clockwise spiralling – which he found significant in that child achievers tended to draw circles in a counter-clockwise direction with either hand. In a Presidential Address delivered at a meeting of the American Psychological Association, San Francisco, in 1977, Blau pointed out that the world's rotation and the majority of living cells displayed dextral rather than sinistral characteristics. Circling in drawing had been found to be associated with child behaviour and handedness, most adults circling in a counter-clockwise direction.

The bad news for left-handers seemed to be that they, together with problem children, frequently mixed left and right circling. His theory was that children who circled clockwise had a defect in the corpus callosum and the resultant mixed dominance prevented them from achieving socially and educationally. He also found that they were more likely to be vulnerable to schizophrenia in adulthood. Blau tested 54 children with no torque and 52 with torque at around 9 years of age. Ten years later, it transpired that 11 of the 52 and 1 of the 54 had developed schizophrenia.

The children were asked to carry out three tests, first with their preferred writing hand and then with their non-preferred hand. They had to copy a simple design, to write their names and to draw a circle with their preferred hand around three 'X's in one row and with the non-preferred hand around three 'X's in the row below. It was the latter test in which he was interested. If one or more of the six circles was drawn clockwise, they were classified as torque – viewed as an external measure of cerebral dominance.

From previous studies, Blau deduced that all very young children, particularly those under four years of age, circle both ways. One study showed that 68 to 90 per cent of kindergarten children tested did so, but it was expected that as children mature and the corpus callosum developed along with laterality, counter-clockwise circling would establish itself in all except around 30 per cent of the population. Those who have not established this pattern by the age of five may experience developmental problems. Numerous studies have shown that handedness, cerebral dominance and maladjustive behaviour are interconnected. Blau's theory was that an inability to lateralise in childhood, which could account for this, could be due to a defect in the brain's connecting nerve fibres and that this could be hereditary.

What Blau was suggesting was that resultant failure to perform or gain acceptance could encourage the onset of schizophrenia whereas support and success would diminish the possibilities. The effects of the defect 'may prevent sufficient and/or appropriate language, cognition, and skill acquisition and socialisation during the crucial developmental years.' This resulted in 'a disposition to lag behind expected stages of increasing competence. This, in turn, may account for an adult pattern of extreme fear reactions, inability to think and communicate adequately, distortion ...', etc.

The good news is that some children displaying torque develop well and even excel (somewhat of a paradox in relation to his main theory). 'If some become eminent, this would not surprise those researchers who have explored outcomes in schizophrenic families. It may be that children who exhibit torque become "unusual" adults – in the best and the worst senses of the word.'

As Blau's tests were conducted during the 1970s, he was not aware at that time of the testosterone theories of the 1980s. The fact that more males (in the 15-to-25 age range) and left-handers were found to be susceptible to the development of schizophrenia and that both groups showed a higher incidence of torque, could equally link up with the hormonal theories of Geschwind and Galaburda.

Playing with circles

An article in the December 1988 issue of the *Reader's Digest* outlined tests taken from *The Hand Book* by Linda Lee and James Charlton in which readers were requested to draw circles with first the right and then the left hand and note which direction they used.

The answer proclaimed that right-handers generally drew counter-clockwise circles while left-handers drew them clockwise with either hand. Those who drew one circle clockwise probably had left-handed tendencies. As a very strong left-hander, my circles, I'm happy to say, are drawn firmly counter-clockwise with either left or right hand. The only peculiarity is that when drawing two circles simultaneously, I display torque with the right hand, possibly indicating that my two hemispheres suddenly move into opposition with one another if I become ambidextrous. Remember how two disconnected hemispheres battled it out in action – one hand closed the door while the other tried to open it. As a measure of handedness, it would show the counter-clockwise circle to be drawn by the dominant hand.

Later, circle drawing in adults was seen to be dependent on the muscle mechanics of the hand, especially the thumb and index finger interactions, not on cerebral dominance, by researchers Jack and Lorrie Demarest, at Monmouth College, New Jersey. They confirmed Blau's findings among children but found that a high incidence of left-handed adults they tested displayed no torque at all. 'It may be that socio-cultural factors have influenced left-handers to behave more like right-handers, and the torque test is a reflection of this influence,' they proclaimed.

As a left-hander, my left hand draws counter-clockwise circles because it follows its natural inclination so to do, prompted more by comfort than any other issue, I strongly suspect. Just to throw a spanner in the works, while trying these tests I found that on the odd occasion, I did display torque with the right hand. Enlightenment came when I noted that, although I always began circling at the top left-hand corner with my left hand, I was inconsistent on initial positioning with the right. As an experiment, I drew four '+'s and placed a dot in the upper and lower left spaces between the lines and in the upper and lower right spaces. With my left hand, I placed the pencil on the top left dot and drew a circle, following suit on each dot on the other three '+'s. I performed the same experiment with my right hand and compared performances.

From the upper and lower left dots. I produced a counter-clockwise circle with right and left hands and from the upper and lower right dots, I produced torque with left and right hands. What was I to make of this? I deduced that the ability to draw clockwise or anti-clockwise circles depends very much on the position of the hand and arm at the starting point and its own personal comfort in relation to the body. In both cases, you are pushing downwards, which, as any skier will verify, is much simpler than climbing mountains.

If the starting point is at the centre bottom, which means climbing either way, the hand will move in the direction of the thumb and first finger, likewise from centre top, not only for comfort but because we are used to going forwards, not backwards. The implement is also important – drawing backward circles with a fountain pen nib can impede progress and, therefore, influence the direction taken. Of course, this is just a lay person's hypothesis and would need to be scientifically verified, grants permitting.

The *Reader's Digest* article urged readers to sign their name with their right hand, simultaneously signing it backwards with the left from the centre of the paper. 'You'll be surprised how much it resembles your forward right-handed writing,' is stated of the latter. This is supposed to indicate a degree of sinistrality inherent in right-handers. Vice versa for lefties, presumably.

Starting with both hands at the centre of the page, as asked, it would be physically impossible not to mirror write with one hand. If one hand drew something entirely different from the other when employed simultaneously, as could Landseer, the artist, it would be far more significant, denoting ambidexterity.

Van Riper Critical Angle Board

Simultaneous bimanual drawing studies, of which there have been many, were put into perspective by C. Van Riper in the 1930s. Because of the unreliability of previous tests, he devised a test aimed at highlighting significant differences between left- and right-handers, indicating varying degrees of laterality and eliminating skills acquired because of environmental pressure. His initial tests showed that both hands drawing simultaneously simply made mirror images, the hand copying the example correctly being accepted as dominant.

His Critical Angle Board test consisted of two upright boards placed on a flat board with the vertical boards parallel to the subjects' chests. They were asked to concentrate on and copy an illustration about 30 degrees above eye contact ahead of them onto two pieces of paper pinned on the outsides of the vertical boards, using both hands simultaneously, as fast as they could. The boards were then rotated through 90 degrees, and to make life more difficult, the angle was increased 10 degrees each time. The exercise continued until one hand produced a mirror image – the angle at that time being the critical one. No mirroring is an indication of ambidexterity. There were, of course, disagreements with this, but it has been widely accepted.

Batteries of tests have been administered to children and adults for decades, including those which might reveal significant data in relation to differences in strength – left-handers were found to have stronger right-hand grips and vice versa – speed and motor performance.

Body language

Left-handers can sometimes be identified by their body language, if you don't spot them writing or identify their right-profiled drawings. Once you are aware of the characteristics, you will find yourself watching people more and more and classifying them into possible left- or right-handers, although it is as well to exercise some caution to allow for cross-laterals who don't conform to any set pattern. As we have already noted, speech accompanied by left- or mixed-hand gestures is one sign to look out for. Generally, they will applaud with their left hand against the right, but they do not always cross the left leg over the right or fold arms with the left uppermost. Another sign is lateral eye movement, which occurs when one breaks eye contact, and looks to left or right when pondering the answer to a question.

Lateral eye movements

The difference in lateral eye movement and its relation to brain function had been noted by researchers in the 1960s and was considered to be a phenomenon of the brain which, like any computer, paused to process additional information in order to respond to the question. The eye focuses towards the side controlled by the dominant opposite hemisphere. Those pausing for thought with their eyes firmly fixed over your right shoulder, providing you are facing them, are likely to be left-handed and vice versa.

Tests carried out at Stanford University using a hidden camera, revealed 64 per cent of the subjects looked rightward when asked for verbal explanations to several proverbs and 31 per cent looked leftward when asked spatial questions involving visualisations, indicating the appropriate hemispheres for speech and spatial awareness were dominating in each case – but only when the questioner was seated behind the subjects. Apparently, face-to-face confrontation was so offputting that 71 per cent of them stuck with their familiar dominant hemisphere and looked consistently in one direction. Try it – it works. Performance under face-to-face stress was said to improve if the habit of relying on old faithful could be broken.

At Harvard University, researchers found that spatial and emotional questions together produced a left-eyed (right emotional hemisphere) response. So the eye is activating the brain as it reacts to different types of questions and the appropriate hemisphere springs into life to deal with whichever type of question it can best deal with, verbal, spatial or emotional.

For the benefit of readers who would like to try these tests, the questions were asked as follows:

What is the primary difference between the words 'recognise' and 'remember'? (Verbal-non-emotional). Imagine a rectangle. Draw a line from the upper left-hand corner to the lower right-hand corner. What two figures do you now see? (Spatial-non-emotional). For you, is anger or hate a stronger emotion? (Verbal-emotional). When you visualise your father's face, what emotion first strikes you? (Spatial-emotional).

The most widely practised 'pop' test for eyedness is to focus on an object in the distance dead ahead and place one finger in front of the face lined up with the object, automatically creating an out-of-focus image. Close the right eye. If you are left-eyed, the finger will remain in the same spot. If you close the left eye, the finger will move to the left of the image. The reverse effect will be experienced by right-eye dominant people.

Another 'trick' is to cut a small hole in a sheet of paper and hold it at arm's-length so that you can see an object through it. Bring the paper back to your face towards your nose and the eye through which you are sighting is your dominant one. You can also test for dominance by noting which eye you prefer to use when looking through a microscope, camera, keyhole or telescope.

Martin Gardner, in *The Ambidextrous Universe*, raises the point that no research appears to have been undertaken yet as to which eye one uses for winking at people. Possibly no research grants have been made available yet for that either, although it is fair to assume, if he is referring to members of the opposite sex, that the dominant eye would be open 'all the better to see them with'. His suggested 'pop' eye test for children consists of rolling a sheet of paper into a megaphone and securing it with some tape. The child peeps through the large end revealing the dominant eye to the tester through the megaphone.

Jaynes' smiling faces

Not only eye dominance but visual perception are dictated by lateral dominance. Julian Jaynes' well-known smiling faces test has been reproduced widely with similar results. Choose which face you think is the happier of these two by staring at the nose in each case.

Each side of the face is perceived by a different hemisphere. Eighty per cent of right-handers out of 1,000 people to whom Jaynes administered the test thought the second face was the happiest. The faces are mirror images of one another and as the right brain tends to dominate non-verbal information and has been seen to show emotion more, it is relating to the happier-looking left side of the face in the second picture. Fifty per cent of left-handers tested responded to the first face, indicating that their left hemisphere was dominating non-verbal perception. The lower percentage would be shown because many people would be cross-laterals with spatial awareness in the right brain.

Facial dyslexia

Some people, however, cannot recognise faces at all. Researchers Daniel Tranel and Antonio Damasio of the University of Iowa College of Medicine have noted a high percentage of left-handers and artistic people, predominantly men, among people suffering from 'developmental prosopagnosia' or 'facial dyslexia'.

When they presented a paper at the Society for Neuroscience in Chicago in November 1989 highlighting the problem, which often arises after stroke or head injury, causing localised brain damage, they found members of their lecture audiences, with no history of brain damage, reporting similar problems which they had always had.

Although their memory may not be affected in any other way, sufferers find it difficult to recognise people's faces, however many times they see them. Many of them have successful home lives and careers, and those who find it a social problem compensate by learning strategies such as recognising voices.

'The difficulty must start early in childhood. If we could identify people with it early enough, we could counsel them to develop alternative strategies,' said Tranel, who believes that connections between nerve cells have not developed correctly.

Foot dominance

Some researchers have found strong interrelationships between hand and foot and eye and ear. The obvious test to determine the dominant foot is to see which one the subject uses first to walk, to mount stairs, to hop or to kick a ball.

Using an escalator is fraught with danger for the left-footed left-hander who would prefer to hang on to the moving rail with the left hand and step on to the left side with the left foot. I always carry shopping or shoulder bags on my right so that my left hand is free for manipulative purposes. As most escalators ask passengers to keep to the right so that others can pass on the left, this can be a terrifying experience, particularly in the London underground where, teetering on to the first step in high heels which are in danger of sticking between the slats (if you are female), you try to mount with your left foot on the right side and hang on to the moving rail with a right hand loaded with paraphernalia. If you transfer that to the left hand, you simply feel unbalanced and insecure. Getting off is a feat of prestidigitation as the top step looms ever nearer and you stagger on the right brink with the left foot poised, praying that you won't miss and be dragged underneath the staircase with the rest of the steps. Never look down.

Ear dominance

Dichotic listening tests are used to define ear dominance, and consist of two separate messages each played simultaneously through each ear. Environmental constraints may play some part in the development of a dominant ear, for left-handers usually hold the telephone earpiece to their right ear so that their left hand is free for writing while right-handers use their left ear. Undoubtedly, the telephone ear will eventually develop at the expense of the less-used ear and before the days of telephones, I am sure the findings of such tests would have been significantly different.

In any event, researchers have found the interpretation of dichotic listening tests to be related to brain lateralisation and the appropriate ear will pick up and relay the appropriate sounds for interpretation by its dominant hemisphere. If speech is in the left hemisphere, the right ear will pick up words better. The left ear will be likely to hear non-speech sounds more clearly, relayed through the right non-verbal, musical hemisphere.

Margaret Clark carried out an intensive study of the laterality preferences of 330 eleven- to twelve-year-old children in the primary VII classes of eight Glasgow schools in the mid-1950s, using a battery of tests for handedness, eyedness, earedness and footedness. In all, she used 18 laterality tests – 8 for handedness, 3 for footedness, 3 for earedness, 4 for eyedness – a writing test and a questionnaire. A full breakdown of the individual tests and their results is given in her book *Left-Handedness* and, for those involved in educational research or laterality testing, the material is invaluable.

The tests and her findings are outside the scope of this book to report, but it is worth noting that she found that a connection exists between foot and hand preference, and between ear and eye, but none between hand and eye. Nowadays it is accepted that foot and hand actions are motor functions, which can be linked to laterality, but ears and eyes are sensory functions, which cannot. Neither did she find obvious differences in speed or quality between left- and right-handed writers. Her recommendation is that left-handers should receive the same attention as right-handers when being taught to write.

* * * *

7
EDUCATION AND THE
LEFT-HANDED CHILD

'Pooh looked at his two paws. He knew that one of them was the right, and he knew that when you had decided which one of them was right, then the other was the left, but he never could remember how to begin.' A. A. Milne, *The House at Pooh Corner*.

Teaching attitudes

Out of ten schools contacted to undertake a small-scale survey of their left-handers − five in Bolton and five in Liverpool − only one from each area responded. The others did not reply to my letters. I had special reasons for choosing these two areas and was curious to know what their attitudes were to left-handedness in schools.

When I launched my left-handed mail-order business, The Left-Handed Company, in October 1988, many of the country's education authorities had asked me to supply catalogues for distribution to schools, acknowledging that it was in their best interests. Bolton told me to consult the telephone book for a list of schools which I could contact myself, adding that they would not want people to think they were promoting a commercial organisation, while Liverpool was one of several north-west authorities which failed even to acknowledge receipt of my letters.

I wanted to know if this attitude reflected that of the schools in their areas so I drafted a simple questionnaire which I asked for them to hand on to their teachers. Only the private schools responded.

Because of the poor response and a discrepancy in the ratio between the sexes, weighted in favour of the girls, it was not possible to gather any significant data other than that only 8.62 per cent of the 406 pupils surveyed were left-handed: 16.8 per cent of the 68 boys were left-handed and only 7 per cent of the 338 girls, showing the higher incidence of left-handedness among boys which could be expected. Had there been more boys in the sample, doubtless the overall percentage would have been higher. During my conversations with several teachers at a recent schools equipment exhibition, the norm for left-handed pupils at some schools appeared to be as high as 20 per cent. Statistics appear to vary from classroom to classroom.

One head teacher surveyed summed up: 'Left-handedness is not necessarily a problem. It has to be viewed in the context of their whole maturity and development. One of the left-handed children has excellent fine motor control and uses left-handed scissors expertly ... in the case of the ... other child laterality was not totally established when he started school and his fine motor control was undeveloped. He now uses his left hand all the time and his fine motor control has developed considerably.'

Although there were few children with apparent educational difficulties, poor hand-eye co-ordination received the highest consideration, followed by clumsiness and stammering. All seventeen teachers were right-handed. Only six thought left-handedness was an educational disadvantage and seven admitted that they made no adjustments when teaching left-handers. The teachers who did make adjustments were normally concerned with placing the left-handers where their writing hands would not nudge their right-handed colleagues.

One teacher mentioned the need for workbooks with the writing page on the left so that written instructions would not be obscured by the left arm stretching over to write on the right-hand page. Another pointed out that in the transition from pencil to ink, some left-handers experienced greater difficulties than right-handers. Another found it difficult to check written work while the left-hander was writing because the work was obscured by their left arm. Only four mentioned the need for left-handed scissors.

One said she gave consideration to handwork tasks, such as cutting out or model-making with tools. When I was in my first term at grammar school in Whitefield, north Manchester, in the 1950s, my geometry mistress consistently threw my feeble attempts at three-dimensional models across the room, declaring them disgusting, which indeed they were.

She occasionally rapped me over the hand with her ruler, and my fingers were covered in red weals from trying to force the right-handed scissors through cardboard, but because I had no idea that my clumsiness was because of the design of the implements, I assumed, as she seemed to do, that I was less able than the other children. I was, unfortunately, the only pupil in the class who had this problem. Apart from finding it impossible to cut card straight because the cutting blades of the right-handed scissors obscured my view, I found it impossible to draw a straight line with a ruler. I had to keep pulling my hand back because it covered the measurements which run from left to right, whereas I draw from right to left.

I was received with even less enthusiasm by my maths teacher who was totally exasperated at my inability to grasp the simplest equations – as a visually orientated, right-brained person I was only able to comprehend when I saw a graph or a cake chart. I suffered from what can only be described as numerical dyslexia. I have always suspected this is an educational problem and now know that there is a dysfunction called discalculia. My fear of maths was so great that I would develop migraine before each session and one eye would black out entirely for the whole lesson. My regular forays into sick bay were received with neither sympathy nor trust, and I possess so little mathematical knowledge even now that I can only run the financial side of my business by translating figurework into graphs and charts and by relying heavily on calculators and the honesty of other people.

A helpful, retired, junior school teacher has specific advice to offer about geometric drawings: 'The left-hander needs to draw lines right to left, thus pulling the pencil. Squares, polygons, triangles need to be constructed in an anti-clockwise direction (the right-hander constructs them clockwise). This anti-clockwise drawing does bring its own problems, of using a protractor and a set-square in a different way.'

Teachers who do recognise laterality problems tend to be more sympathetic. One teacher sends out questionnaires to determine her left-handers when they begin school and Derbyshire Education Authority issues guidelines to junior school teachers on how to help left-handed pupils, but, as far as I know, it is the only authority to do so.

Neil Gordon, honorary consultant paediatric neurologist formerly at Booth Hall Children's Hospital, Manchester, told me that it is the pathological left-handers who are most likely to experience learning difficulties. He recommends that they should be identified as soon as they start school, and that their progress should be monitored. He recommends the tests outlined by Dorothy Bishop (1980) which reveal abnormal clumsiness in the right hand.

A left-handed supply teacher complained that most teachers do not understand the problems and needs of left-handers, and that even those teachers who supply left-handed scissors usually mix them in with other scissors, rendering some right-handers clumsy. 'I would advocate that one teacher in every school be invited to a meeting to learn about ways of helping left-handers ... obviously reception teachers are the most important, so that the correct habits can be encouraged right from the start,' she said.

One head teacher in a Group Two primary school who had researched left-handedness for his Advanced Diploma in Education, decided to pursue his research further on discovering that 25 per cent of his next class were left-handed. 'The more I went into it the more I realised that very little had been written about it and many teachers knew even less than I did,' he stated.

Research material

This complaint crops up incessantly from people who feel inclined to study left-handedness and who find that lack of available information prevents them from so doing. My own research reveals that in fact so much has been written on handedness and laterality that it is impossible to consult all the documentation. It is simply a matter of knowing where to look. But it is true that not much can be found on the popular bookshelves which can add to such studies.

The head teacher did what he could in limited circumstances, carrying out tests with groups of children in different types of schools in the area. As is usually the case, figures varied from class to class but the average was around ten per cent. 'There was a special need because of the different styles. I found four variations of the "hook". They were generally very bright children who were not progressing particularly well,' he told me.

'It is very much a right-handed world. If there is not something set aside for these children, they are on a loser to begin with. In every class, teachers had not taken them into consideration. It takes no expertise and no organisation but every class I went into had a left-handed child sitting next to a right-hander on their left-hand side. When I pointed this out, they hadn't thought about it. If I asked some teachers to fill in a questionnaire and asked how many left-handers there were, some said they didn't think they had any or they wouldn't know.

'Since doing this, we developed our own policy for left-handed children. At a very early stage, we worked out the correct positioning of the paper and the best place for children to sit in the class. We already had scissors.'

Rural folklore

The school was in a rural location and it is important to realise how, in some areas, even in the 1980s, folklore continues to view left-handedness as a sinister subject. 'I had a child lower down the school who developed obvious left-hand tendencies from the age of about three. Before he was due to start full-time school, his father forbade him to use his left hand for writing. This continued during his first year in school.

'I heard about it the year after – everyone had kept quiet about it. The child used his right hand but he fell and broke his right arm. It came to my attention because the teacher showed me the piece of work and it was just as neat with the left as the right. I approached his mum but his father wouldn't listen. His attitude was archaic. He thought it was unnatural and that retarded children were left-handed.'

Did the child stammer? I wondered. It transpired that he did indeed and that he had been having speech therapy. His father, who didn't view this with any significance, said that he had also stammered when he was a boy. It would have been no surprise to find out that his own father had prevented him from using his left hand too.

'The only people of any use were in the area of special needs education, because they said that overall they tended to come across a higher percentage of left-handed children,' continued the head teacher.

Not only are some rural schools behind the times. One plea for help with her son's handwriting came from a woman who had been warned when her son was at nursery school that, because he wouldn't join in painting activities, he might experience a handwriting problem later. Now aged eleven, the boy – a left-handed writer – produced spidery, untidy writing riddled with spelling mistakes. His mother complained that he was seated next to a right-hander who constantly bumped elbows with him. 'Some teachers didn't notice this problem, although teachers were informed D. was left-handed and found handwriting very difficult and I did ask for additional help. Very little help if any was given.'

A left-handed teacher in a sixth form college made a point of observing left-handers when invigilating examinations over a twenty-five-year period. He found that 10 per cent of the examinees were left-handed and that 3 per cent of the left-handers wrote by making the hook. The other 97 per cent turned the paper and held their pens in the mirror image of the right-handed position to avoid smudging. 'Marking scripts ... I have the very strong impression that left-handers usually write more slowly for their scripts are generally shorter, and perhaps this is because to push a pen is harder than to pull it.' Observation alone is not always acceptable to researchers, some of whom would doubtless disagree with the view that there is any difference in performance between left- and right-handed children.

As a left-hander, I must put my oar in here again and admit that exams were a nightmare, for to sit for long periods writing interminably with a pen clutched tightly in the pushing position creates cramp and muscle fatigue in the left hand, index finger and thumb not experienced by the right-hander. If the left-hander's examination scripts were seen to be shorter, it may not have been because they wrote more slowly – I scribble very quickly – but because they were sitting as much a physical endurance test as a test of any mental ability and the sooner it was over, the better.

Case histories

'As a baby and toddler, we noticed J. held things differently and all the families thought it was terrible. It was as though she had an illness. They were all keen to tell us that *no one* was left-handed in their families and even wondered if the postman was left-handed! We had eight postmen in eight, weekly, shifts,' said one mother.

Many parents suffer anxiety over their children's learning difficulties, but none so much as those whose left-handed children's problems have been overlooked or incorrectly diagnosed. The mother of a 13-year-old boy sent me his assessment report from the Service for Special Educational Needs, from which I gathered that his reading accuracy and spelling were that of a 10-year-old and his reading comprehension that of a 12-year-old. His handwriting assessment revealed that, as a left-hander, he wrote very awkwardly, mixing lower case and capital letters. His pencil was held with the thumb crossing the first finger, his paper was not sloped to the right and he formed the letters o,a,g,d,e,y,p,r,H and R incorrectly.

He was slow in answering questions and carrying out instructions, although he eventually came up with the goods. It was suggested that he should continue into the normal secondary school curriculum on a trial basis.

His mother told me that the report omitted to mention that her son had an IQ of over 100. 'His slowness is possibly due to having done most of his work backwards in primary school, where they never explained to him he was doing it wrong until he was over eight, when we all gave him a crash course in reading.'

Her husband died when the boy was ten and she had to go out to work to support him. 'When he started senior school it took me a year with his homework to get him completely forwards with his maths. I've had him jumping up and down, saying he was a failure at eleven and kicking and screaming on the floor because his pen wouldn't write properly – it kept stopping. He is still not very good at using scissors ...'

Eighteen months after his assessment, her son was still printing in the remedial class, after a few handwriting lessons. 'He is still a lovely, caring boy with a lot of common sense. When I had him privately assessed, they told me, not only was he very bright but he's brilliantly talented with his hands,' his mother wrote to me.

The parents of a nine-year-old boy had no idea how their son was doing at school because he had had no headmaster for nine months and consequently there had been a teachers' strike and no parents' nights. They realised he was slower than other children and had been told at the last parents' night that he had a problem of sorts that the teacher couldn't quite put her finger on.

'He is a normal child and very polite. He tries his best and doesn't fit into the mould of disruptive child. The school didn't want anyone going in because of their reputation,' his mother told me.

'It first appeared as "a slow reader" (almost into the remedial class) although his teacher was never convinced he was "slow". She suggested further investigations, first with the doctor. Our doctor said there was nothing wrong with him. Because we insisted that it was not just a small worry, he put us in contact with the out-patients department of the Gartside Street Clinic in Manchester to check for physical defects. At this point we were convinced he suffered from dyslexia.

'They recommended a child psychologist. She was surprised to find that he had a high IQ. She said he was above average intelligence but had a rotten memory. When he was young and started to write his name, he wrote it with the left hand and then put the pencil in his right hand and wrote mirror writing. He was totally confused as to which way he should be writing.

'He was four at the time and we were told he would grow out of it. We thought he was ambidextrous and were not aware that he was left-handed so we left him alone.'

The child psychologist also thought her son might be dyslexic, particularly as he confused 'b's and 'd's and wrote 'saw' for 'was'. The child struggled with his work every evening at home and was referred to an occupational therapist. 'She said he had an imbalance. When he tried to write, all his muscles would tense up and he would grip his pen so hard, his face would curl up and his tongue would come out. She did simple tests with him, including one for laterality,' continued his mother.

When she discovered he was left-handed, the occupational therapist contacted the school, which was not prepared to offer any help and wanted to leave him a little longer. His mother was ready for blasting them out, but when she mentioned that she had consulted a doctor, they relented, although they told her they couldn't find an occupational therapist for him.

The boy's own occupational therapist began visiting him at school once a week, to see him do some exercises which would help improve his co-ordination and make him relax more. Eventually the family found another tutor to help with their son's reading problem and a third therapist to help with remedial work.

'There are thirty-six children in the class – they would never have one hour each reading a week normally. Also, he was writing at school and told he was doing the letters the wrong way. "We don't do the 'g's like that at this school", he was told. The occupational therapist had taught him to do it that way,' continued his mother.

'I think he feels special. At school, he gets upset because he wants to be like the rest of them. He kept crying because he wanted to be on the same work as his friends and he knew he couldn't be.' His parents also told me that their son was not alone with his problems and they could identify ten other children with similar learning difficulties.

He was lucky, for not all parents would take the time and trouble to persevere so that their child received adequate attention, particularly in the face of such apathy from both school and doctor. From letters I have received, however, it would appear that not only some teachers but several doctors have strange attitudes to sinistrals.

One parent was amazed at her doctor's attitude when she had her two-year-old daughter examined after she had broken her left arm. At the time she had not lateralised although she was predominantly left-handed. Now she had to use her right hand. 'I was virtually called a liar, as if I was making excuses for her being a slow developer. It was not until the little girl drew recognisable features on a "face" that the doctor drew that she believed my daughter was left-handed.

'It broke my heart the other week when I stayed at her playgroup to see her struggling so much to cut and paste when the other children were doing it with ease; and I think in her own way, she felt frustrated that she had to wait for the teacher to cut her bits of paper up for her; and I am worried about when she starts infants school or nursery that she will feel even more left out as they tend to be left to their own devices more.' The playgroup did not supply left-handed scissors and most parents do not know where they can obtain them because there are so few outlets.

The inconveniences may begin at playgroup, but they don't always end there. A 25-year-old librarian remembered her college days when 'there was one room with the most infuriating study-desks – they consisted of a chair with a book-rest projection attached to the right arm of the chair. Not only could I not use this for writing purposes, it made any other position very uncomfortable.' A common complaint this and surely one that could be rectified with a bit of ergonomical foresight, although according to the experts I tackled in that particular area, left-handers do not need any special equipment.

The 'which-handed' child

Youngsters who have not lateralised and who do not receive adequate guidance may face the biggest problems. 'Take a bewildered, shy child of five or six pitched into a noisy, crowded world of education and given an implement for writing and told to copy what is a) in the book or b) on the blackboard. When that implement is taken firmly from the left hand and replaced in the right, the bewilderment increases.

'From then on, the battle of switching hands begins and carries on through life. Whilst most will argue that no teacher will force a child to use the non-dominant hand, they perhaps forget that some children may not know which is the preferred hand and, trying to keep up with an increasing demand for written responses, begins the devastating disaffection with writing implements.

'During the early years and throughout school life, the "which-handed child" is increasingly reluctant to commit anything to paper, and poor handwriting is often coupled with spelling/writing mistakes ... uneven lines, illegibility and untidiness, and the more the writer's attention is drawn to these unacceptably untidy and seemingly unnecessary failures, the more the reluctance to write, or to show that writing for comment and correction.'

Written by a left-hander, now middle-aged, who was beset by such problems herself. Among the subsequent learning difficulties she experienced were rote learning, logic, visual short-term memory, word-searching, resulting in 'malapropisms', problems with hockey sticks, laboratory instruments ('I remember reaching around a titration set-up in chemistry with dire results'), musical instruments, geometrical instruments, rulers, drawing tools, right-handers either telling her to do things the opposite way or simply ignoring her, poor spelling, disorientation, difficulty making conceptual connections 'particularly when translating from right- to left-handedness ... enormous difficulties when working with partners who are right-handed particularly in practical situations, e.g. starting from a different position or direction in, say, cutting, tracking, etc.'

The writer concludes: 'I am suggesting that many left-handers may have to go through different and additional thought processes to arrive at the same point as right-handers. Some may manage without undue concern but for others, there can be confusion, distraction and failure.'

We are beginning to see that some (not all) left-handers do experience educational problems, due in the main either to inadequate equipment or to an ongoing battle with different thought processes unrecognised by some parents, teachers and the medical profession. The writer eventually found 'success and confidence' in discovering that she was good at physical education, maths – under a patient teacher – and reading for pleasure.

Blackboard problems were conquered by beginning with the left hand at the left of the board and switching to the right hand half-way along. As a special needs adviser, she observed that not all teachers know how to help left-handers or have the time to do so. 'Often solutions appear as generalisations such as "see that the child is sitting correctly", or "make sure the lighting doesn't throw shadows on the page". I am suggesting that each left-hander needs an individual solution based on their own self-concepts as a left-hander, difficulties and particular motor-patterns, particularly hand functions ... when teaching PE I was able to demonstrate techniques both right- and left-handed – there was/is a difference. I strongly believe in giving the child time, not just to practise exercises but to listen to their own interpretations of their difficulties – but then this applies to all, young and old.'

As mentioned earlier, the isolation suffered by some left-handers often lies in the child's ignorance of his own laterality, because parents and teachers fail to communicate this fact. There is also a conviction among right-handers – and researchers are often the worst, most biased offenders – that left-handers merely have a problem of adaptation in this right-handed world, and that adequate equipment for their use is now available.

Need for guidelines

Weak statistical analyses and recommendations based on inadequate questionnaires have determined very little. What is needed initially is an individual, large-scale survey to pinpoint the real problems of left-handed children, to determine how best to equip them, and discover what these children feel as individuals. Where do their strengths and weaknesses lie? In which areas do they need special help? How are their brains organised? Do they solve problems in a different way from right-handers? My attempts to obtain backing for this project have so far met with no success, even though the expertise is available.

Whenever I managed to work out mathematical problems successfully, my maths teacher would be incredulous because I arrived at the same result as the others by a totally different path; one which she had never thought of using herself. I now know why, but would have benefited far more from this knowledge at that time.

Researchers ought to stop regarding left-handers as statistics to be tested mechanically to prove that they react one way or another and begin looking at them as individuals with feelings, perceptions and possible problems which may only become apparent in repeated practical situations and where observation over time may be more revealing.

Left-handed problems must be considered on an individual basis because of environmental and personal factors. It would be simpler if the problems were uniform but they are not. Some left-handers have reading and spelling problems, while others do not – they may have writing difficulties, or problems with numbers, with left-right orientation, memory, clumsiness or speech – the combinations are endless. Vivian Sherman, an advocate of integrated learning for schools, believes that the traditional left-hemisphere learning systems are biased and that the real need is for creative learning with more emphasis on the arts.

Right-brain teaching

In one of the poorer areas of Doncaster, Yorkshire, where unemployment is high, a remarkable method of teaching, based on developing the whole child, is the norm. Children at Rossington Grange Lane First School are taught line drawings from the age of three. By the time they are five years old, they are able to produce ink drawings of cockerels and barn owls of a high standard. From the age of four, they learn to paint in three primary colours, mixing their own paints so that when painting grass or trees they produce their own shades of green.

At assembly, the headmistress, Margaret Horbury, encourages a few of the pupils to show items of interest they have chosen to the other children, and conducts assembly singing to the accompaniment of her guitar. At lunchtime the teachers serve lunch and sit at the small tables with their pupils. Margaret Horbury is firmly convinced that schools must provide a caring environment where fear of school or teacher is nonexistent and where the learning experience is stimulating and beautiful. Her child-centred approach is based on the belief that if the children are presented with quality materials and good experience, they will develop high standards and recognise quality in their outside environment.

'You should not judge a person purely on their academic ability or just educate the academic. You must teach the whole person. I believe we have got to allow our children opportunities to communicate in other ways. They should not just communicate through writing – very young children can communicate far more than they can write by body language. From the age of three, our children work with basic materials that they can develop for the rest of their lives,' she said.

Apart from language, movement and mark making, her pupils work through five basic materials: line drawing ('writing is symbolic line drawing'), powder paint ('materials have got to be experiential'), fabric and thread ('communicating the essence of something through sewing'), clay and box modelling/craft design and technology. 'The children can have success in this way that they might not get in an academic sense. Children learn through their senses and we all learn through our own experience, not by someone telling us,' said Margaret Horbury.

Craft, design and technology

Many left-handers find craftwork difficult at school simply because of the right-handed layout of workbenches, or because they prefer to put screws into wood anti-clockwise. They also have difficulty with electrical equipment, such as drills which have function buttons on the wrong side and flexes which get in the way. Fortunately various cordless electrical tools like drills and screwdrivers are now on the market. Geologist Alan Cook experienced many problems as a left-hander, especially in craftwork. He adopted a 'sort it out yourself or be precluded from all sorts of pursuits' philosophy by experimenting with tools and utensils until he had adapted them for his own comfort.

'Before you seek to alter things, you need to find out how they work and what the principles are. When that has been resolved you can then decide how much to alter and whether it is viable. Many tools that are right-dedicated can be used successfully by the left-hander with care and practice; those that cannot are the problem. You either make purpose-built ones or find some one who can, or take the least satisfactory option and convert.'

Martin Bennett carried out a research project into teaching left-handed children in the secondary age range craft, design and technology, in conjunction with the University of Loughborough, for a university dissertation because he found equipment for left-handers in CDT sadly lacking.

Left-handed scissors

A right-hander himself, he found that 8 per cent of the girls and 12 per cent of the boys in the sample he tested were left-handed writers. His final conclusion was that, although designed for the right-hander, most equipment was adequate for left-handers. He was adamant that right-handed scissors with left-handed grips are sufficient and cut perfectly well in left hands. He insists that it is the comfort of the grip that is most significant, and that some left-handers grip scissors in their right hands.

He fails to see that traditionally the only way for a left-hander to use scissors was with the right hand. Some even turn their left hands upside down to produce an efficient cutting edge. It is, however, illegal to advertise right-handed scissors with left-handed grips as left-handed scissors. 'Ambidextrous' scissors, advertised by some manufacturers, unless the blades rotate 360 degrees are no more ambidextrous than they are left-handed. Right-handed scissors in left hands will not cut textiles effectively. The cutting blade, which should cut upwards from the bottom, cuts downwards and obscures the cutting line, which is an essential in CDT tasks, I would have imagined.

Nowadays, some right-handed scissors are honed sharply enough on both blades for left-handers to use them without difficulty. In fact, some of them are so sharp they are positively dangerous, especially in tiny hands. One of the frequent complaints I hear from parents is that the scissors provided by some schools are too sharp and should have round-ended blades for safety. While trying out several kinds of 'ambidextrous' scissors supplied by manufacturers, I continually cut straight through the finger tips of my right hand, which held the material, because the downward cutting blade is on the wrong side for a left-hander.

As a left-hander, ergonomics experts notwithstanding, I prefer to use left-handed scissors with reverse engineered blades biased together, rather than apart, so that while cutting my line of vision is not obscured; so that I don't have to force the blades apart to prevent the material from slipping between them; and so that the cutting blade cuts upwards, not into me. There is also the psychological factor involved of feeling 'at one' with a pair of scissors made especially for left-hand use. This factor is not taken into consideration by ergonomics experts but it should be noted by marketing people – many left-handed consumers empathise more with special-design utensils, in addition to finding them more efficient. Right-handed scissors, with or without left-handed grips, are designed for right-hand users and are unsatisfactory for us.

'I have a ten-year-old son who is left-handed. I bought two pairs of left-handed scissors – one for home and one for school as his teacher (who was a bit thick and didn't understand his problem) had been complaining about his art and craft work being a mess, especially the cutting ... the school got burgled and they were stolen – there is probably a right-handed yob somewhere complaining that the new scissors he took won't cut!' said one mother. And from a left-hander: 'A few Christmases ago I had a gift of a left-handed scissors, and what a godsend they are. If a right-handed person uses them, they can then appreciate our difficulties.'

One misleading factor of the surveys is that left-handers who have had to 'make do' and adapt to right-handed utensils often say something suits them because they have no concept of how left-handed implements actually work and differ. And if they have managed to adapt to right-handed implements, naturally they are then likely to find initial difficulty in using left-handed ones. With scissors this is basically because people are so used to forcing the blades apart to make right-handed scissors work that they continue to do so with left-handed ones, which prevents them from working effectively.

Left-handed teachers

With all our problems, though, we sinistrals do have areas of marked excellence. Chris Moore, a retired head teacher and a left-hander herself, found that her sinistral pupils were highly developed in spatial awareness – credited as a right-brain function.

They were able to place together easily piles of bricks, blocks or jigsaw puzzles, and could do it more quickly than the right-handed children. With more abstract tasks, especially some aspects of maths, unless they could solve problems visually, they had difficulty explaining themselves, even in cases where they knew what they wanted to do or to write. Switching from concrete to abstract concepts presented difficulties.

She noticed particularly that they suffered from right/left confusion with balanced equations and that with fractions, they were able to solve problems practically and visually, using models, but not mentally. They were able to express concepts creatively and imaginatively but not in mathematical terms.

'I can lay crazy paving like nobody's business – I did the garden path with two and a half tons of stone. I can see just the piece I need and just how I want it. If you gave several children and a left-hander a set of bits and pieces and showed them what you wanted them to make and made one with them, or a jigsaw, the left-hander would see an easier way of doing a time and motion study on it. They would turn things just the way they needed to work in the most economical way, although they are clumsier.'

Clumsiness with tools and toys results in breakages. Chris used to wind clockwork toys the wrong way until she had the idea of putting little arrows on them, to indicate the correct way to turn the key. Locks are often broken for this reason, too.

And if little consideration has been given to left-handed pupils and their problems, the drawbacks of being a left-handed teacher in a right-handed schoolroom are almost totally ignored.

One left-handed high school deputy head found blackboards a big challenge. 'Notice how many are off-set to the side of the classroom, so that a "righty" stands in the corner of the room and can easily write on the board and also see the pupils without obscuring their view. The same board means that us lefties are standing between the board and the class and really do need eyes in the back of our heads! It would also help the class if we were transparent. Such adversities have no doubt improved both my teaching techniques and my discipline!'

A Welsh 'proud left-hander' noticed many 'small' things over the years that prove the extent to which our world is built around right-handers: '... our school photocopier feeds out paper to the right with all the controls on the right ... If I write words to copy from the board, I get the complaint "you're in the way, sir. We can't see!" and, of course, I have to finish and get out of the way to allow them to start! Drawing and diagrams can pose problems. If I say, for example, 'copy this map' and do some hatching, a right-hander does this:

but, of course, left-handers do this:

'If I train a child to use a ruler neatly, I always begin my line at the right-hand end of the ruler and move left, but the natural instinct of a right-hander is exactly the opposite, so I have constantly to remind myself to "correct" myself ... It would help if the numbers began at the right-hand end ... In craft work if I teach skills like weaving, knitting (which I try to do!) and plaiting straw or paper, I find it almost impossible to teach the children as I can't do it right-handed myself!!'

Another left-handed teacher remarked on the difficulty of marking pupils' books in the conventional way with the tick at the right, because their left hand obscures what is being marked. 'If you are looking ahead, striking out across the body is not as natural as an oblique stroke outwards would be. A left-hander prefers to mark to the left of the answer,' she stated. Left-handers' ticks – a reversed symbol – usually slip through the net when children learn to correct their mirror writing. 'Such ticks are seen in rather a dim light by pupils, colleagues and especially parents. They probably feel that a wrong example is being set,' she complained.

Should we have to conform or 'should not left-handers "come out" and insist on acceptance on equal terms? What are the implications for us as teachers?' she continued.

I once held up someone's operation by fifteen minutes while two nurses in the corridor outside my hospital bedroom battled it out with the doctor as to why my ticks were written back to front on that morning's menu. Finally, they gave up and came in for enlightenment, enabling some poor soul prostrate on a trolley in the corridor to get on at last with her life-saving surgery.

A paper for paediatricians

In Burnley, Dr Maung, clinical medical officer at Colne Health Centre, noted many left-handers in local schools and produced a paper for paediatricians much in line with Dorothy Bishop's assessment that all left-handers are not brain damaged or defective. As it is routine practice to assess hand, foot and eye preferences in school medical examinations, he tested 129 schoolchildren between the ages of ten and a half and eleven and a half to discover the relationship between hand dominance, eye-hand crossed dominance, hand-foot crossed dominance and reading and motor abilities.

He found two types of crossed dominance — eye-hand and hand-foot — and that 15 had changed hand preference for writing since school entry. There appeared to be no significant differences between left- and right-handers and of the 15, none showed any definite motor impairment or neurological abnormalities. 'The change probably reflects motor and/or cognitive functions having matured over the years. The results do not indicate that sinistrality is in any way sinister ... most individuals with mixed hand preferences, like left-handers, appear to be cognitively and neurologically normal ... Mixed hand preference can be an indication of immature motor or cognitive development in children who change hand preference not only between tasks, but from trial to trial within a skilled task.'

Nor does eye-hand crossed laterality play any significant role in indicating abnormality. Some children with mild abnormalities affecting hand function may find their skills shifting between hands and these children are the ones identified by Bishop, because of poor performance with their non-preferred hand, as pathological left-handers.

'It is important to test handedness not only at school entry but also repeated at about seven to eight years of age when handedness is thought to be well established. It should not only be confined to the use of pencil but a few other tasks should also be included, like using a spoon and throwing a ball, and testing the performance of the non-preferred hand,' he concluded.

A variety of researchers have discovered no significant differences between left- and right-handers in terms of educational performance but other reports have conflicted, mainly on account of the small numbers of subjects or samples tested. Even estimates of left- and mixed-handedness in Europe and the Western world differ, ranging from 2 to 16 per cent (Hecaen and de Ajuriaguerra, 1962), 6 per cent left and 10 per cent 'inconsistent' (Douglas, Ross, Cooper, 1967), and 10 per cent left and 5.8 per cent mixed (Calnan, Richardson, 1976), to mention a few. The latter found that left- and mixed-dominant children were behind right-handers in general ability and reading comprehension, although they were in broad agreement with other researchers.

A dissertation on left-handedness

Kate Sladden experienced no difficulty finding research material on handedness when she wrote her dissertation, 'Left Handed in a Right Handed World' for her BEd Honours degree in 1987. She looked at handedness and associated specific learning difficulties in school and society. She believes strongly that a great deal can be achieved at little cost to improve the present situation and lays down her own guidelines.

She also believes that too much emphasis has been placed on right-handed thinking with the emphasis on skills and knowledge and that left-handers, whose thought processes are different, are consequently not realising their full potential. To favour one hemisphere over the other is to limit the individual and impede progress. While she advocates the continuation of left-brain thinking skills, reading, writing and arithmetic, she believes that right-brain creativity should also be encouraged.

'One way schools can be seen experimenting with rightist thinking at present is in the problem-solving approach to science, where the child is encouraged to collaborate, experiment and view problems holistically. Education at present channels people into scientific or artistic directions comparatively early in their lives; by doing this, I believe we are losing the potential of many people via a policy of single-mindedly perpetuating the reason/intuition divide.'

Kate noticed over a three-year period, a high proportion of left-handers among those attending her father's practical furniture restoration course. The year before she wrote her dissertation she noted 5 out of 12. Dyslexia seemed to be common among them also. It made her wonder whether left-handers were attracted to professions requiring spatial or practical skills of this type because it gave them the opportunity to work independently without having to write or attain qualifications in practical skills.

The Warnock Report

The Warnock Report (1978) gave a broader overview to special education, estimating that one in five children would need special education during their schooling. While children with 'specific learning difficulties' described in the report may be perfectly intelligent, some may succeed in one area but fail in another. 'The only evidence of their problem tends to exhibit itself firstly in the classroom ... in my opinion Warnock helps to recognise this group but offers little in practical terms to help teachers help children in the classroom. The report recommends more attention be paid to special needs in teacher training and in-service training courses, and to an extent this has been implemented.

'At the present time those children suffering from dyslexia, poor hand/eye co-ordination and other like conditions are all too easily missed in assessment and struggle through school frustrated and demoralised by their inadequacies,' stated Kate. She added that caution should be taken between labelling children and recognising their difficulties: '... there is a danger not in enlarging the number of children categorised as needing special help but in extending the multiplicity of terms used to describe them.

'The Warnock Report changed the definitions of handicap and disabilities but little appears to be changing in terms of what goes on in classrooms for children with specific learning difficulties. I am hopeful for changes as more teachers with at least a smattering of knowledge about special needs come out of training.'

She doesn't regard left-handedness as the cause of learning disabilities but recognises that connections between left-handedness and dyslexia, clumsiness, stammering and maladjustment can create additional problems for left-handers. 'I feel strongly that too little is done to help the left-handed child in the classroom. Sinistrals may not be in difficulty but they may be using valuable time and initiative in working out how to cope with their very specific view of the world, which could be very much better used in furthering their learning in other directions ...

'Whether the left or right [hand] is dominant, all children should be given instructions and encouragement to utilise their preferred hand to its full potential, particularly in the field of writing, which though it may have less relevance in a technological age is still of vital importance today ... I feel the time has come for education to accept the existence of left-handedness and to teach with it in mind.'

Kate followed up her theory that left-handedness was ignored in the majority of classrooms with a small-scale survey of three local schools, issuing a questionnaire to which 21 teachers responded. Of a total of 357 girls and 318 boys, aged between four and eleven, she found 15 per cent were left-handed, showing a ratio of 1 in 10 boys and 1 in 6 girls. The results revealed that few teachers were aware of their pupils' laterality preferences.

Policy for teaching

'I think that more information needs to be available to teachers about the establishment of handedness, particularly that many [children] take a while to establish preference and that there are crucial periods when children need additional help, or need to be steered into making a decision. I think it is not generally understood that hand preference may vary from task to task, which is important, and most teachers focused heavily on writing in their discussion of left-handedness ...'

Kate felt that the variety of responses was indicative of the personalities of individual teachers as much as of the problems of children. Overall she felt that the teachers may have interpreted more severe specific learning difficulties than she would have done, therefore overlooking and lowering the number recorded.

In her four years of teacher training, left-handedness was mentioned only once. Accordingly Kate drew up her own policy for teaching left-handers:

1) An observation of each child for laterality and specific learning difficulties, foremost in writing and sequencing.
2) Place children in appropriate seating positions in class to alleviate problems during written work. Also make sure there is appropriate equipment, e.g. scissors for the left-handers and that children know where to find these.
3) At appropriate intervals group left-handers for special help with writing and other problematic tasks.
4) Bearing in mind my own left-handedness, ensure that I am demonstrating activities clearly to the right-handed majority particularly in written demonstrations. If it is to be valuable, acceptance of left-handedness must be a two-way process for teachers and pupils.
5) Continue to view not just the verbal and analytical as valuable. Keep room for intuition and artistry as well as reason.

6) Above all, view children as individuals and avoid categorisation!

Kate Sladden, intrigued by the testosterone theories of Geschwind and Galaburda, asks: 'Can levels of hormones be seen as a determinator of strength of handedness? It is also interesting to imagine a time when a clear theory is formulated and verified. Will we then have the capacity to engineer handedness in the womb? If so, would parents show a preference of handedness for their children?' – an intriguing thought ...

* * * *

8
WRITING LEFT-HANDED

*When I was at school, for two terms I was not allowed to use my
left hand, and as a result of that I can't do joined-up writing to this
day ... I am not just left-handed – my whole total outlook is left
of line – I cannot do anything with the right side of my body. I
can't kick a football with my right foot ...* Derek Jameson.

Left-handers may be ignored in some classrooms, but behind the
scenes a great deal of research has been carried out by handwriting
experts to help left-handed children. While this material has been
readily available for years, it is surprising that so many teachers
are either unaware of it or make no use of it. Children who may
have an educational problem may be struggling along with their
disability, growing used to the persistent complaints of parents and
teachers, totally unaware that there are particular reasons for their
problems, which could be overcome with some guidance and a little
understanding.

Handwriting probably presents one of the major areas in which
left-handers experience difficulty, although that by no means
precludes the fact that so do some right-handers. What appears to
be happening is that right- and left-handed children are being looked
at en masse, and that left-handed problems are not being recognised
as a separate issue. Many left-handers' difficulties may arise as a
direct result of our own man-instituted right-behavioural polarity
problems which society itself has inflicted upon left-handers and
which are not experienced by right-handers.

As the majority of teachers are right-handed, it is no wonder that
many are oblivious of the needs of left-handers, that they do not
distinguish between right- and left-based problems or recognise the

131

need to differentiate between left- and right-brain organisation and characteristics in order to encourage strengths and help overcome weaknesses. Perhaps today's teachers should become more market-orientated in the classroom and carry out SWOT analyses on their pupils, identifying their strengths, weaknesses, opportunities and threats at an early age.

History of handwriting

Ancient writing evolved according to the usefulness of the materials available at each period in history. The individual letters and the direction they took depended on how easy or difficult it was to write on stone, metal, clay, parchment or paper with whatever implement was in vogue. The angular style of our capital letters was easily produced by stone-cutting implements, prevalent in right-to-left Semitic and Arabic writing. Brushstrokes favoured the Oriental vertical line and the pen produced an easy left-to-right rounded European style.

Our own alphabet is descended from the Semitic Phoenician right-to-left script, a tradition continued by the ancient Greeks. Their boustrophedon ('ox-turn-like') writing read from right to left and vice versa on alternate lines, with the former lines reversed as in mirror writing, until our traditional western method was adopted. To date, history has failed to reveal whether or not the majority of writers who employed this curious script were left-handed and whether a minority of right-handers had the writing problems of today's left-handers.

Eye, hand and brain are the prime factors in written communication. The fingers, hand and arm are guided by the eye in a co-ordinated visual and manual sensory-motor activity. Writing evolves from drawing, representing the child's perception of what is seen and understood, and eye dominance plays an important role in lining up the eye, hand and paper.

Correction techniques

The main problems for left-handed writers include lighting and seating, the hooked pen/pencil hold (inverted hand posture), letter reversals and inversions, and even total mirror writing, which may result from the more purely physical problems, inadequate writing tools, incorrect hold, techniques and posture. These problems can be overcome with a little guidance – indeed many left-handers write perfectly well and some make excellent calligraphers. So what can be done for those who do not?

Some writers sit with their noses practically touching the paper. This may mean a simple adjustment of lighting – a left-hander should have the light coming from the right shoulder to avoid the shadow of their hand obscuring their page. Bad posture is often the result of bad paper positioning – the paper should be placed to the left of centre, slanted clockwise towards the right. This way, the problem of the left hand moving across the body is eliminated and the writing is not obscured.

Rosemary Sassoon is a recognised authority on handwriting and has worked with applied psychologists in the Medical Research Council Applied Psychology Unit, Cambridge, and as an honorary consultant at a London hospital. She has also lectured and written extensively on the subject. She recommends that the left-hander should sit to the right of the desk so that there is plenty of room for movement on the left, unless the child is sharing, in which case the child should share with another left-hander or sit on the left and use a higher chair. She also suggests using a free-flowing writing implement, such as a fibre-tipped pen, to avoid the usual problem of hard-tipped pencils and fountain pen nibs digging into the paper and making holes.

Correct writing implements

Nowadays, there is a whole range of ink pens for left-handers, and standard rolatip or italic writing nibs for fountain and calligraphy pens have reverse oblique nibs. In my schooldays, ballpoints and left-handed nibs were unheard of and you could always recognise the left-handers by the inky shirt cuffs. My own schoolwork was always covered in blobs of ink which were carried across the page with my hand as I wrote, the wrath of my maths and geometry teachers being carried through to the English mistress via the pages of my essays. I also went through a variety of fountain pens, snapping every nib, until I found I could write on the back of a Parker 51 nib with ease. I do not recall anyone recognising these difficulties as left-handed ones – they were simply put down to my own inadequacy, untidiness and clumsiness.

Pencil grips can help to provide a more comfortable hold. Both triangular grips and grips specially moulded to the shape of the fingers and thumbs are now on the market and these simply slip onto the pencil or ballpoint. Triangular pencils and ballpoints are also comfortable to grip, although psychologist and special educator, Jean Alston, observes that pencil grip becomes established very early in a child's drawing/writing career and is then difficult to change. A natural wooden (non-shiny) bevelled triangular pencil may help in the early stages of writing. However, some seven- and eight-year-olds show that a grip established with a six-sided pencil remains adapted to that shape and is not easily changed by the use of a triangular pencil later.

She conducted her own survey in 1986 on eight-year-olds who tried out triangular and six-sided pencils because she felt that some writing tools were being marketed without adequate research or reference to the requirements of the children themselves. The six-sided pencils won for reasons ranging from: 'It helps me to write neater' to 'I can hold it better'. She concluded that children ought to be given a choice of writing tools rather than having the choice made for them by the 'experts' and that more market research should be instituted before producing such products.

Left-handers often grip their writing implements too hard and hold them too close to the end. This can sometimes create calouses on the middle finger. The implement should be held in a gentle, pincer grip between thumb and first finger, using the middle finger to rest against, and positioned at least one and a half to two inches away from the point so that the writing can be seen. Jean Alston believes this to be a deterrent for children making the inverted hand posture which she believes they do in order to avoid obscuring their writing. Rosemary Sassoon's antidote to this is to encourage pupils to practise writing on a vertical blackboard. The fashion for sloping desks, recommended by the Victorians, may well return for experiments being made with them by Brenda Brown and Dr Sheila Henderson, research lecturer at the University of London, at present show that they may be beneficial to young writers, and may also discourage the inverted hand posture.

Gay Hall, head occupational therapist (paediatric) at Preston

Health Authority, writing in *Handwriting Review* (1988), points out the psychological effects and behavioural problems of children whose writing incapacities are not recognised in the classroom for what they are. Such sufferers may be seen as classroom clowns or may experience peer isolation, which disciplinary measures only exacerbate. Sometimes they are classed as lazy by teachers and parents and disagreements drag the child into an atmosphere of conflict. If they are treated like losers, they will become losers. Gay Hall emphasises that it is imperative to display understanding and compassion to instil security and confidence to the child, before the writing problem can be worked on. She does, however, highlight a valid point – with classes of over thirty children, how can a teacher give individual attention to each pupil or probe more deeply into the complexities of one child's dilemma?

One American left-hander, writing from America, said that her anti-lefty teacher continually accused her and the only other left-hander in her class of cheating by copying their classmates' work because their papers leaned in the opposite direction to the others. Jean Alston suggests that teachers would gain a deeper insight into left-handers' problems if they were to try mirror writing and letter reversal for themselves.

Better techniques for writing

Ruth Fagg, a Chislehurst head teacher, writing in *Good House-keeping* (1969) on the handwriting problems experienced by many children, points out that children are happy to scribble but may be reluctant to graduate to handwriting. She points out that free scribbling is more pleasurable for an undisciplined infant than the structured rhythmic muscular movement of writing and while some children adapt easily, others do not. She recommends a more relaxed approach for those children who experience stress, such as playing the child's favourite records while she/he stands to create large coloured patterns on big sheets of paper pinned on the wall.

She also recommends large, thick crayons as they require a lighter grip for control. I found that fat pencils actually hurt my grip and strained the muscles in my hand. My personal preference would be for slimmer pencils for small hands, particularly for children who do grip tightly.

Fagg's philosophy is to develop rhythm, hence the music. Even singing is recommended. Eventually the child should be able to face writing seated. She believes that writing begins with the feet – in other words, if the child's feet are correctly positioned and supported, by a stool, for instance, the body will be well balanced. She recommends beginning by writing in coloured patterns, joining letters together to create shapes, the idea being to stimulate the child's interest. Whatever the problem, the body must first be relaxed, not just the hand.

Burt, in the *Backward Child*, recommended trying, gently and subtly, to change the left-hander over to the right hand, without forcing the issue. If this didn't work, he pointed out that the left-hander needed more help and should not be left to his own devices or he might try to copy the right-hander's posture which would hinder his movements and could produce mirror writing. According to Parson (1924) in New Jersey, it has always been normal practice to change left-handers. Blau in *The Master Hand* recommended doing this from primary school because left-handers were at a singular disadvantage in a right-handed world. It would have to be done with caution, he added, for fear of exacerbating the left-hander's unfortunate negativistic personality difficulties such as resistance to learning, obstinacy and reticence. Both Burt and Blau were convinced that there was no connection between changed left-handedness, stammering and other speech defects.

In the United States, Luella Cole theorised that left-handers wrote less well than right-handers and predicted that most left-handers would emerge from elementary schools producing awkward and illegible handwriting. She reasoned also that they had difficulty writing quickly enough to finish exams because their discomfort affected their concentration.

Margaret Clark's research is not alone in revealing that there is little difference in the speed of left- and right-handers, although left-handers first learning to write are said to be slower. As they grow older, the gap between the two tends to decrease, some left-handers catching up and taking over in speed. To study quality differences, 615 left-handed and an equal number of right-handed children in two California suburban school districts were asked to write the opening of Lincoln's Gettysburg Address. The only significant difference found was that right-handed Grade 6 girls scored higher than their left-handed counterparts. Left- and right-handed girls from all grades, however, scored higher than the boys in the same grades.

Patrick Groff of the San Diego State College, in *The Elementary School Journal* (1964) wrote that since no difference between the quality of right and left handwriting was found from between Grades 4 to 6, there was no need to institute a different teaching method for left-handers. But boys, in general, probably did need better instruction. Groff also noticed the marked deterioration in quality of writing today and asked not only why, but whether standards are high enough and whether teachers are being prepared well enough to give adequate instruction. Preparation is important, but much of the frustration of those left-handed writers who experience difficulty stems from a lack of specific guidance in adapting to right-handed orientation and inadequate instruction in letter formation. Left-handed boys are thought to outnumber left-handed girls by about two to one in the general population and about 40 per cent of left-handed boys as opposed to 20 per cent of left-handed girls curl their hand round to make a 45-degree right-handed pen angle, indicating an attempt to counter left-handed difficulties.

Evaluating writing methods

Enstrom in Greensburg, Pennsylvania, placed left-handed writers in Grades 1 to 6 at 11 per cent in 1957. He made an extensive study of references to handwriting, teachers' manuals, instruction books and handwriting courses dating back to 1847, and only found the first reference to left-handedness in 1915 – by C. P. Zaner in the *Zaner Method Writing, Arm Movement, Teacher's Manual No 4*. Later literature revealed six different approaches, covering a range of recommended letter slants from backwards through vertical and forwards.

Armed with a camera and sketch pad, Enstrom attempted to do what previous researchers had failed to do and noted the various handwriting methods used by the pupils with a view to evaluating the most efficient methods of left-handed writing. For two years, he studied children in the higher grades whose writing patterns were already established, and found not six but fifteen different handwriting methods frequently in use – a first-rate example of how first-hand observation can contradict testing for statistics.

He looked at the two obvious main groups – those with the hand below the writing line and the 'hooker'. He found six variations in the former and nine in the latter. Looking at quality, rate of writing, neat, smear-free papers and healthy body posture, he listed 1,103 subjects.

Enstrom found that 69 per cent of the first group produced the only three techniques he could recommend from his findings. Of the other three techniques, one was most frequently recommended, although it was very low in quality. This was the reverse of the right-handed position with the arm axis at 90 degrees with the paper lines. The downward strokes were directed towards the elbow – 'into the sleeve' – with the writing approaching a vertical slope which he found 'somewhat irregular'. Of the second group, Enstrom found only one technique – used by 20 per cent – approaching acceptability and about this he had reservations. The remaining 80 per cent were using methods he found unacceptable. He recommended that teachers should favour the group one approach from day one and that already established 'hookers' should be persuaded to adapt to the one acceptable technique, where the paper is turned leftward and the wrist turned on edge sufficiently to allow maximum flexing.

One left-hander wrote to tell me how annoyed she had been on reading an article by a handwriting expert who said that a slant to the left meant a person was devious and sly. 'Being left-handed, I am unable to slant to the right. I'm certainly not sly,' she proclaimed indignantly.

The inverted hand posture

A 1984 study of writing postures in left-handers by Guiard and Millerat found that the hook had nothing whatsoever to do with laterality or any neurological quirk but was a direct result of the counter-clockwise position of the page, the horizontal position of the writing forearm on the page, and the positioning of the non-writing hand below the start of the writing line and nearer to the left edge of the page than the pencil tip, so that as they wrote, their hands were actually crossing. They conjectured that the hook, which usually developed from a non-inverted style, resulted from the left-handers' inability to stop the page from moving as they pushed the pencil. By holding the paper down under the pencil the left forearm would be placed horizontally to the paper which would then have to rotate counter-clockwise, resulting in the pencil being pulled along the paper in the familiar 'hooked' position.

Dr Jean Alston has produced an excellent booklet entitled *Writing Left-Handed* in which she answers some often-raised questions in relation to left-handed writers and suggests an antidote to some of their problems, including a ten-point roundup of rules. Jean is the editor of the *Handwriting Review*, the journal of the Handwriting Interest Group formed in November 1983 with the help of Dr Ronald Davie and staff of the National Children's Bureau. Its launch came as the result of growing concern about handwriting standards and the needs of pupils with fine motor and co-ordination problems.

Its stated aims are to raise standards in handwriting teaching in schools, to develop assessment techniques and teaching programmes for pupils with handwriting difficulties, to disseminate teaching ideas and methods and to encourage and co-ordinate research.

The need for improved standards

Writing in the first issue of *Handwriting Review*, membership secretary Janet Tootall reviewed the report on the 1986 CSE English Examination – Folio of Writing – from the North West Regional Examinations Board which criticised the poor standard of north-west teenagers' writing. She suggested that a more positive approach should be adopted in secondary schools. 'Rather than writing "Your handwriting is untidy" at the end of a child's piece of work, analyse the errors and suggest methods to rectify them,' she wrote.

Reports from the Northern Examining Association's GCSE examiners in 1989 (*Times Educational Supplement*, 27 January 1989), indicate that chief examiners for physics, biology and geography all complain about the poor quality of scripts with regard to handwriting and general legibility.

Calligraphy

Those children who do receive the correct guidance in handwriting skills may have no problem producing neat and legible work. Many go on to master the art of calligraphy, although it can be difficult for the left-hander to learn this with inappropriate materials and tools. Margaret Shepherd, an American calligraphy teacher and designer, has produced an excellent guide for the left-hander using a group of specially adapted alphabets which she outlines in her book, *The Left-Handed Calligrapher*. Even the guideline sheets, with much foresight, are positioned on the left so that practice work can be carried out without covering the instructions, and a choice of alphabets is geared towards the left-hander's preferred hand position. Nowadays, a range of ink pens for left-handed calligraphers is available for basic or master calligraphy and easy-change nib units come in a variety of styles.

Although not a left-hander herself, Margaret Shepherd discovered, by deliberately using her left-hand, that the left-hander uses a variety of different writing positions, not just one, and that some alphabets are much easier for them to use. She consulted several left-handers for advice, among them Dr Albert Galaburda, learning at the same time that, unlike the usual bad connotations of 'left' found in most languages, in calligraphy at least left-handers can be the aristocrats – in Greek the word 'aristo' means left, 'kali' means beautiful and 'graphos' means writing.

Shorthand and typing

Some left-handers complain that they experience problems writing shorthand and that the action of having to turn over the page with their right hand slows them down. There are many successful left-handed shorthand writers – including Mrs Nancy Hall of Wimbledon, the Perfect Secretary for Britain, 1965. As with learning handwriting techniques, poor teaching methods could be at fault rather than laterality problems.

Having flunked out of grammar school with only 4 'O' levels to my credit and no particular career in mind, due to the lack of any guidance from either school or home, I opted for a secretarial course at Miss Wilkinson's School for Gentlewomen in Manchester. This was as much a surprise to me as to everyone else. When my plans for a musical career were scotched for family reasons, I was left with no future career plans in mind. It was only when our form mistress went round the class demanding to know what each of us in turn was going to do when we left, that I realised with some embarrassment that everyone, apart from me, had mapped out their futures. Because I was too ashamed to admit to being a failure and a dropout, I simply followed the lead of the girl in front of me who announced she was enrolling at Miss Wilkinson's.

As things turned out, it was the best choice I could have made for at this excellent school, on being treated as a normal human being by the instructors, I managed to excel in everything, including the dreaded bookkeeping, to my astonishment, and was one of three pupils given a free session because our spelling was so good. I left with the top speeds for shorthand and typing, and later pushed these up to 140 wpm and 98 wpm respectively.

The typewriter is an ideal instrument for left-handers because the majority of the most-used letters are on the left, including the much-punched 'a'. As one Birmingham leftie wrote to me: '... letters must be typed (however badly) as the average left-hander's writing cannot be read, only made up by the local chemist.'

In any event, having trained as a pianist from the age of five, I had a head start on my colleagues because my fingers were already supple. I found the shorthand outlines much easier to write neatly than handwriting and found they contained far more artistry. The basic strokes are, in fact, similar to those employed in calligraphy. Our teaching included copying pages of shorthand outlines every night which helped to produce good writing and clear outlines which could be read by anyone if we were absent from work. It is curious that my shorthand outlines were beautifully formed and my cursive handwriting appalling. We were encouraged to write with shorthand nibs in ink as pencils can break at crucial moments, and taught how to push up the page gradually as we wrote so that it could be easily flipped over when we reached the bottom.

Shorthand note pads are spirally bound at the top so there was no problem of my left hand getting stuck against the inside binding of the book and, since we were pushing the paper upwards as we wrote, my writing was not obscured by my left hand and I did not produce any ink smears. Surely it would be a simple matter to introduce this type of notebook for left-handed pupils in schools. It would constitute a small step in the direction of progress.

Much of my success at Miss Wilkinson's was due to the self-confidence I gained through the interest and guidance of the teachers

– something I had not known at school – and my left hand went unnoticed, or was never remarked upon. This experience indicates to me that, had my schoolteachers been more helpful and understanding about my educational shortcomings, left-handed or otherwise, I would have flourished equally well in their hands.

Teaching requires two-way communication, and it is as much the manner of imparting information as the information itself which creates mutual understanding between teacher and pupil. It is, in effect, a public relations exercise – the teacher's attitude, in turn, reflects on the school, and how the pupil perceives the school depends on her/his opinion of the teacher.

A good teacher will instill in a child a feeling of pride for the school, and a desire to do well and achieve. A poor or unpleasant teacher will gain no respect from the pupil and may inspire a desire for retaliation – so a circle of conflicting wills is created. Unfortunately, when we are young we don't realise how this situation can affect our future lives. The teacher will continue to teach, though the classes change, whereas the pupil is likely to face a bleak future.

All good things come to an end and the advent of computers was bound to bring changes. The news that the familiar Qwerty keyboard may be phased out in favour of the Maldron keyboard, intended to reduce RSI, or repetitive strain injury, may not be as well received by left-handers as by right-handers. The Maldron comes in three banks and spreads the workload between the fingers more evenly than normal typewriter keyboards which favour use of the left hand. There are special versions for the one-handed (left or right) and the disabled and it can be fitted on to electric typewriters and computers.

Shorthand, too, has seen some changes. 'I have had difficulty in mastering the right-handed Teeline shorthand system used by newspaper reporters. A trainee reporter has to attain 100 wpm before being eligible to sit the proficiency test set by the National Council for the Training of Journalists. If they pass the test they are entitled to 'senior' reporter service and a rise in salary. It took me between ten and fifteen attempts to pass the shorthand examination,' came the complaint of a left-handed reporter from Cheshire. Pitman's would have presented him with no such problems.

A campaign launched, in 1988, by educationalist Andrea Innocenzi to institute a type of shorthand based on Leonardo da Vinci's mirror writing has fallen on deaf ears in Italy, where around 13 per cent of the population is said to be left-handed. Innocenzi formed his idea when trying to teach left-handers to write conventional shorthand because mirror writing eliminates the need for those who make the hook in order to see what they are writing. The Italian government has now agreed to recommend rounded script instead of the traditional vertical kind.

Mirror writing and reversals

She puzzled over this for some time, but at last a bright thought struck her. Why, it's a Looking-glass book, of course – and, if I hold it up to a glass, the words will all go the right way again. Lewis Carroll, *Through the Looking-Glass*.

Lewis Carroll was thought to be a left-hander. He certainly seemed to have had a fascination for mirror images, for not only did many of Alice's adventures take place through the glass, but he was known to have written letters in mirror writing to his young friends. Carroll's work, like da Vinci's, smacks of genius and much of his writing is too subtle for the average child to appreciate fully. Certainly Alice failed to appreciate it.

Many of the letters I received are written from right to left on the paper, in mirror writing, the writers claiming that they can write more easily from right to left than from left to right. Along with many left-handers, mirror writing was one of my early writing problems, together with letter reversal. The most commonly confused letters were 'b' and 'd', 'p' and 'q' – possibly the origination of the phrase 'mind your ps and qs' – 'n' and 'u', reversed 's', 'S' and 'N' and number reversal and confusion, particularly '6' and '9', '2' and '5'. Some children, although I cannot recall doing so myself, reverse words like 'was' and 'saw'. Another tendency is to add columns of figures from left to right.

Some handwriting experts recommend bringing the left-hand margin to the writer's attention by marking it in coloured lines or shapes or simply with an 'X' to ensure that they begin writing from the correct direction.

As mentioned earlier, I stayed behind at school each afternoon to copy rows and rows of letters until I got the letter formations (literally) right. Perhaps someone should have told me why I was doing this, because it might have lessened the confusion I remember feeling at the time. I am not totally convinced about current research which states emphatically that it is a small percentage of mixed-laterals, or those who are late in determining hand preference, who are more likely to experience educational difficulties. None of the majority right-handers in any of the schools I went to had the same type of problems as I did and, as I am left-handed, -footed and -eyed I can hardly be classed as a mixed-lateral. I am sure that most left-handed children are slower to respond to teaching initially, until they adapt to right-left orientation, that some are slower than others at doing so and that others experience severe difficulty.

Margaret Clark's explanation for mirror writing is the natural inclination to write away from the body. The left-hander will find it more comfortable to push outwards, from right to left. She adds that some adults, particularly right-handed writers who would, if left to themselves, have been left-handed, can do this with ease because, if they have been forced to use their right hand, mirror writing would never have been corrected in childhood and would occur spontaneously if attempted. It could also be an indication of left-eyedness but those who cannot read it back may also have a reading problem or a low intelligence quotient. She doesn't see the characteristic as abnormal, or of any pathological significance, unless it continues into adulthood, bearing in mind that the right-left direction would be the norm in other cultures. Neither Carroll nor da Vinci could be classed as mentally retarded despite the fact that the habit followed them into adulthood.

Mirror writing was normally noted among people who had had a stroke affecting the opposite side of the body to the affected hemisphere (hemiplegia). Blau thought that mirror-writers often had reading, spelling and speech difficulties. He pointed out that Beeley (1918) discovered one to every 2,500 children in Chicago and that Gordon (1921) found 0.5 per cent of them in normal children and 8.5 per cent of them among feeble-minded ones. Endless theories have attempted to account for mirror writing over the years, including mental deficiency, heredity, eye, hand and brain abnormalities. Blau thought it was due to a developmental eccentricity connected with preferred laterality. Another of his theories was that it constituted a mirrored action between the two hands.

Several people have mentioned to me that they learned certain skills – particularly handicrafts – by sitting opposite the right-handed teacher and mirroring her actions so that they carried out the task with their left hands. Blau mentions a report by Critchley (1928) in which Ugandans learning English writing were seated around a low oval table. The only copy book they possessed lay in the centre and they ended up by writing in it whichever way they faced the copy – one upside down and the others at a variety of different angles.

Blau thought that reading reversals were due to left-hand directional gaze not having been established and that poor visual imagery led to reversed handwriting. His antidote was for the teacher to use a pointer against the blackboard as a guide for the pupils' eyes. This would graduate to the child using a finger when reading from a book, writing drills and word tracing. He stressed that teachers should be especially sympathetic, patient, reassuring and sensitive to emotional reactions, with the emphasis on correction rather than quality.

Burt assessed mirror writing as 'a quaint peculiarity, found especially among backward and left-handed children ...' The earliest recorded sample was found by Critchley in medical writing in 1698 by Rosinus Lentilius, referring to an epileptic girl. Critchley himself thought that it was the result of defective vision. Burt's own survey produced a sample of 1 in 500 children, mostly aged between five and nine, and 93 per cent were left-handed. He thought it was caused by the nervous centres for motor control and visual control working independently. Mirror writers were motor types writing by muscle sense without the normal visual sense to check the orientation. The eye had to learn to guide the hand as well as observe. This is usually corrected when the child watches what he writes.

Burt also noted that mirror writing could occur in a state of lowered attention such as under hypnosis, intoxication, mediumistic trances and hysterical dissociation. He was told by a left-handed teacher that she wrote her diary every evening in mirror writing solely due to tiredness which caused a relapse into what had been a childish habit. Burt also attributed it to neurotics – left-handers being 'self-assertive ... disposed to stubborn obsessions and compulsions ... intolerant of social criticism, and react[ing] against social conventions.' Trust them to adopt a contrary fashion in writing.

He recommended that the child should practise repeating isolated letters, like 'p', in a stream of joined-up writing so that there was no chance of individual letters being reversed and beginning with a downward stroke because it was the upward stroke − difficult for left-handers − that started the mirroring.

People changing hands because of accidents have often been observed to produce mirror writing. Hecaen and Ajuriagueira (1964) noted that 86 per cent of right-handed adults and 80 per cent of left-handed adults could do this with their dominant hand. And it appears to be easier with the non-dominant hand if the dominant hand is writing forwards at the same time. If you place a piece of paper across your forehead and write your name on it, you are likely to produce mirror writing. Apart from left-handers, women appear to be more adept at it than men.

Corballis and Beale in the *Psychology of Left and Right* explored the subject and saw it as a spatial rather than a motor skill. They thought that memory traces from one hemisphere were recorded reversed in the other, although conflicting evidence showed that the information could equally as well be transferred from one hemisphere to the other during writing and that it would be most likely to affect mixed-laterals.

Reading and spelling

Most of the letters I received from left-handers concerned writing and mastery of right-orientated stroke directions in cursive writing. Many mentioned reading or spelling difficulties. My own spelling was excellent from infant school onwards, so much so that I was regarded with some amusement as the school dictionary and teachers used to constantly ask me how to spell words. I only understood later from my father that they had been doing this because at the time I thought I was being tested and it made me uncomfortable. I was also reading fluently when I began school at five, was held back by the rest of the class who were at the 'cat sat on the mat' stage and raced through library books on the day my sister brought them home, agonising for a week until she replaced them.

However, not everyone is that fortunate. One nineteen-year-old's mother wrote to tell me of his mirror writing in primary and junior school where his teachers told her she was worrying unduly. When the boy was eight years old she attended an open day at school and was horrified to see his school books were illegible. His teacher said that he was the first to put up his hand in class and answer questions correctly but his written work was non-academic. His mother remarked that this seemed hardly logical, to which she received the reply, 'You mothers are all the same and think your children are brighter than they are.'

The boy's mother promptly insisted, against some opposition, on seeing an educational psychologist. It eventually transpired that he had a very high IQ but was a mixed-lateral. When she explained this to her son, he replied, 'I'm so glad, I thought I was thick.' For two years a psychology graduate helped him to spell phonetically but when he moved on to comprehensive school he suddenly took sick for no reason after about six weeks. He was sick each morning before attending school and sent home on arriving. After six months of visits to doctors and specialists, they removed his appendix, which it was discovered, had absolutely nothing wrong with it.

Because he had lost so much schooling, his mother sent him to a small private school with a pupil/teacher ratio of 5 to 1 and although she noted a drastic change, after a few weeks she heard complaints from his headmaster that her son wasn't doing any homework. It transpired that his previous comprehensive form teacher had ridiculed his spelling and passed round his homework for the class to see and laugh at. He had also been told that if he didn't improve, he would be put in the remedial stream. After this was brought into the open, her son progressed with no problem and even achieved the highest ever marks in maths in the Common Entrance Exam in his area, shooting straight up the academic ladder afterwards.

Once he was enlightened, given reasons for his inabilities and treated with sensitivity, he changed from 'an immature cry-baby who showed no sign of competitiveness and gained self-confidence and determination and also began to excel in sport ... after eleven years of battling with the authorities who refused to acknowledge the problem, it frightens me to think what would have become of him if we could not have afforded to opt out of the system and worries me to think of how many other children have been placed in a remedial class because they were thought to be "thick".'

The writer came from Swansea. The following day, another Welsh mother wrote about her left-handed thirteen-year-old: 'nobody in the educational system here in Clwyd will recognise that the left-handed child has a problem.' Because her daughter was experiencing typical left-handed smudging, she had obtained some literature which helped, only to find that 'not one teacher would take it seriously ... including nursery and junior teachers, two head teachers, the director of education (who offered remedial teaching) and the former Headmaster ...' 'Leave her to work it out herself,' she was told.

Slightly more helpful was one teacher who found herself with half a class of left-handed five-year-olds. 'She had never known anything like it. She had to have two display boards on which she formed letters and words – on one with her right hand – and on the other with her left hand.'

Orthoptics

Dr J. F. Stein of the University Laboratory of Physiology, Oxford, and Mrs S. Fowler, orthoptist at the Royal Berkshire Hospital, Reading, conducted a survey among children showing dyslexic tendencies, particularly lateness and/or excessive difficulty in learning to read. Many showed a discrepancy of two years between mental age and reading age. Many had spelling difficulties and reversed letters and words in reading and/or writing.

Often, they performed perfectly well on a normal distance eye test. When required to view writing at close proximity, as in writing or reading, however, they often perceived more than one image. This is because the requirement that both operate independently but focus together with precision is too much for their immature visual systems. Using a variety of equipment and the Dunlop Test – which orthoptists use to determine eye dominance – Stein and Fowler defined two symptoms: their eyes could not be held steadily and the images were variable. Also, the children may not have developed a 'leading' eye – the eye which gives the reliable image when a choice between two visual images has to be made.

A page from the notebook of a nine-year-old left-handed boy who had received no guidance at school. His teachers complained to his mother about his poor handwriting and said he did not try hard enough.

2 7th February

How the Earth was made

Our planet Earth was born more than 4,500 million years ago.
(4500000000 years). Our sun and its nine planets were all formed at the same time. The Earth was a ball of hot gases, much larger than the earth is now. As it cooled into solids and liquids it shrank. No life was possible yet but after about 1000 million years the earth had cooled enough for water to form.

Remember that when you write less slanting, it is easier to read.

It was after this incident that she discovered the following note in his rough book, quite by chance, and the mystery was solved. She realised that he had been unable to see his own handwriting because he was left-handed.

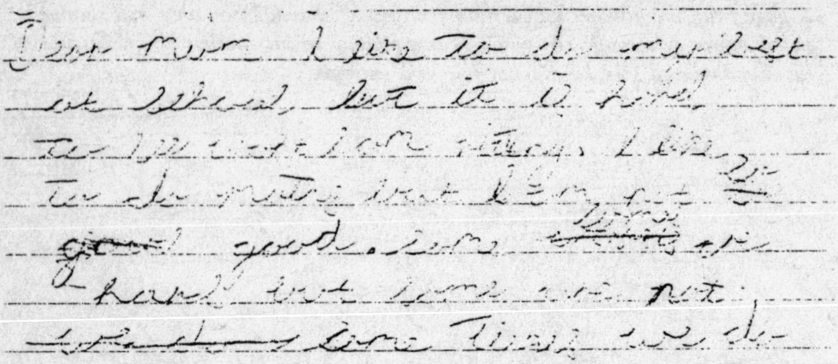

Some common mistakes made by left-handed children are illustrated below, by kind permission of Dr Jean Alston. They are taken from her booklet, Writing Left-Handed.

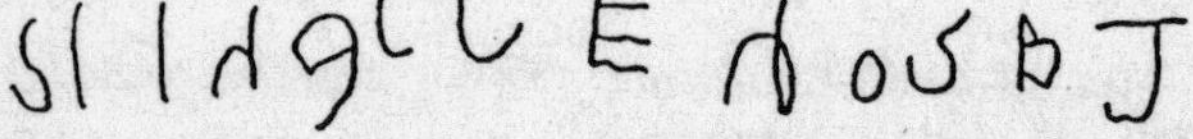

Figure 1   *A five-year-old writes his name in mirror writing*

Figure 2   *A six-year-old reverses letters and numerals in his spelling test*

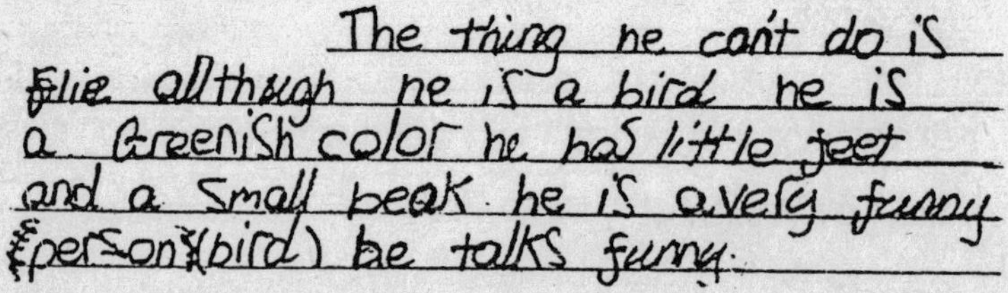

Figure 3   *The handwriting of an eight-year-old left-handed boy shows variable slant*

> Lee Majos (allway) always wears a checked
> shirt and brownish trousers. Once Lee Majos was
> in there own areoplane and he was with his friends,
> when He told thies bady and his pater to June

Figure 4 The handwriting of a nine-year-old left-handed boy shows poor alignment

ι	like	the	part	(were?	were
the	little	girl	puts	a	wig
on	ET	and	a	hat	that
part	.was	very	funny		and

Figure 5 Word spacing is a problem for this left-handed eight-year-old girl. She compensates by making the spaces unduly large

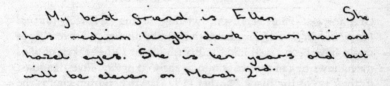

> My best friend is Ellen   She
> has medium length dark brown hair and
> hazel eyes. She is ten years old but
> will be eleven on March 2nd.

Figure 6 This ten-year-old left-handed girl has adopted a backward sloping script

Children who reverse letters and/or words at the age of seven, should be referred, through their general practitioner or the clinical medical officer from the Child Health Service, for eye assessment for binocular stability under conditions of near-vergence and for Dunlop Testing. The orthoptic departments at many hospitals now administer these tests also.

Connections with dyslexia

Sometimes left-handers and dyslexics share the same problems, and these conditions appear to be associated (this is denied by some researchers but not by others). A typical dyslexic child may be clumsy, disorganised, inconsistent, erratic and distracted; he or she may have problems with reading, spelling, letter formation, reversing or inverting letters and mirror writing. Some suffer from short-term memory and an inability to comprehend instructions or distinguish left from right. The term 'dyslexia' comes from the Greek for 'difficulty with words or language'. It is estimated that about 10 per cent of all children have this problem, which stems from the arrangement of their brain cells; an arrangement which is different from that of other children and which prevents an efficient connection between the two hemispheres. Many are left-handed or mixed-laterals.

Some people – not all of them left-handed – are more comfortable reading newspapers or magazines from back to front. A survey carried out in 1963 by *Newsweek* magazine among 5,800 people revealed that 43.9 per cent did this but of them only 13 per cent were left-handed.

Graphology and the criminal

Graphologist Paul Ferguson, writing in the *MENSA Journal International* (1984), suggested that public money and several lives might have been saved had the British Home Office taken note of the handwriting of certain criminals early on in their investigations. In the case of the Black Panther (1975), Mr Ferguson claims the police had samples of the suspect's handwriting early in the case but, as no handwriting tests existed, forensic handwriting experts were unable to recognise his left-handedness. In the course of their investigations, the police interviewed 50,000 people, many of whom could have been eliminated early on had such a test been available.

Most manuals on graphology declare that the left-hander cannot be identified by his/her handwriting. Apparently we are on complicated ground and Mr Ferguson and members of the British Institute of Graphologists who have studied the phenomenon recommend the following:

1) Tracing over the sample with left and right hand to test for comfort, although the tester would need to be ambidextrous to a certain extent to come to a meaningful conclusion.

2) Ink trails should differ, because of the left-hander's push of the pen. This wouldn't be foolproof because not all push – some hook and pull.

3) Studying the sociological approach involving stress factors apparent in the writing (which Paul Ferguson believes is experienced more in the left-hander coping in a right-handed world).

I know some very stressed right-handers. The present-day fashion for healthcare, involving stress-relieving therapy such as meditation or yoga, must be playing havoc with such research, for some left-handers will no doubt have become far more laid back than their left-handed predecessors. I am not aware of any proof that left-handers are more stressed than right-handers but it is thought that they deal with stress less efficiently.

Franks and Davis at the University of Birmingham's Department of English Language and Literature and Grove at the Department of Statistics combined with Totty and Hardcastle of the Home Office Forensic Science Laboratory in 1985 to look at the differences in pen movements between left- and right-handed writers, recognising that significant characteristics might be crucial to document examiners in eliminating suspects and speeding up the investigation process.

In 1975, Fryd discovered that 63 per cent of left-handed writers produced horizontal letter strokes from right to left in a capital 'T', a trait not observed in right-handed writers, findings which were backed up by other researchers. Where horizontal lines were seen to have been drawn from right to left or circles in letters drawn clockwise, the handwriting was more likely to be that of a left-hander. Although not all left-handers did this, right-handers did not.

Franks, Davis *et al.* looked at the direction of marks (or burr striations) shown in the ink line made by ballpoint pens, assuming them to be the most used writing implements today. As the ball turns, the imperfections in its housing may produce white streaks running along the ink line. Previous researchers in the 1950s had already noted these but Snape, in 1980, proved that they could be useful in showing stroke direction, providing they could be observed, since the marks only show on curved lines.

Franks, Davis *et al.* found discrepancies in the circular movements.

None of the right-handers tested made right-to-left straight lines but between 16 and 76 per cent of left-handers did so on some target letters. Eighty per cent of left-handed writers used a clockwise circle or a right-to-left horizontal on one or more target letters. After much deliberation and theorising on odds-on of writers producing either feature being left-handed, it was deduced that the clockwise circling in the letter 'o' would not indicate for sure if the writer was left-handed but that a right-to-left cross on a 't' or 'T' would be a strong indication that this was so.

One more tale is worth the telling, for if only a minority of left-handers or mixed-laterals is accepted as having educational difficulties, it must be a large one. A left-handed woman who used to mirror write and invert letters at school, left as a semi-literate. When she was nineteen, she decided to attend a course at her local college of adult education: 'The class was made up of men, aged between twenty-one and forty years and women nineteen to thirty years old. The class was made up of 42 students and *all* were left-handed!!!' They learnt the basic skills of writing, learning to recognise their names and addresses and basic maths. 'I was on the course three years and learnt to re-read and write,' she wrote, in clear, legible handwriting. Another woman, working with an Adult Literacy Project, told me: 'I was amazed to find that in educational circles left-handedness was thought to be a cause of illiteracy. The students I taught were right-handed.'

* * * *

9
ARTS AND THE
RIGHT BRAIN

When I was a kid I seemed to do everything back to front. I used to write backwards, and every time the masters at my school looked at my book, they used to throw little fits. I had difficulties outside school, too. I couldn't learn to ride a bike because I would insist on pedalling backwards and was quite convinced that mine was the right way, and everybody else's was wrong. I do everything with my left hand, and no matter how hard I try I can't alter the habit. Paul McCartney.

If I have painted a somewhat bleak picture for the left-hander so far, it should be remembered that, whatever they may lack in orientation, many of them make up for it in other directions and some become great achievers. Perhaps left-handers try a little bit harder to compensate for any disabilities they may experience, although that is true of positive thinkers in every section of society. Certainly, many of them excel on the sports field and it has been suggested that those who do not achieve academically may strive harder in this direction. The right-brain approach has also spawned some talented artists and musicians.

But before looking at some famous creative and sporting sinistrals, there is one further area we have not touched upon that is sorely neglected in schools and where the creative left-hander in particular is badly handicapped. The gentle art of needlecrafts has struck terror into the heart of many a left-handed maiden in the past. My own experience was as follows:

Handicrafts

At the pre-primary stage, my sewing teacher recognised that I sewed from left to right of the work and reversed the stitches. She found it confusing to teach me but never complained and my work wasn't too bad. At primary level, all I remember making was a tapestry in basketweave stitch moving from the top left-hand corner using diagonal left-to-right stitches. The teaching was clear and I do not recall my handedness being made an issue by the teacher. I have made many tapestries since and derive great pleasure from working them. Lefties who have problems following right-handed instructions are usually given the simple antidote of holding the illustrations up to a mirror or turning them upside down. Life, however, is never that simple because this means the written instructions are also back to front or upside down and so ensues a series of frenzied cortortions while the book is moved backwards and forwards in an attempt to follow two sets of instructions, at the same time grappling with material in one hand and needle in the other.

At grammar school, as soon as the eagle eye noted the left hand, I was moved to the back of the class, where I languished until the day I left. If I was spoken to at all, it was with sarcasm. I was berated for clumsiness and messiness but generally I was ignored. I remember once sitting for the best part of ten minutes with my (left) arm up waiting to ask a question. The needlework teacher deliberately avoided making eye contact, perhaps in the hopes that I would go away, but I remained, as stolid as a stalagmite, until I was noticed. Eventually, she tutted in irritation, glared at me and remarked: 'You're still there are you?' to which the rest of the class tittered. I couldn't cut material with the scissors and the sewing machine, apart from the treadle, was designed for a right-hander. The bulk of the material, which for a normal person hung over the edge while they sewed, was always scrunched up in a ball on the left of my needle.

This was a great letdown because I was very design conscious and interested in fashion and this could have been a possible career area for me. I always avoided darning socks by throwing them away and buying new ones. Today, it is rare that I sew on a button without it falling off ten minutes later and my stitches are decidedly 'dog's'.

Many similar stories poured through my letter box – one of the worst came from a woman who, when aged between ten and thirteen, was asked the inevitable question by her needlework teacher. As she was the only left-hander in the class who responded she was immediately sent to the back. 'She made me use right-handed scissors and I was always allocated the machine that was noted for breaking down.

'She used to make me stand next to her when she demonstrated something and this made it very difficult for me to figure out how to do something, because I had to watch opposite from her to see her going backward – so to speak. Apparently she did this to all her left-handed pupils. It became so bad that I ran away from school because of it and I used to literally shake with fright before her classes,' she said.

My right-handed sister-in-law taught me to knit by standing behind me and guiding my hands, consequently I have always knitted right-handed, although – a common complaint from many of my contributors – I have to pause after winding the wool round, thereby losing time and the rhythm, because I can't quite keep the needles together. One woman told me she had to dig the ends of the needles into her ribs to balance them. I certainly would never dream of wearing anything I had knitted. I once made a distorted sock which my mother used as a duster. Using four needles is confusing for left-handers because they tend to knit in the opposite direction.

Knitting left-handed is carried out with the stitches on the right, not the left needle. The tip of the left needle is placed under the first stitch and the yarn, held by the left hand, is carried behind the point of the left needle and brought round to the front. The new stitch is moved to the left needle by pulling the top loop through the old stitch from the right needle with the tip of the left.

To crochet, I reversed the instructions in a library book. Although it worked, I was only ever able to make a chain and single crochet. I had imagined making delicate lace curtains and elegant Victorian chairbacks. How deluded, we left-handers. I immediately set to work to make the handle for a china biscuit barrel which promptly crashed to the floor when I proudly picked it up.

A left-hander holds the hook in the left hand, wrapping the ball of thread around the little finger of the right hand once, then under and over the other fingers. The chain stitch is made by catching the thread from the right forefinger and pulling it through the loop. The work should be held near the top chain stitch with the thumb and forefinger of the right hand. The instructions need to be illustrated but perhaps this is the subject for another book.

Tessa Halfpenny runs her own needlework shop in Clitheroe, Lancashire. A left-hander in her forties, she had her knuckles rapped many a time at school for doing her work incorrectly. 'The teacher thought I was doing it wrongly for bloody-mindedness,' she said. Tessa persevered against all odds, learning 'by trial and error', even studying for her City and Guilds in the subject, despite being the only left-hander in a class of eighteen. 'I don't like to be beaten, I thought, "No one is going to say I can't do it",' she said.

'I think a lot of left-handers avoid the hobby unless they are really keen. They don't persevere because it isn't made easy. Yet it is so easy – I would like to get that through to children in school. It seems to be a fairly common complaint from left-handers who hate sewing that their aversion originated from their needlework teacher's hostility. Given the encouragement and correct guidance, left-handers ought to make good seamstresses, given their dominant right brain's talent for spatial awareness and creativity.'

Right-brain creativity

John M. Peterson of the University of Cincinnati noted that the arts attracted more left-handed students than the sciences. In a paper presented at the American Association for the Advancement of Science's annual meeting in Texas in 1979, he revealed that of 1,045 undergraduates attending an introductory psychology course, 9.38 per cent of them were left-handed. Only 4.35 per cent of them were majoring in the sciences compared to 14.89 per cent in music and 12.24 per cent in the visual arts.

The behavioural sciences attracted 8.89 per cent, humanities 9.80 per cent, business administration 9.54 per cent, engineering 10.67 per cent and nursing 4.23 per cent. Two other interesting statistics surfaced: in a category labelled 'others' in five colleges totalling 14.66 per cent left-handed students, 18.18 per cent of them had no major and 13.33 per cent were 'undecided', and the results revealed a high proportion of left-handed women – 9.13 per cent compared to 5.9 per cent found in other studies.

Peterson's higher percentage of women following the arts appears to be at odds with the recognised psychological view that women are poorer on spatial awareness than men and men poorer on verbal abilities than women. It might fit Jerre Levy's theories that left-handed women who wrote without making the 'hook' and right-handed women who made the 'hook' when writing, were better on spatial awareness. These subjects had language in the right hemisphere, spatial ability in the left. Hence her theory, that if you were female, whatever was programmed into the left hemisphere would be enhanced relative to whatever predominated in the right. In males, it was the other way around. In children, she theorised, the left hemisphere developed first in girls and the right developed first in the boys. The hook, incidentally, has only been noted in writing, not in drawing or painting.

Thomas Blakeslee in *The Right Brain* looks at creative thinking processes and how the visual thinking of the right brain complements the verbal left. Mathematicians rely heavily on their ability to visualise abstract concepts. Einstein used the two stages of thinking characteristic of creative people, invoking creative visual imagery which he translated into logical verbal concepts. The intuitive right brain operates first in the formulation of any new invention or theory before the scientist can translate ideas into acceptable mathematical formulae. If this were not so, all left-handers would be creative and all right-handers logical. What seems to be apparent is that there tends to be a higher percentage of left-handers among creative people than the percentage in the general population because of their enhanced right-brain activity.

Art and the left-hander

In our Western culture, our eyes follow a left-to-right direction in reading and writing. The same is true in art where the traditional composition is laid so that the viewer perceives the detail in a left-right direction. According to Blau, art historian Heinrich Wolfflin discovered, while lecturing, that when his accompanying lantern slides were reversed in error, an entirely different effect could be seen together with a change of emphasis in the detail which evoked a totally different feeling for the viewer. This propensity to feel 'right' about absorbing the mood of a painting, or, as Rodin also observed,

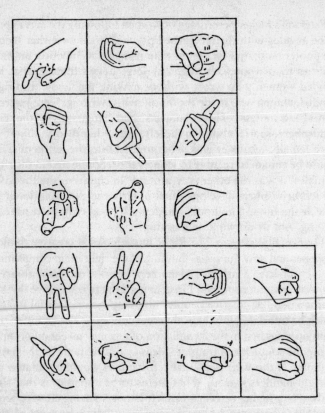

Thurstone's Hand Test. This exercise in spatial awareness is a right-brain task. Can you tell which are left hands and which are right hands? To work it out, the right (visual) brain passes the answer to the left (verbal) brain.

a sculpture, by sweeping the gaze from left to right can be noted in interiors, landscapes and portraits and is thought to be a peculiarity of Western civilisation.

Primitive art has generally yielded evidence of a high proportion of left-handers. Anthropologists studying the remains of aboriginal North American Indians in the United States in the late nineteenth century found about 33 per cent of primitive rock drawings to be left-handed ones. Some felt that there was an equal mix of left- and right-handers among primitive peoples. Perhaps the development

160

of speech lessened civilised man's natural creativity and intuitive powers to provide a verbal home in the left brain for the majority, thereby creating a balance between visualisation of images, on one side, and interpretation, on the other, which was unnecessary for primitive man.

One of the characteristics of right-brained people is their holistic perception. In an art gallery with others, I am always the first to finish viewing – I walk around quickly, absorb what I have seen with appreciation and can discuss the paintings with others afterwards who have stood back and stared intently at each and every work, admiring every detail. What happens is that I take in the whole painting at a glance. I find it impossible to stand and dissect each detail to gain an overall appreciation of the whole – all I gain is confusion. I would be a hopeless witness to a crime or accident unless I wrote down the details immediately – observation of minutiae is not my strong point.

This may not be so surprising when we reflect on the split brain experiments of the 1960s which revealed the right brain's ability to recognise a face in a crowd or piece together a jigsaw, and the left brain's tendency to recognise a face by its individual features.

Right-brain drawing

Earlier, I mentioned Ann O'Hanlon, the American artist who finds that her students produce better work using their left hands. This idea has been taken a step further by Californian art teacher, Betty Edwards, who has written two books outlining her techniques for using the right hemisphere in art.

Drawing on the Right Side of the Brain was written after ten years of searching for a method which would make art easy for all the pupils she taught at the California State University, not just some. She noticed that out of a class of over 30 students, only a few found drawing easy. Those who did improved dramatically and suddenly, rather than gradually but she could find no reason for this.

While lecturing, she found that her concentration on the drawings she was demonstrating would be broken if she spoke at the same time and she concluded that it was impossible to draw effectively while speaking. She also noted that her students produced better pictures if the drawing they were copying was upside down or if they were looking at the space around a drawing, instead of the drawing itself.

It was while reading about Roger W. Sperry and his associates' split brain experiments at the California Institute of Technology during the 1950s and 1960s that she hit on the reason for these phenomena. She deduced that one's ability to draw depended on a shift from the verbal, analytic left hemisphere to the spatial, intuitive, holistic, processing right hemisphere, what she termed 'left mode' and 'right mode'.

Consequently, she developed special techniques for art students which involve dipping into the right hemisphere, setting tasks which can only be performed in 'right mode', so that all her students could learn how to draw with ease. The results were amazing, even with some of her less promising students − testimony to the theories that our ancient intuitive and creative abilities may have been impeded by the advent of speech. A sequel to her book, called *Drawing on the Artist Within*, was published in 1986.

Among the world's famous left-handed artists, in addition to da Vinci and Landseer, we can include Pablo Picasso, Paul Klee, Hans Holbein, Albrecht Dürer, Mozzo of Antwerp and Adolph von Menzel (whose autopsy revealed a larger right cerebral hemisphere). Michelangelo, whose laterality has for many years been the subject of controversy, was thought to use both hands (which he did when painting the Sistine Chapel ceiling), but, as we have seen, this was a Renaissance characteristic. Raoul Dufy, although a right-hander, painted with his left. *The Spanish Singer* by Edouard Manet, in the New York Metropolitan Museum of Art, holds and plays his guitar the left-handed way. So does François Janinet's female *Guitar Player* in the National Gallery of Art, Washington.

Music and the left-hander

Several noted twentieth-century guitarists play specially constructed left-handed instruments, notably Paul McCartney and Jimi Hendrix. Bass guitarist McCartney uses a Martin acoustic guitar upside down which appears to work perfectly well. Some, like Dufy the artist, feel more comfortable operating the opposite way around. Reversing the strings on a right-handed guitar is not sufficient, for the entire instrument must have all its parts reversed to produce an acceptable tone.

Nicholas Clarke, an Englishman now resident in the United States, has produced an instruction manual and special chord chart for left-handed guitar players, now in its fifth printing, which is circulated to schools and libraries all over America. It is available in the UK from the Left-Handed Company in Manchester. Clarke is currently preparing a similar manual for ukelele players. Many people would argue that with any stringed instrument the right hand has to be pretty dextrous so it shouldn't make any difference which way round the instrument is played. For folk or classical guitar playing, the argument goes against this theory because much of the control is carried out by the right hand, which left-handers might find difficult.

As with most left-handers, finding a patient teacher who can instruct in reverse is almost as difficult as finding a left-handed instrument, for most teachers are right-handers. Left-hander Bob Callaghan, a professional guitarist, bought his first guitar for ten pounds in a second-hand shop when he was fourteen years old. It was, by coincidence, strung for left-handed playing. All the teachers he approached simply refused to teach a 'cack-handed' pupil, until he found 'a broad-minded musician who spotted my enthusiasm for the instrument ...' His solution was to seat Bob opposite him. '... it was like looking into a mirror, except that in my case, the "reflection" was doing it right, and seemed a quick way of learning.'

Finding an instrument

Bob commented that left-handed acoustic guitars were pretty rare in music shops and that solid-body instruments were the most abundant. Left-handed jazz guitars appear to be a rarity. 'As far as availability of up-to-date technological advances are concerned, left-handers drag behind yet again. Guitar synthesisers are not readily available to us as easily as conventional players so, yet again, I gaze in awe at these new instruments with longing and "itchy fingers",' he mused. Difficult to obtain, left-handed guitars are also difficult to sell when their life is over. One advantage is that other musicians cannot play them or borrow them.

The Guitar Workshop in New York made a detailed study of left-handed guitar playing and found that it took three to six months for players who changed over to regain their previous level of attainment, after which they improved even further.

Composer and guitarist John Duarte, a 'changed' man, said: 'Now I would not encourage a lefty to learn right-handedly, and when I inherit a student who does play that way round, I advise him to change if he does not appear to be reaching his potential ... I think there has been much irrational prejudice against lefties ... and such things die hard.'

Nicholas Clarke recalls seeing one left-hander simply playing in mirror image with the strings unreversed which meant he had to read the chords upside down. Another held the chords upside down over the guitar neck which meant using the little finger to play bar chords. Bob Geldof, Albert King, Bobby Womack and Otis Rush find it easier to play with the bass string nearest the floor.

Some workshops make left-handed guitars to order, others are imported from the United States but they come expensive. Most companies add a surcharge of ten to fifteen per cent – sometimes as high as seventy-five per cent – and a long wait for delivery. This is on account of the extra attention to detail involved, for the structure is assymmetrical and must be reversed. The bridge, fingerboard and pick guard must all be changed over, and the work is done by craftsmen used to constructing the instrument the opposite way round, so greater concentration is essential.

Gordon Smith Guitars appears to be the only British company which makes left-handed models at no extra cost, usually carrying several in stock on the off chance. Orders from left-handers amount to around ten to twelve a year compared to around four hundred right-handed instruments. Prices range up to around £700 for a left-handed model. Peter Cook Guitars, a left-hand guitar supplier, said: 'We always wondered why they had so little choice? Our research shows that pressure put on wholesalers for left-handed products gets results.' The company imports their guitars from Japan and the USA.

Andy's Guitar Workshop in London specialises in electric conversions, simply changing over the strings and bridge saddles and turning round or remaking the nut. On demand, they will also move the knobs and switches over and fill in and spray over the original holes or put in a new cutaway.

Although I feel happier playing a guitar right-handed. I found it impossible to play a violin that way; much preferring the feel of bowing with the left and fingering with the right hand, but the chin rest gets in the way. Patrick Park is a right-handed violin and viola teacher from Stafford who often receives enquiries from the parents of left-handed children. 'As both hands are required to play the instrument, the fact that they may be right- or left-handed really makes no difference,' he tells them.

'The bowing action of a mixed grouping of violins strung and played in different ways would make an already difficult instrument even harder to teach, and the violin/viola is built in such a way that the lowest strings are on the left as you face the instrument and the highest on the right. The sound post is placed, critically, just behind the bridge on the right part of the bridge. I suspect reversing the strings to accommodate a "left-handed" approach would seriously affect the sound and timbre of the instrument,' he told me.

String players

For convenience, non-solo string players have to play right-handed to avoid not only breaking up the symmetry of a group but knocking their fellow players' eyes out — ever seen a left-handed string player in an orchestra? The City of Birmingham Symphony Orchestra boasts the only one — a viola player who was obliged to change to the left after an accident to her right hand. Charlie Chaplin played the violin left-handed in the film *Limelight*, creating not a little confusion for his audience. From the age of sixteen Chaplin practised several hours a day. His violin was strung in reverse, as was the bass bar and sounding post. He finally gave up when he realised he would never be a great virtuoso and turned his (right) mind to better things.

Turning the pages presents some problems for left-handers who say they don't have sufficient control to hold the bow and turn the page quickly with their right hand. 'I speedily transfer the fiddle to under my right arm and turn with my left hand,' said one left-handed violinist.

One left-hander who contacted me played viola and violin right-handed and the viola da gamba left-handed, the former because everyone told her she *couldn't* bow the wrong way round as it looked so odd and the latter because she found it so much easier, despite years of right-handed playing.

Three major compositions have been provided for the left-hander: Ravel's Concerto in D Major for the Left Hand for piano and orchestra, written for Paul Wittgenstein after his right hand was blown off during the First World War, Prokofiev's Concerto No 4 for the Left Hand, and Britten's concerto for Harriet Cohen, whose right hand had been injured. Ravel's dedication to a work which demanded extreme virtuosity to perform, was: 'This is not so much to show what the left hand can do, but to prove what can be done for the appendage that suffers from sinistral stigma.'

The Disabled Living Foundation operates a music advisory service which issues a vast list of piano music for one hand, some written specifically for the left hand. It includes carols, Old Time Music Hall, jazz, duets and classical works by many composers, including Bach and Britten.

Pianist Cyril Smith, the late husband of Phyllis Sellick, with whom he played duets, wrote about his work as a one-handed pianist in *Duet For Three Hands*, published by Angus & Robertson. Theodore Edel, while at the Manhattan School of Music, even wrote a thesis on *Piano Music For the Left Hand Alone*, in 1980.

A musical Savant

Darold A. Treffert describes a blind, left-handed Savant, aged 38, institutionalised in Ontario, who is epileptic and profoundly retarded with a severely spastic paralysed right arm and hand. This extremely handicapped young man has a very low intellect and cognitive skills, yet, aged two and a half, he developed an interest in music which became obsessive. He would practise the piano all day and often during the night.

Even more amazing, as his right hand was impaired, he played the melody with his left hand and the bass with the heel or toes of his left foot, until he developed his own techniques for playing both parts with his left hand. At the age of eight, his talent was outstanding and he subsequently mastered the organ, melodeon and harmonica.

His vast repertoire ranges from jazz to opera, he can improvise, transpose and embellish and he can play in many different styles with ease, and imitate other performers and instruments. Researchers have tested him relentlessly to find out whether he is simply mimicking others or whether he has an understanding of the rudiments of music. Treffert's equation summed up their conclusions as 'brain injury + prodigious memory + neural circuitry that allows encoding into and access to a cognitive sense of musical systems + intense practice and repetition = the musical Savant'.

Keyboard players

Keyboard players, and percussionists generally, have their work spread between the two hands – left-handed pianists often noting that their left hand needs subduing from time to time because of its predominance over the right in terms of volume. When learning music, I experienced the same confusion with the pedals as some left-footed motorists, at first confusing the piano with the forte pedal. Typically, I displayed a total inability to comprehend the rudiments of music, playing perfectly well intuitively and instinctively in my own right-brained fashion.

I ignored the shorthand, had no concept of what key I played in, never understood time signatures or note length, and reversed the lot when writing manuscript. Consequently, aged eleven, after passing Grade 5, I could progress no further because Grade 6 was the gateway to the advanced examinations, heralded by written theory, my knowledge of which was non-existent. My piano teacher had for six years visited our house on a Sunday afternoon, the only purpose it seemed to me being to sample the contents of our tea caddy and my mother's excellent baking as she listened to my endless repetition of the same exam pieces for six months (which I never practised during the week), after which any child who failed such a meaningless test of virtuosity must surely have been mentally retarded.

After her tea, she marked my theory with a row of crosses, indicating failure for every exercise and left for home, without further explanation. She finally admitted defeat – on her part, not mine – and recommended professional training, which meant beginning from scratch and learning such hitherto unheard of skills as technique and repertoire, something which my ongoing exam preparations had impeded to a quite considerable degree. The theory book was thrown away.

At the grammar school, I turned down the offer to be the school pianist out of shyness and fear of being noticed, and became a marked woman. Beryl Wynne, with ginger plaits and freckles and Dilly Dream granny glasses – who was two years behind me in her musical studies – became the school heroine. I was admonished for conducting back to front, with my left hand, had the usual problems mastering anything remotely theoretical, could never remember the names of anything I played and passed my Music 'O' level. Had I not had a high profiency in composition and harmony, I might have failed. After missing one lesson through illness, the music mistress told me not to bother catching up as the subject would be optional in the exam. It wasn't and the only question I could answer was the composer's name.

For keyboard players in today's synthesised world of music, controls over on the right must be a nightmare. Over-the-shoulder keyboards designed for one-hand operation present no options and manufacturers will not produce left-handed models for a minority market. Roland are known to have made a left-hand GR500 guitar synth for McCartney and Elliot Easton of The Cars was noted on Live Aid playing a left-hand GR707, but keyboards have a long way to go.

But think of the brain power which must be employed by many keyboard players, particularly harpsichordists and organists where not only both hands but both feet are performing completely independent and different tasks simultaneously, while the eye is interpreting treble and bass musical notation written on two levels and noting musical shorthand indicating tempo, rhythm, mood and key changes, with peripheral vision, all at lightning speed. Both brains are working in harmony.

Science and art in music

Sensory messages are delivered to the brain which commands the appropriate motor function. The musician's skills are not only based on the ability to interpret music skilfully, involving eye-hand co-ordination, but on the personal interpretation of the composition, dictated by the right brain's translation of it into emotional concepts. The left brain, meanwhile, is adept at recognising musical symbols. Not everyone has the required motor abilities to master musicianship, in whatever form, but of those who have, not all of them have the requisite musicality provided by the emotional, creative right brain – something we can hear in the 'soul' music of jazz musicians or the intensely personal experience of the so-called 'romantic' composers, Chopin, Liszt and Tschaikovsky, who can be heard practically crying between the lines (depending on the interpreter).

For example, several girls in my school music class had a better understanding of musical theory than I did but were not versatile musicians. One bright girl couldn't even play a musical instrument. They were obviously left-brain dominant. I find many music teachers fall into this category, including the one described earlier – in all the Sundays she sat by my side I never once heard her play the piano. My school music mistress thumped and banged until the flesh under her arms shook and wobbled along with the poor piano – highly qualified she may have been but she was certainly no musician.

Mozart, who was playing the piano at three and composing at five, heard music 'walking' into his head. The initial melodies were followed by passages which linked his themes together. He could also hear the notes to be played by each instrument – the counterpoint – different notes which he could distinguish at one and the same time. He 'saw' images in his head. Mozart was also known to be able to hear a piece of music once only before being able to sit down and perform it perfectly and to be able to play music backwards.

Interestingly, Hans Von Bülow conducted Stanford's First Symphony without a score after reading through it once on the train from Hamburg to Berlin the same day. There seems to be a pattern of extreme right-brain activity among highly precocious children who frequently show signs of genius from an early age, in contrast to trained talent which tends to emerge at a later age.

Some other instruments

Harpo Marx is said to have been a left-handed harpist. How this can be is difficult to say unless he played the bass with the right hand and the treble with his left. It would be inconceivable to string a harp backwards because of the shape of the instrument. The strings would not fit. Other instruments can create problems for left-handers. One girl studying the harmonica told me: 'The harmonica has to be held the wrong way around and so the notes are consequently the wrong way round.' Paavo Berglund is the only left-handed conductor I have heard of.

Left-handed drummers are sometimes put out because their shiny badges face the wrong way on their kit. Some manufacturers put them on both sides of the drums or sell them separately – most drum shops stock them. 'Nick' La Rocca (1889 – 1961) was the leader of the original Dixieland Jazz Band formed in 1914. Rocca was a left-handed trumpet player who composed the famous Tiger Rag and other well-known jazz numbers. When the Band played in London in 1919 at the Hippodrome, they gave only one performance because of George Robey's jealousy of their success. Playing trumpet left-handed didn't appear to be a problem. Interestingly, the French horn is valved for the left hand.

In mediaeval times, the recorder was played with the right hand uppermost – the opposite to the way it is now played. Tony Evers plays guitar, dulcimer, mandolin and fiddle left-handed and recorder, flute and tin whistle right-handed, all of which feels perfectly natural to him. Tony, an instrument maker, makes three-string dulcimers that can be adapted for left- or right-handers. Recently, he made a hammered dulcimer, which he believes favours the left-hander. 'It uses wooden hammers in a way similar to, say, a glockenspiel. The layout of the strings is rather odd, with strings passing over bridges so that you play on both sides of the bridge. The higher notes are on the left. In most cases, in duple time, the left hand plays on the beat ... triple time requires ambidextrous alteration of the hands.'

A test to discover whether language spread over both hemispheres might limit both the normal spatial and musical abilities held by the right hemisphere, appears to have created some conflicting results. Brian Byrne at the University of New England, Australia, tested mixed- and right-handers and deduced that musical ability and handedness was an independent issue and that, although some spatial ability might be reduced, music was unaffected. His findings, however, contrasted with a low ratio of mixed-handers found in musical groups tested by Oldfield five years earlier. A point not usually considered in such tests, is that the left-hander may find music-making easier because of the necessity of using the right hand for some day-to-day tasks, whereas right-handers are not as dexterous with their left hand.

A female Beethoven

Why is there no female Beethoven, asks Blakeslee? Lack of opportunity and acceptance in a man's world no doubt, but why then, now that barriers have broken down, is there no female Andrew Lloyd-Webber? Women do achieve certain recognition but never make it to the top. Genius is absent. Blakeslee theorises that as women mature faster than men, their brains tend to work like 'a pair of generalists', while a man's brain is more like 'a pair of specialists' and generalists don't breed geniuses. Einstein was apparently a late maturer.

The last word on the subject comes from a thirteen-year-old guitarist: 'I would like to say how disgusted I am with people who treat left-handed people as "aliens". They call us awkward and unimportant. I had a teacher once who refused to teach me because I was left-handed and insisted I played right-handed. So, of course, my dad told him "what to do" with his tuition.' That's tellin' 'em, lad!

* * * *

10
ADVANTAGE LEFT

One of the biggest strokes of luck has been the land of my birth. For its population, there are more left-handed golfers in New Zealand than anywhere else in the world. I was not discouraged by others for being left-handed and no one tried to change me, because I was not seen as an oddity. I was among many left-handers.
Bob Charles, *The Bob Charles Left-Hander's Golf Book.*

Scoring on the sports field is one way a non-academic left-hander can hit back at the right-handed majority, and many, as we well know, excel, although Professor Stanley Coren estimated that they were 20 per cent more likely to suffer sports injuries than right-handers. But other factors may play a significant part in their success. Heightened spatial awareness may be a contributory factor in strategic placing of the ball. It can also place a right-handed opponent at a singular disadvantage, particularly if she or he is not used to playing against a left-hander. The left-hander will certainly be accustomed to playing against right-handers and is likely to be adept at changing hands for different tasks. Some left-handed tennis players can switch the racquet from one hand to the other with ease. Many left-handers bat with the right and bowl with the left.

Golfer Bob Charles

Left-handed champion golfer, Bob Charles is not, in fact, left-handed at all. He is completely right-sided. Like his parents, he simply feels more at ease playing two-handed sports like baseball, cricket and golf 'on the wrong side of the ball'. One-handed sports, like tennis and squash, he plays right-handed. He was the first left-hander ever to win a Professional Golf Association tournament.

His home country, New Zealand, boasts 10,000 left-handed players out of 100,000 golfers. In America, 250,000 out of 14 million golfers play on the left. There are approximately 10,000 left-handed golfers in the United Kingdom. An ancient Highland game of *Camanachd os Shinty*, a twelve-a-side field sport, similar to hockey and played with a stick intended for use with left and right hand, is said to be the basis for the unusually high forty per cent who play golf left-handed in Badenoch in Scotland's Spey Valley, where left-handed foursomes are quite common.

The true percentage of actual left-handers among the world's golfers has never been assessed, for many right-handers, like Charles, prefer to play on the left and many left-handers prefer to play on the right. Steve Cram plays tennis with his left hand and golf with his right. Most magazine and newspaper articles refer to 'left-handed' players of sports like tennis boasting a high preponderance of left-handed champions, all of which can play havoc with laterality statistics, for many are not true lefties and many true lefties are swallowed up with the right-handed players.

Jack Nicklaus credits Bob Charles with his fine method of play, his 'intelligent, well-controlled, well-paced approach to golf', regardless of his left-handed play. In the past, it was always thought that playing left-handed would be disadvantageous. It didn't impede the game of Charles's mother, Phyllis, who achieved a handicap of six and represented the province of Canterbury, or his father, Ivor, who, with a handicap of two collected many district titles. Charles himself – rated as one of the world's greatest putters – boasted a scratch handicap at the age of sixteen.

South African champion A. D. (Bobby) Locke said of Charles in the early days of his career: 'I do not consider that Charles's development will be restricted because he is a left-hander. That, in golf, is a common fallacy. I don't agree with the argument that because a man is a left-hander he cannot reach the heights.' When Charles finally did so, he was acknowledged by press and peers to be the finest example of left-handed play in the history of the game.

After his success at the 1963 British Open Championship at the Royal Lytham and St Anne's course, Pat Ward-Thomas of the

Guardian had this to say: 'No left-handed golfer in the history of the game has achieved eminence in any way comparable to that of Charles, whose position now is quite unique. All over the world when children grasp the club the wrong way round, parents henceforth may think again before insisting on the change. Left-handers are common in other games, but in golf they are rare birds who, with notable exceptions like P. B. Lucas, look strange and often ungainly.'

Lucas, author of *The Sport of Princes – Reflections of a Golfer*, recalled how left-handed golfers were treated as outcasts in the 1930s. Bob Charles believes that handedness makes no difference in golf, other than that certain holes can be awkward for the left-hander. The 13th at Augusta National, home of the Masters, is one. Some, however, can be an advantage, like the Titirangi course, New Zealand, the Royal Lytham and St Annes and Scotland's St Andrews course where many holes have out of bounds on the right, relegating any problems to the right of the left-hander's back.

Playing golf right-handed entails holding the left hand uppermost on the club and swinging to the right of the body. But right-handers normally hold their right, stronger hand at the top of implements such as brooms, spades or rakes. We can now see why Charles and other right-handers are more at ease playing one-handed sports with the right and two-handed sports with their left. The opposite is true, of course, for left-handers. Left-handed American Val Skinner is a right-handed golfer, as was the late Pam Barton, who was killed in 1942 in an air disaster. Jessie Valentine, winner of six Scottish and three British titles, is another. Ben Collier of Callender is the first left-hander to win the Scottish Boys' Championship.

In Kristianstad, Sweden, right-handed lady beginners are being actively encouraged to play left-handed instead, the theory being that right-handed housewives play better golf left-handed because they can use their stronger right side more effectively. The side in relation to the swing is immaterial for research shows that the hips and legs provide the power, while the arms and shoulders merely transmit it. The experiment was launched by golf pros who noticed that the women showed no resistance in the left arm, which bent just when the ball was hit and now around six out of every ten beginners play left-handed.

Left-handed golf clubs

De Linke Jongens was a fraternity of left-handed golfers, formed in the 1950s, which, like many left-handed fraternities, died a natural death. Roughly translated, links meant 'left' and link meant 'clever' – 'Clever, daring boys'. For the Linke Jongens of today, Barend Agterhorst a Dutch golf writer, gave me the following tip: 'Watch the TV in a mirror. All right-handed golfing "tracks" hit the ball perfectly with a left-handed swing.'

Left-handed golf societies exist in around 15 to 20 countries. The British Left-Handed Golf Association was re-formed after a lapse by 12 London golfers. It is now run by Tony Kirkland, who took it over in 1977. Of its 500 members, 90 per cent are right-handers who play on the left. They meet 12 times a year, three times in Scotland.

In June 1990, The National Association of Left-Handed Golfers hosted the sixth biennial World Left-Handed Championship in Galway with a round over four courses. It was won by Peter Read, an Australian. This is an amateur event which has been held previously in the USA, Canada, Australia and New Zealand and this was its European debut. With no restriction on handicap, it attracted an entry of over 300 players. In 1992, it will be held in Taiwan.

At one time, left-handers had to play with right-handed clubs turned the wrong way but nowadays left-handed clubs and putters are made by most manufacturers and sold in golf-pro shops. The dearth of equipment was probably a contributory factor for left-handers playing on the right but, if the Swedes are correct – and this is not an entirely new theory – it may be no bad thing.

Hockey

Other sports, however, are not so accommodating. Left-handed hockey does not exist for the game does not permit it, although ice hockey does. But left-handers on the hockey field have their uses – a scoop from the left is one of their specialities, along with the jab and the left-hand wing. Many use reverse stick stops, sometimes dribbling that way with left hand only.

Elizabeth Hunter, who once played for Scotland, has also taught and lectured on the subject. 'The proportion of left-handed players at a high standard is, I am sure, much greater than in the normal population. Mentally, because it is a right-handed world, left-handers have to "work things out" and I consider that this pays off. I would expect a higher proportion of left-handers among those who have probably retired from playing than from the players of today,' she says.

If she is correct, what we are probably seeing is a display of good spatial awareness, as on the tennis court, the left-hander's mind putting the pieces of the jigsaw together and envisaging the strategic solution in a flash with the holistic approach of the right brain. Even the goalies have a chance to shine for they can glide out and dive for the ball on their stick side, making tackling easier because their reaction is automatic and faster. Gill Prime of Burgess Hill Ladies Hockey Club in Sussex said, 'When faced with a penalty my natural preference is for the ball to go to my left, which it invariably does, as most strikers assume a goalkeeper's weakness to be their non-stick side ... I feel as though I can cover the goal area with more confidence, as I am strong on the side which most people aim for when trying to get a goal. Sometimes I become too confident and leave my left side rather unguarded and a few goals slip past as I leave too wide a space for inviting shots.'

Most believe it to be an asset. Pam Rogers, a strong left-hander, played centre half for England about seventeen years ago. 'I was able to stop-field many balls on the reverse stick side, which right-handed people found more difficult. Many was the time when my left-hand stick would be reaching out to rob the player of the ball, in many cases when they thought they had beaten or passed me easily.' Now a hockey teacher, she makes a point of trying to strengthen her pupils' left hands to improve their reverse stick play. 'This was very much frowned upon in my day and, in fact, I was frequently "blown up" when the umpire obviously did not like my reverse stick play. Now, of course, this is very much the pattern of play and features a lot in coaching young hockey players.'

Polo

Another sport out of bounds to lefties – at least in the UK – is polo. In the United States, only left-handed players registered before

1964 can use their left hand but only three of them exist, including Skee Johnston, Chairman of the Polo Association, who plays on a three-goal handicap. He has his own team, Tennessee Polo. Michael Hogday, editor of *Polo Express*, told me, 'I think people accept he has got to play by the rules as if he was a right-handed player but bearing in mind his nearside is his offside. When you ride against somebody from different directions, you have to meet stick-to-stick. In his instance, he would have to meet stick-to-offside-stick.'

Other left-handers must play right-handed and learn to adapt. Both the horse and the stick are important and it means that their left hand must be fully occupied handling the reins while the right hand is at play, whereas it would be easier if the left were idle. One of Argentina's top polo players with a nine-goal handicap, Martin Zubia, was a nagsman who played right-handed. At one time he turned to training, including the Queen's polo ponies, because his left-handedness impeded his progress at the game. In England, he worked hard at it and after a very short time developed into one of the world's greatest players.

Athletics

Throwing a javelin is impossible for a leftie because it has right-hand grips. One youngster's mother told me, 'No one at his school has been able to show him how to throw the discus or hammer as it is too dangerous to hurl these things about going the "wrong" way.'

Not only hands, but eye co-ordination and foot dominance play a vital role in sports. It may well be that again, mixed-laterals experience drawbacks, in addition to the left-hander's usual 'right-hand world' handicap. Does this mean that certain sports inhibit some children who would otherwise perform perfectly well? Few surveys relating to handedness and sport are known to have been carried out, which leaves a wide open field for research. Track racing, for instance, can present problems to left-footers as right-legged runners have their strongest leg on the outside which helps them corner on the anti-clockwise track. So far, no one appears to have undertaken a survey to see if left-footed children run more slowly than right-footed ones round a curved, anti-clockwise track.

Football

Football does, however, favour the left-footer, the most well-known being John Barnes of Liverpool Football Club, who can play and score goals with either foot, as can Tony Dorigo of Chelsea, Stuart Pearce of Nottingham Forest (second and first choice England left-back respectively) and Ian Rush, also with Liverpool. Nigel Winterburn, Arsenal's left-back, is completely left-footed and is unable to kick with his right foot. Other famous left-footers include Bobbie Charlton and Brazil's Pelé. At least half of each team operates predominantly on the left-hand side of the pitch and not many are left-footers. Players on the left wing or full back find it advantageous to kick with the left towards the centre of the field. On the right-hand side, they can cut inside and strike with the left foot, although crossing a ball from the right with the left foot is virtually impossible.

Target sports

Hand-eye co-ordination is the key factor in target sports such as snooker, darts, shooting and archery. Any attempt to assess left-handers would be fearfully inaccurate as right-handers with dominant left eyes play left-handed and vice versa. Left-handed player, Patrick Chaplin, holds the darts in his left hand but lines them up with his right eye and throws in an arc from the right-hand side – a mixed-lateral by all accounts. The most famous left-handed darts player in the UK is Alan Glazier, who turned professional in 1975, long before the game was popularised by the media.

Known as 'The Ton Machine' because of the frequency with which he scores 100 or more with three darts, and dressed all in black, he once placed three darts into the centre of a Polo mint which was swinging in front of the dartboard. In the Isle of Wight in 1976, Alan competed against thirty local players at 1001 each and won 30-nil. He played for England in the 1970s, losing his place in 1978 but retrieving it in 1981.

The left-handed snooker players Jimmy White, Tony Meo and Dean Reynolds are among the most successful players of the 1990s. Right-hander Dennis Taylor uses both hands, changing over to deal with each shot.

It is estimated that around 10 per cent of all archers are left-handed and sinistrals account for half of the United States 1988 Olympic archery team. Champion Alan King won the Sussex County Championships – the York – in 1988. Although a right-hander, he is left-eye dominant and finds he must shoot left-handed for maximum effect. When he took up the sport four years previously, the archery shop handed him a bow which he took in his right hand but the salesman immediately changed it to his left. 'He understood I was left-handed – all he had done was look at me. It was the eyes which told him.'

Alan shoots a compound bow which, at full draw, is weighted at 26 lbs. He plays with Cuckfield Bowmen, Sussex, and is rated about third in the county. He has broken twenty-five club records, three country records and in 1986 won the county indoor championship and several tournaments. 'I get odd looks shooting a right-handed bow left-handed. It is peculiar to me and a few other people. I shoot with a release aid as I couldn't shoot using my fingers on the string. Now I have right and left-hand bows with a left or a right handle,' he said. One disadvantage is that left-handers sometimes find themselves relegated to the end of the row. 'Sometimes, if you happen to be on the left hand facing the target, you are looking at nobody,' said Alan.

Rifle shooting

Rifle shooting has always been one of the most complex of hand-eye co-ordinated sports and in times of conflict could have cost lives and not necessarily those of the enemy. During the Second World War, one left-handed soldier could only shoot if he placed a patch over his right eye. 'I don't think he ever shot a German but he must have frightened quite a lot of 'em', one of his comrades told me.

In the army, the standard .303 SMLE bolt-action rifle had the bolt and the loading port on the right-hand side. Shooting off the right shoulder, the left hand would have to support the far end and reach right over it to operate the bolt. This upset the alignment and it had to be re-aimed each time it was fired. Although accuracy was probably unaffected, the rate of fire would have been as lefties were not allowed to shoot it with their left hand. The now defunct semiautomatic SLR rifle had to be cocked, whereupon a fresh round was passed into the breech for firing after each discharge. The cocking lever was on the right but once cocked, the gun could be used by left- or right-handers.

Infantry regiments were delighted to find a left-hander among their ranks because it meant he could cover a field of fire to the right better than a right-hander. When laying out infantry patterns, they always covered the arc of fire against the enemy advancing from the front. One man would be given a point to watch in his arc of fire without having to turn to fire one way or the other. He would take the first quarter and the next soldier would take the next quarter, covering a semi-circle, and they could cover a wide field of fire this way, forming a fan shape. The left-hander would be asked to cover the arc on the right. Shooting could be done with the left or right hand but parading was right-foot dominant, with the left foot starting off and the right for standing easy. The left foot did the stamping and the right marked pace.

The British Army recently developed a new rifle – the SA80 – which is significantly shorter than its predecessors and which has been used for the Changing of the Guard. Unfortunately, it cannot be fired off the left shoulder. 'A good soldier in combat is encouraged to be ambidextrous for taking advantage of cover. I tried a prototype at Bisley and if you shoot off the left, the cocking handle would hit you in the eye when you pull the trigger,' commented Mike George, assistant editor of the *Sporting Gun*. Because the cartridges are expelled on the right side, left-handers are in danger of being hit in the face. This means that they have no option but to use the right hand. It also means some soldiers must use their non-dominant eye and it is very difficult to train someone to use a rifle which depends on such quick reactions of adaptation because, once again, the issue of brain organisation has been overlooked.

'The Austrians make a much better rifle and that can be converted from right to left in the matter of a minute. People should be taught to shoot with both hands but will never shoot as well with the wrong hand,' said Colin Greenwood, editor of *Guns Review*.

Right-handers who are left-eye dominant automatically shoot left-handed. Steve Barrett has shot for fifteen years for Lancashire and is on the Great Britain Squad. 'I hold the rifle with my strong arm, sight with the left eye and pull the trigger with the left hand.' The

Cross-Eyed gun has a butt which fits into the right shoulder and is bent so that a man who shoots from the right with a left crossed-eye can shoot without blanking off his strong eye.

Around 5 to 10 per cent of national championship shots in the UK are left-handers and the numbers are growing. National champion Barry Dagger is an Olympic shooter but other left-handers find competition shooting difficult because they have to dismount the rifle, which is supported by a sling. Some club competitions are based on the old Army training of fifteen well-aimed shots per minute at 300 yards, which means that the left-hander will lose vital time. The self-loading rifle, banned on 1 February 1989 by the Home Office as a result of the Hungerford Massacre in 1988, would eliminate the time-loss factor because the shooter would be able to retain the point of aim shot after shot.

Said Colin Greenwood: 'Hungerford was the only incident in which a self-loading rifle has been used in a crime. If the Home Office can ban a particular class of firearm on the basis of one incident without thought or enquiry as a hysterical reaction, they can do the same to every other class of firearm. The type of rifle used and its emotive name – the Kalashnikov – was responsible for much of the hysteria. As many people were killed with a pistol but those have not been banned.

'There is a broader fear in the business of what this Government intends to do. Target shooting in this country has been with the military weapon of the day because its roots are with the volunteer movement – one of its priorities was to train people in the defence of the realm. It now means that a whole series of competitions for which self-loading rifles were essential have had to be discontinued in the UK, although there are no restrictions anywhere else in the world.'

A left-hander must push the top lever of a shotgun to the right to open the gun whereas the right-hander would pull, which is easier, and this can make a substantial difference in re-loading rapidly. 'In shotgun shooting, there are more left-hand shotgunners than you would ever believe. I remember standing at a shoot last year and watching the shooters go through and I was surprised at the number of left-hand shots,' said Mike George. Some of those are quite likely to be right-handers with a dominant left eye.

'A lot of people who design layouts for clay pigeon shooting tend to forget to cater for left-handers in terms of range shooting. It is easy to set up a shooting stand so that a right-hander can't possibly fire in the wrong direction. They should remember left-hand shooters or they can create a special stand for the right-hander which is unsafe for the left-hander.'

Even revolvers have their cylinders swinging out to the left and are designed for right-hand use. Pistols with moulded stocks must be specially made and are expensive to buy second-hand. In pistol-shooting, both eyes remain open and the leading eye always looks down the barrel. It is impossible to shoot with the right hand using the left eye and vice versa.

Kitting out

Three-position match leather jackets, waistcoats and shooting gloves can be bought in left-handed versions at no extra cost. Rifle manufacturers do seem to provide for them nowadays also, with mirror-image versions, although some add an extra ten per cent surcharge. Some make adaptations for match rifles with an extension to the bolt handle which curls round underneath the rifle and over the top so the bolt can be operated with the left hand. A left-handed stock alone can cost over £100 which makes a left-handed conversion expensive. Some makers charge anything from £250 upwards for them. The second-hand left-handed gun, like the left-handed guitar, is difficult to dispose of and has to be sold off at a loss because there are so few takers.

British manufacturer Swing Target Rifles in Kent make left-handed rifles for the same price as right-handed versions but they can still run to around £1,000 or more. Royal gunmakers James Purdey & Sons have built custom-made guns which shoot from the left shoulder for many years, although many of their customers prefer not to have the mechanism changed as they feel that the standard of opening will maintain the value of the gun if it is sold. Other British gunmakers are not so accommodating, preferring the comfortable view that it does not take a lot of practice to adapt.

In Germany, Feinwerkbau, together with fellow manufacturers Walther and Anschutz, carried out a survey which revealed that between 5 and 10 per cent of German target shooters are left-handed. Consequently, 10 per cent of their total production is left-handed.

Anschutz makes at least ten true left-handed rifles and six right-handed action guns with left-handed stocks, although from their actual sales, they found that only 2–3 per cent of customers bought left-handed versions. Perhaps British industry in general could take a leaf from their book instead of adopting the general attitude that left-handers are a minority not worth troubling themselves over.

Fencing

Fencing is another sport in which left-handers excel, reported by Azemar, Ripoll, Simonet and Stein in 1983 as 35 per cent male and 32 per cent female. In the late 1950s to 1960s, five out of the six-strong national foil team were left-handed. In the 1966 Commonwealth Games in Jamaica, four of the individual British champions were left-handed, namely Alan Jay (foil), Bill Hoskins (*épée*), Janet Wardell-Yarborough (ladies) and Ralph Cooperman (sabre). In the 1984 Olympics the first eight places in the men's foil went to left-handers. Alan Jay was the Olympic captain at the 1988 Seoul Games and Cooperman has competed at three Olympics and four Commonwealth Games.

As in tennis, although the proportion of left-handers in relation to right-handers is small, lefties make it to the top. 'Left-handed fencers play against right-handers more often than right-handers do against left-handers. Like southpaw boxers, they have a slight advantage as they have more practice against right-handers and it puts their opponents off,' commented Ralph Cooperman.

His opinions are borne out by the famous French *epéeist*, J. Joseph-Renaud whose book, *Traite d'Escrime Moderne*, devotes several pages to a technical discussion on left-handed fencers and how to deal with them. He states that left-handers learn fencing more quickly than right-handers and are more successful. The most serious injuries in most of the real duels at which he assisted were caused by left-handers, apparently. When he wrote the book, in 1928, he mentioned that left-handed fencers were becoming rare. It wasn't until after the Second World War that left-handed British fencers became more common, possibly because of changing attitudes towards them.

Left-handed fencers accounted for around fifty per cent of gladiators in Roman times. In those days, they fought with a sword and short dagger, the latter held in the left hand by most gladiators, although right-handed versions existed.

'The first time I ever fenced against a left-handed person was during my first competition, where my first-round pool contained four left-handers (in a pool of five). The reaction of right-handers to my on-guard position ranges from eyes raised to heaven to double takes and even to refusals to fence. I've had someone resign at 3−0 down saying it was too difficult to fight a left-hander and someone who said (after losing 10−0): "Oh, you're left-handed − I wondered what was wrong",' stated one left-handed fencer.

The biggest problems facing opponents are an exaggerated sixte position (for angulated attacks), an exaggerated height on the leading arm during a lunge and standing on guard in quarte. 'Standing on guard in quarte is also my favourite remedy for facing a left-handed opponent. On these rare occasions I feel that my target area has suddenly increased ten-fold and that I am completely "open" (something that right-handers don't feel against right-handers),' he continued.

One teenager had suffered severe psychological problems which had held him back in his schoolwork because he had been forced to write with his right hand at infant school. His problem was not diagnosed until his mother took him to see an educational psychologist at the Great Ormond Street Children's Hospital in London. Despite any educational drawbacks he excelled at fencing in which he noted two distinct advantages: 'Many right-handers in *epée* go for the outside stop-hit (that would be the inside stop-hit on the fellow right-hander). It is a natural instinct to "claw" the other fencer's hand with the weapon and most right-handers get their moves mixed up because an inside stop-hit to a right-hander is an outside to a left, so while they are working this out I give them an under arm stop-hit.'

For left-handers, the sabre and *conquille* or hand guard are offset slightly off-centre where the blade protrudes. The left-hander's must be set the opposite way round. The *epéeist* must have the armpit and arm protected on the left arm. If the beginner joins a club which makes no provision for the left-hander, it will mean wearing a right-handed jacket and using a right-handed foil. As in most sports, coaches have great difficulty in reversing their lessons, unless they happen to be left-handed or ambidextrous.

Reg Snepp is a left-handed fencing coach from Jersey who had to learn right- and left-handed fencing because in the Channel Islands 90 per cent of fencing takes place between left- and right-handers. 'Right-handers are confused by a left-hander on coaching courses and nobody wants to pair up with me. When we change partners I make them all move round one so everybody gets to grips with a left-hander. If we have five left-handers doing an *épée* course we can do things we couldn't do before when fencing right-handers.

'I coach the youth service. When they see I am left-handed they get confused. There is a psychological disadvantage – which way do I engage the blade, what do I do? – this is where it falls to bits. Right-handers fight left-handers very carefully and quickly. The left-hander must be taught from the word go how to engage the blade and attack,' he said.

Unimanual sports

In unimanual games like lawn tennis, squash, badminton and table tennis, heightened spatial awareness is an undeniable advantage. Left-handed champions abound, dating back to the days of 'Little Mo' Connolly, women's champion from 1952–54, a left-hander who played tennis with the right. Pancho Segura and Beverley Fleitz were ambidextrous champions. Those who won with their left include Kay Stammers, Ann Jones, Jaroslav Drobny, Rod Laver, Neale Fraser, Tony Roche, Mervyn Rose, Roger Taylor, Mark Cox, Martina Navratilova, John McEnroe, Jimmy Connors, Sara Gomer, Bill Knight, Roscoe Tanner, Guy Forget, Mark Woodforde, Guillermo Vilas and Henri Leconte – an impressive line-up. Even the late King George VI played with his left at Wimbledon in the men's doubles in 1924. At Wimbledon in 1978, 15.6 per cent males and 9.4 per cent females played left-handed tennis.

Richard Lewis, Men's 18 and Under national training director for the British Lawn Tennis Association is himself a left-hander who played Davis Cup tennis for six years and Wimbledon for fourteen years. He was ranked No 2 in Great Britain and reached the world's top 60. He listed the possible advantages for left-handed players: 'A change of angles for the opposition to cope with: inexplicably left-handers seem to be able to hit heavy slice serves much more easily than right-handers, possibly because they constantly practise to right-handers' backhands. Interestingly, in the current men's world ranking list there are less than ten players ranked in the top hundred who are left-handed.'

Pam Bocquet, secretary of the Professional Tennis Coaches' Association of Great Britain listed a few more advantages: 'There are less left-handers; right-handers have to adjust their game; left-handers practise more often with right-handers; right-handers dislike the spin coming from left-handers and left-handers are useful to have in a match, especially when it is game point and no one likes a left-hander's service from the advantage court, spin drawing one out.'

On the 'off' side, left-handers play mostly right-handers so dislike playing other lefties, and beginners find copying or shadowing a stroke quite difficult in a group. Left-handers are rarely considered by tennis coaches – one told me that some thought of them as 'a bloody nuisance'.

Beating Navratilova

Right-handed player Steffi Graf experienced problems with left-handed servers. Her solution was to hire left-handed players to practise against on tour so that she could better deal with opponent Navratilova's vicious slice and improve her backhand. At Wimbledon, she hired Australian lefty Mark Woodforde and finally broke Navratilova's successful run to become 1988 and 1989 Champion. This was some achievement as her opponent had been the Queen of Wimbledon eight times, including a six-year stretch from 1982 to 1987.

'The spin and angles which a left-handed player uses are exactly opposite those used by a right-handed player. Playing against a left-hander is like playing a mirror image of oneself. Many players get used to the spin, angles and tactics (hitting a ball to a right-hander's forehand is the same as hitting a left-hander's backhand) through practising with left-handed players,' a member of her management team told me. In 1990, Martina returned to victory, leaving Steffi far behind. Navratilova is one of only two left-handed women Wimbledon champions since women were first allowed onto the hallowed courts in 1884. In 1969, Birmingham-born Ann Jones beat Billie Jean King 3–6, 6–3, 6–2. After her 1990 win, Martina became the second woman to achieve nine victories there, including a run of six from 1982 to 1987. Monica Seles also plays with the left – what an interesting final that would have been.

In the men's singles, Connors took the title in 1974 and 1982 and McEnroe, dubbed the 'superbrat' by the media for his aggressive outbursts on court, held sway in 1981, 1983 and 1984.

One complaint came from a competitor who serves with his left hand and plays with his right. 'It does require me to play in a pair of shorts with large pockets, as having served, I change the racquet on my down swing from my left hand into the right. If my first serve has gone in, I have no time to lose the second ball.' Another found playing doubles confusing. 'When I was on the right and a right-hander on my left, if the ball was returned centrally, we would either both go for it and bang racquets or both leave it, thinking the other would get it.'

Table tennis

Playing opposite a left-handed table tennis player is equally confusing for a right-handed opponent. One man said that he had to change his whole game when playing against his left-handed team captain because he normally concentrated on the back-hand side. Phil Vickers, a left-hander, is ranked around the 70–80 mark in England and plays in Division One North for Ruston ML, and Desmond Douglass has ruled English table tennis for the past decade, having only recently been topped by right-handed Alan Cooke. Douglass was England's best player at the Seoul Olympics, beating six players before losing to the World No 1, from China, and Eric Lindth from Sweden.

Former Sheffield Veteran Champion (1969) and Open Veteran Champion Alec Head remembers a Table Tennis League dinner during which the treasurer came over to greet three YTTA officials. After returning to his own table, he continually glanced over until Head passed by, when he said, 'You're that so-and-so that coits them'. Head answered: 'You're that so-and-so that switches your bat from one hand to the other.' When playing one another in the Yorkshire League Veterans, Head played high top spin returns, his opponent countering those that were wide on the backhand side by playing a powerful left-handed drive, despite playing right-handed normally. 'This shock tactic had won him many points but it had never bothered me,' he remembered.

Another anecdote he tells concerns left-handed Crown Green bowlers. 'Playing against a very experienced player one day in a competition, I was giving him some trouble and as he stood on the mat, he growled, 'They should drown left-handers at birth.' This was a joke, because he himself was a left-hander and almost of County standard.

'Players had to declare the bias on sending out the jack to make a mark and this was either "thumb" or "finger", but it was the opposite for a left-hander. Visiting players sent out the first jack to start the game. Four pairs of players on the green, they would declare the bias and you would tell them you were left-handed so each declaration would have to be translated, and the comment audible for all the other players and the spectators: "I've got one of them left-handers".'

Cricket

Bowling of quite another type can create havoc by a left-hander – on a cricket pitch. John Barry Ismay, as a teenage leg-spin bowler in the 1950s, played in a match against Derby Crown China Works Team. The firm's managing director at that time was the opening bat, a left-hander who soon saw off the opening fast bowlers. 'Eventually I came on to bowl slow spin and set my field. Part way through my short run-up, I realised that he had turned round and was now batting right-handed. I reset my field and got on with the game.

'For the remainder of his innings, he batted right-handed against me and left-handed against the quicker bowlers. When he got down to my end, I asked him about this and he replied, "I play a straighter bat left-handed against the quickies, but can hit harder right-handed against slow bowlers".'

Roughly one in four first-class cricketers are left-handed. Former England captain David Gower throws, bowls and plays tennis and golf with his right hand but bats with his left. In 109 Test matches, he made over 7,500 runs, gaining 15 centuries. 'I can remember one or two passing occasions when my left hand scooped a low and fast slip catch,' he says. In 1989, Test Match cricket was faced with two left-handed captains – Gower and Australia's Allan Border – as well as England team member Chris Broad. Australia fared well in 1909 when Warren Bardsley was the first Australian in Test cricket to make two separate centuries. Wilfred Rhodes, one of England's greatest bowlers, boosted Yorkshire into prominence with his left hand in the early 1900s. Former England captain Brian Close, from Yorkshire, and former West Indian captain Gary Sobers both play left-handed. In 1989, Paul Pollard (21) was the youngest-ever batsman to score 1,000 1st-class runs in a season.

Most cricket teams find it desirable to have a right- and a left-hander batting together when opening and one or two left-handers in the opening five batsmen. This tends to upset the opposition bowling line and length because they keep having to change the attack from one side to the other. Some bowlers find bowling to a left-handed batsman difficult. Despite the advantages, left-handers have to cope with the ball slanting across them, which calls for some spritely footwork across the crease.

When batting, the left-hander finds the fielders are all on the wrong side of the pitch. One rounders player commented, 'When I go in to bat, all the fielders move round to the left side of the pitch and are always glad to get a left-hander out. Even the referee has to move to the left side. The annoying part is that when I do hit the ball, I'm nearly always out at the first base because I hit it straight to them.'

Baseball

But the national American game of baseball boasts more than its fair share of southpaw pitchers and portside catchers. Pete Gray, a natural left-hander known as the 'One-Armed Wonder', during his five-year professional career, included a stint with the World Champion Saint Louis Browns during the Second World War. 'After catching a fly ball, Gray, using one swift, fluid motion, would bring his glove up to his right armpit, letting the ball roll down his wrist and across his chest. With his glove tucked under his right stump, he would then drop his left hand in time to catch the ball and then rifle it in,' wrote sportswriter Jack Cavanaugh in *True Magazine* (1975).

One normally associates the term 'southpaw' with boxing but it was coined by a Chicago sportswriter to describe left-handed pitchers who played in the old West Side Stadium and who would face south when going into their stretch with a runner on first. The term was first used in the UK in a 1934 *Daily Telegraph* article on boxing which featured the then American World Featherweight Champion, Freddie Miller, who won 213 out of his 237 fights.

Around 30 per cent of all major league baseball pitchers, 32 per cent of batters and 48 per cent of basemen are said to be southpaws. Baltimore's 'Babe' Ruth (1895–1948) was probably the most famous left-hander in the game, playing with the famous Red Sox and the Yankees. His record was sixty home runs in 1927. It seems to give an advantage to pitchers, who can see first base more clearly, and to basemen, who have good coverage of the infield with their gloved right hands. Of left-handed catchers, there are none.

Boxing the 'southpaw'

The southpaw has always been a formidable contender, leading with the right foot and hand and causing confusion to his opponent. At one time, left-handed boxers were discouraged and forced to fight with the right. One of the disadvantages was that they are vulnerable on the right-hand side although, in the main, they can confuse their opponents, who find them awkward to fight. In the original *Rocky* film Sylvester Stallone portrayed a young 'downer' whom no fighter of merit wanted to take on, because he was a southpaw. Consequently, his only use in the fight game was as a sparring partner. And very few southpaws have hit the heights. But among them are Marvin Hagler, the undisputed World Middleweight Champion between 1980 and 1987, an American who is adept with both hands; the former Middleweight Champion Michael Nunn, also from the USA; and Herol Graham, British and European Light-Middleweight and Middleweight Champion. Scotland's Jackie Patterson was World Flyweight Champion from 1946–48 and there have been several others but left-handed heavyweights have never picked up the title.

Right-brain sports

Thomas Blakeslee, commenting on the 'dialogue' between left and right hemispheres, vis-à-vis sports, in *The Right Brain*, echoes my earlier comments about the arts. Some sportsmen talk incessantly about the tactics and theory of sports (left brain) but are poor on the actual sports field because their right brains may be impeded by left-brain activity. Some berate themselves after performing badly, particularly in golf or tennis. Can this be the left brain telling the right what it thinks of it, as a coach tells a player? Blakeslee maintains the verbal left brain is too slow to act during play so it takes over before and after the action, spurring the player on but also criticising – the right brain plays an active, non-verbal role. This may elucidate tennis champion, John McEnroe's aggressive behaviour on court, not only towards himself but also towards the umpire.

Because some people suppress the creative applications of their right brain by heavy reliance on their verbal left brain, many people are not making the best use of their abilities. In *The Inner Game of Tennis* and *Inner Skiing*, author Tim Gallwey highlights two mental compartments – a verbal Self 1 and an active Self 2. His theory is that Self 1 should become a spectator while Self 2 performs.

He suggests non-verbal visual and kinesthetic techniques to encourage a more natural and improved performance. During play, Self 2 comes under constant criticism from Self 1, urging on during shots and berating afterwards. How many of us have said to ourselves, 'You twit, what did you do that for?' We know we are talking to ourselves but we never ask just who is doing the talking and to whom they are talking.

We are looking at the same dualism mentioned earlier in relation to Leonardo da Vinci – a dualism of scientist and artist. Both are within us and when the scientist takes over, inevitably the artist must suffer. Don't be analytical, is Gallwey's message. To perform well, whether in tennis, fencing, skiing or boxing, the answer lies in co-ordinating the two brains so that they get on well; in training Self 1 to stop berating and impeding Self 2; to hold Self 1 back and allow Self 2 to perform freely.

Some of the phrases used to describe players at the peak of their performance include: 'he's out of his mind, he doesn't know what he's doing'. That is precisely what is happening – the player is losing himself in the game totally, forgetting to remind himself of the rules and conventions – of how the knee or elbow should be bent and so on. Athletes often describe the 'high' they feel when adrenalin is flowing and they have smashed through the finishing line – a similar high can be reached through meditation, where the bounds of consciousness are transcended. As soon as thought comes into the picture, this feeling goes.

One technique Gallwey uses to keep Self 1 under control is to train the player to say 'bounce' and 'hit' to himself, at the appropriate moments, so that his attention is occupied and Self 1 cannot move in and take over. Other techniques teach him to concentrate on breathing, or counting breaths, or on singing a song silently to prevent verbal thoughts from flooding the mind – rather like using a 'mantra' in meditation.

Self 1 and Self 2 are, of course, the left and the right cerebral hemispheres. If the left-hander's Self 1 is unable to shine in the classroom, the unfettered Self 2 may well take over on the sports field.

* * * *

11
THE RIGHT CAREER?

We left-handers are victims of dextrism – an assumption of superiority which litters the English language with such discriminatory phrases as 'right-hand men', 'left-handed compliment' and 'two left hands' as a symbol of clumsiness. The Rt Hon Gerald Kaufman, MP, Shadow Foreign Secretary.

In a survey of left-handers in sport conducted by the *Sunday Times* in 1988, forty-one out of three hundred professional snooker players, footballers, rugby players, basketballers and orienteers approached agreed to be tested for handedness. Most of them scored zero because they were found to be right-handers which more or less killed the view that left-handers were good on spatial awareness on the sports field.

We have already seen that it is virtually impossible to collate statistics on handedness in sport because many players prefer to play with the non-dominant hand, either because they have been taught that way or because the type of game calls for dexterity from the opposite side or because of visuo-motor factors. We have also seen that some researchers claim that spatial awareness can be impaired if speech is in the right hemisphere and that, even if speech is in the left hemisphere it can hold back the creative right if not properly controlled. We know that some left-handers simply confuse their opponents playing tactical games.

Spatial awareness in sport

A massive investigation into spatial awareness on the sports field was carried out in 1989 by Charles Wood and Dr John Aggleton at the University of Durham's Department of Psychology. They discovered a high proportion of left-handed bowlers in professional cricket over the last forty years but no significant figures for top batsmen. Neither was there any evidence of an excess of left-handers among 500 men and 252 women tennis pros or 167 professional soccer goalkeepers. They concluded that any excess was simply due to the nature of the game and not to any neurological advantages.

What it all boils down to is a question mark against the old chestnut that left-handers make good architects, computer designers and chess players because of their ability to visualise where the next piece or shot should be placed in juxtaposition to the overall picture. Many people have the ability to do this but, again, we are dealing with brain organisation, not handedness. The whole complexity of laterality is based on the individual, which is what makes it so impossible to define.

Left-handers do appear to be more attracted to chess but are as likely to excel in it as right-handers, according to Bill Hartston, writing in *You* magazine. Mostly thought of as an 'egghead's' pastime, Gareth Lewis, chairman of the Greater Manchester Children's Chess Association, finds that about 75 per cent of players come from working-class backgrounds. 'I think people with high stress jobs live on their nerves at work and are sometimes intellectually stretched so they like to relax at home. Those who work on machines or the assembly line all day are using their hands rather than their brain. They like to get out and be stimulated after work. A lot of deprived children walk in their plimsolls in the winter three-quarters of a mile in the snow to come to the chess club,' he said.

Some researchers might deduce that as these enthusiasts were working in tactile jobs all day, their right brain might be more active for such spatial activity.

Chess players

A left-hander himself, Gareth plays chess with his right hand. Stewart Reuben, director for Congress Chess with the British Chess Federation, states that serious left-handed players equal the proportion of those in the general population. 'As the chess clock is always placed to the right of the player who has the black pieces, it gives a small advantage to a right-handed player which offsets the disadvantage of the black pieces minimally,' he told me.

'This administrative nicety is not in the rules. We make the clocks all face the same way for the arbiter. I have never had any complaints concerning this from left-handed players. When they have white – they then get the advantage. When a left-handed player plays a right-handed opponent, the clock can be placed to their mutual convenience. Often there is little space on the table and the space for recording moves is aligned to the right-hand side. Again, I have never received any complaints. Thus either left-handed players are long-suffering or the difference is negligible.'

Jonathon Wilson, a sixteen-year-old left-handed international player and one of the UK's strongest chess players tells me that a higher than normal proportion of left-handers can be found among weak players. Among top players, the percentage is the same as in the general population. Could it be that left-handers are attracted to the game initially because of its spatial attraction but, as working out complex moves would probably be dictated to the player by Self 1, the verbal left, there is no room in the game for Self 2? For there is no creative skill in moving the pieces round the board as in sport or the arts and short-term memory retention is not on the plus side for right brains ...

Orienteers

As for orienteering, which scored an average of 0.75 points for each person tested by the *Sunday Times*, many left-handers suffer from extreme right/left polarity problems and make lousy navigators. Say right and they immediately turn left. As for map reading: 'My husband and I used to tour abroad a lot and I was supposed to map read. This caused some ghastly strained silences when I waved my right hand and shouted "turn left here" and vice versa. Occasionally my husband would turn opposite to the waving hand and everything would be OK – but not always. In the end, I wouldn't be able to stick the grim silence in the car and I would weep. He just couldn't understand why I could be so stupid – I didn't either,' says one left-hander.

'I truly believe that my mind sees things differently. I drive a car and I never ever use a road with a "no left" or "no right" turn because

I can't make out quickly enough which the sign means. Of course, I had no bother whatever with the "NO LEFT/RIGHT TURN" we used to see – it is these new signs. I look at them and panic … but I dare not trust myself and unless I can see the red no entry signs on the side road in time for me to indicate, I sail by,' said another.

Not noted for my own strong sense of direction, it was several years before I could find my sister's home in Southport without first circumnavigating Liverpool or Wigan or, in one extreme case, losing myself in a labyrinth of old train tracks in the Trafford Park dock area for one hour before arriving in the centre of Manchester where I had begun. 'Where have you been this time?' is the usual greeting. Once, on my way to Congleton in Cheshire, I found myself heading out to North Wales and missed an excellent Christmas lunch. Maps are always facing the wrong way and I have to contort myself to make any intelligible sense out of them, so I tend to rely instead on road signs and arrows.

Do we make good architects?

So do we make good architects? Do we really have the ability to visualise a high-rise building just from looking at the plans on paper? Personally, I am as confused by the sight of an architect's plan as I am by a road map, and am a hopeless sportswoman, indicating that my spatial abilities may be impaired. What do the researchers have to say?

Peterson and Lansky speculated from casual observation during the 1970s, followed by some rigorous testing, that architects and architecture students were more likely to be 'left-handed' than would normally be expected and that all the left-handed students they tested could follow complex instructions on spatial maze drawings, whereas only 50 per cent of the right-handers tested could do so. Peterson, a left-handed architect himself, noticed that many of his colleagues were left-handers. Using 10 per cent as the norm, the two architect-researchers tested seventeen full-time male faculty members in the Department of Architecture of the University of Cincinnati and found 29.4 per cent to be left-handed. Of 484 full-time male students tested, 16.3 per cent were left-handed.

A later study revealed that between 1970 and 1976, 73 per cent of left-handers graduated, compared to 62 per cent right-handers. The 1976 entering class contained over twice the amount of left-handers expected by chance. They also noted that 21 per cent of the men were left-handed, but no women entering that year were.

Charles Wood and Dr John Aggleton found no evidence of a surfeit of left-handers among 236 qualified male architects and 78 male architectural students surveyed in Newcastle and London, or in a backup study on 1,017 university students.

On the strength of observation, many architects report there is a high proportion of left-handers among them, ranging from 40 to 60 per cent. At Kingston Polytechnic, one tutor of architecture noted a 50 per cent pass rate among left-handers in the postgraduate year. (He also noted that left-handers predominate in the upper echelons of microbiology.)

On the minus side, architects may find a dearth of left-handed equipment. One draughtsman feels handicapped because some companies use draughting machines which can be turned over for left-handed use, but the angle graduations remain reversed. 'Once or twice I was moved because the board would not convert to left hand. I was always afraid of dismissal if the company had no left-hand equipment, and expected me to use "standard" equipment, so I never complained,' he said. A frequent admission this and one which may account for the common opinion by employers that left-handers have no problems because they have never complained. Perhaps lefties should complain a bit more often.

Left-handed draughting machines are available, although they cost more. The new breed of electronic attachments seem to be made for right-handed machines only. 'When writing vertical dimensions on a drawing, I write from top to bottom when looking to three o'clock. Right-handed draughtsmen write bottom to top when looking at nine o'clock, which is almost impossible for a lefty. When working on a project with other draughtsmen this causes inconsistencies that spoil the overall presentation,' commented another.

'In the days of tee square use on a drawing board, now largely replaced by drafting (sic) machines or parallel rulers, there was no difficulty in obtaining left-handed tee squares but one was faced with odd looks in drawing office supply shops when one asked for a left-handed sixty degree set square – they thought you were pulling their legs. But with a bevel-edged set square, a left-handed one was essential when drawing with inks,' said one architect, a diocesan surveyor. He also commented that when inspecting churches, he always went round in an anti-clockwise direction. 'There is an old superstition which I believe comes from the west country – that if one walks three times anti-clockwise round a church, one will meet the devil (known as walking widdershins). I must keep my guardian angel very busy.'

Accountancy and figures

Left-handers have been sighted in growing quantities in several other professions, including librarianship, banking, public relations, building society telling, the world of entertainment and accountancy, although I am not aware of any research supporting these claims. TV weatherman Ian McCaskill has confirmed that a large percentage of weathermen have been left-handed. However, the reason they always stand on the left of the screen is because there are more viewers in the East, whose view would be obscured if they stood on the right, than there are on the Atlantic side.

One accountancy student, having noted a high percentage of lefties among physics undergraduates at his university, found a similar phenomenon when he joined a firm of accountants. In 1987, while sitting his final examinations he surveyed the class of seventy graduates employed by large accountancy firms.

He delved into their family backgrounds for hereditary connections and set them handedness questionnaires and found 19 per cent were left-hand writers. Only 17 per cent of the lefties failed their exams whereas 40 per cent of the right-handers did so.

C. J. Harris, head of finance at the Polytechnic of North London, noticed a high proportion of lefties among his colleagues during the 1950s and 1960s, both in chartered accountancy and educational finance. 'My own theory on the phenomenon of left-handedness in accounting is that when we are first learning to *write* we tend to cover (and hence smudge) our work due to the left-to-right nature of European written languages. The lack of skill in writing which at this age we display to our teachers and parents, not leading to praise and encouragement, turns us towards other subjects in which we do not have this natural disadvantage in order to display our skills and hence receive praise,' he hypothesised.

'Basic arithmetic meets this need, in that very simple arithmetic in one column, and even more complex junior school arithmetic, work from right to left. Our teachers and parents, therefore, see *something* we seem to be able to do fairly tidily and so reinforce our learning of this skill. From these marginal differences in our apparent learning skills we become known as "good at sums", and so through reinforcement tend towards maths throughout our schooldays – leading in turn to our looking for careers in a number-orientated profession ...'

A plausible explanation perhaps and one that has already been expressed in relation to sports. One accountant commented that lefties were perhaps more numerate – 'or are they more *inquisitive* (e.g. auditors)?' Yet another expressed the view that maths was not the strong point, but the attraction had to do with looking at an overview of the entire business, rather than calculating figures – the left-hander's holistic right-brain approach, perhaps? One accountant, with an interest in practical art and design, actually claimed that she felt 'a conscious switch from left- to right-hand side of brain when transferring from art to accountancy'. Another accountant proposed that a lobby be made to improve the lot of left-handers, adding 'It goes without saying that I have always found left-handers unusually bright and intelligent and far superior to any common right-hander!!' He was, of course, left-handed!

'I am a left-handed accountant. The only advantage in being left-handed is in the ability to do mirror writing fairly easily. However, I regret to tell you that there does not appear to be an overwhelming demand for left-handed accountants who are very good at mirror writing,' mirror-wrote one wag.

Proving a point

Management Accounting published the results of some research conducted by Herbert Brain, BSc, FCMA, who was intrigued by the proficiency of some accountants. His observations led him to believe that left-handedness played some part in this and that it was beyond the realms of mere chance. He believes that accountancy is right-brain dominated because that hemisphere is responsible for processing data creatively and intuitively.

Water, a precious commodity in Egyptian times, was checked and distributed using highly sophisticated methods by the high-ranking royal priests and scribes – civilisation's first accountants. Brain's theory is that, although hieroglyphics were normally written from right to left, they were reversed for royalty, as found on royal tombs, which must surely indicate sinistral scribes. He believes that during right-brain activity, creative functions are at their best for solving complex problems. Brain also commented that if changed lefties were to reactivate their right hemispheres, their abilities and career expectations might be greatly improved.

Computer design

As far as computer designers go, it is claimed that three out of five Apple Computer designers are left-handers, which doesn't say a lot for their foresight – one of the complaints that occurs most frequently is that the numerics pad is always on the right of the keyboard (except in Sweden where it comes separately). I prefer to place the VDU of my word processor to the left of the keyboard. This causes problems because the flexes are set up with right-handers in mind, and in order to position the screen where I want it, I have to cope with cables stretched right across my keyboard. Cash registers and checkout scanners present problems, so much so that one enterprising left-handed clerk sued an Illinois grocery chain for discrimination and won $136,700.

The Jewel Food Stores in Naperville had insisted that 24-year-old Crystal Sagen check out groceries with her right hand after they changed over to computerised checkout scanners in 1981. As a lefty, she had been one of their quickest clerks but after the switch she was forced to sign an agreement that she would work with her right hand. This proved too much and she soon returned to her preferred hand. After numerous arguments over this with the manager, she left the firm, then sued them. The right-handed jury awarded her $18,323 in lieu of lost wages and the rest in punitive damages. One British left-handed cashier, seeking part-time work, told me she could not apply for a job as all the cash-out designs seemed to be geared for right-handers.

Comptometer operators may be at risk too. One office worker was sent for training and found the machines set in a well in the right-hand side of the desk. She had to remove the machine and place it in front of her until she had mastered it with the right-hand, when she could move it back into its place. 'Luckily, everyone was patient with me,' she said.

In June 1989 left-handers writing to the *Daily Mail* revealed frustration over the design of ticket barriers in the London underground – obviously the 'brainwave' of right-handed designers – which entailed a stretchover for the left-hander which the complainants compared to the equal irritation of cleaning one's teeth with the cold water tap on the wrong side.

Cheque-book counterfoils

Another complained about the new credit card facility which placed the signature space in an area difficult for the left-hander to reach. Banks, despite various claims that a high proportion of their employees are left-handers, are particularly insensitive to their more gauche clients, for one of the most common complaints concerns the cheque book stubs which get in the way when writing cheques and while bookkeeping. The Bank of New Zealand issues a personalized left-handed cheque book at no extra cost, despite the fact that only 2 out of the nation's 10 per cent left-handers use the facility. 'The primary reason for the introduction of a left-handed cheque book was to counter the introduction of similar products from our competitors,' Roy J. Borgman, their marketing manager, told me. While their consideration is admirable, I am not so sure about the motive. But it appears that that country's banks, in general, are taking a positive approach to marketing. The Bank of Melbourne followed suit in 1990.

What are the friendly, listening, UK banks doing for us? The Midland appreciates our problems and for this reason produces a non-counterfoil book with record pages at the front for cheque details and transactions. The TSB finds the proposal 'interesting' but as cheque books are so expensive to produce and they have to keep their costs to a minimum, the cost would be prohibitive. Barclays have already thought about a left-handed cheque book several times in depth, but have rejected it because of the high cost of adapting their printing system. Besides, their left-handed customers are satisfied with the present system. They also produce an optional cheque book with no counterfoil.

The Yorkshire Bank points out the difficulty of issuing a cheque book to joint account holders, only one of whom may be left-handed. Their general manager, a left-hander, points out that left-handers are, on average, far more intelligent than the population at large and should not, therefore, find it too difficult to cope with such a problem. Recent research into the relationship between left-handedness and intelligence, carried out by T. J. Harvey at the University of Bath School of Education on 800 fifth formers, 1,000 sixth formers and 400 university science undergraduates, indicated that left-handedness did not appear to be a function of intelligence at all. Controversy, however, has been raging for years on whether intelligence tests are an adequate measure of intelligence in any event.

The National Westminster Bank has apparently received requests from left-handed customers for this facility but finds it cannot adapt its existing machinery. It carried out an extensive pilot exercise on counterfoils for use by left- or right-handers which involved turning the counterfoil layout by ninety degrees but this had an unfavourable reaction. It also issues a non-counterfoil style cheque book with a separate wallet register for recording transactions.

The Royal Bank of Scotland considered the issue fairly recently but research revealed that its left-handed customers experience no problems with the existing design. The Bank of Wales has not considered the issue and is not intending to.

Bank employees

One could argue that they do spend a great deal of money on advertising and promotion, some of which could perhaps be diverted to better customer services. Perhaps a large-scale research project might either confirm their findings or produce a quite different picture. How do they look after their left-handed employees? One left-handed clerk found she had to work her computer keyboard and the tills with her right hand. (She also complained about the cheque stubs). 'It was like being "brainwashed against the grain" when learning. I count money out "my way" and "cack-handedly" sort and file items away,' she said.

A Scottish bank clerk found learning to flick bank notes difficult. Right-handers found it impossible to teach her. Stamping counterfoils, paying-in books and cheque stubs were among her other problems. 'Holding the teller's stamp in your left hand, you have to turn the pay-in book upside down to stamp it. In a cheque book of thirty cheques, when you get down to the last few, it is difficult to hold open the used counterfoils to write on the next one,' she said. The machines are all geared towards right-handers, the terminal keyboard has the function keys on the right with the printer on the left. 'A special L-shaped desk was designed to go with the machines, which left a space at the corner of the L on the left, for placing entries once they had been keyed. But as I key with my left hand, my right hand is used to turn over the keyed entries, therefore I need space on the *right* to lay my entries.

'As the special desk has holes cut into its top for wires to go through to the terminal, it was not possible to move the actual terminal over to leave space on the right. We have three such machines sitting side by side and I can only operate the right-hand end one, with a desk moved up next to it on the right for me to place my finished entries,' she complained. Further, the note dispensing machinery has a keyboard on the right of the desk, as does the foreign till keyboard which has the electric socket on the right wall with a lead which is too short to allow its relocation.

Left-handed offices

Many office workers complain that the positioning of equipment is inconvenient for the left-hander. One business equipment firm geared some of its marketing towards minorities. Its brochure, entitled *Left-handed Office, Please*, highlighted the bright, eager and productivity-orientated employee assigned to the office space that doesn't fit either because of his height or because of his left-handedness. In addition, there was no place for his computer. They were prepared to tailor their furniture systems to suit the individual. But the drawbacks are apparent – what happens when the left-hander leaves?

But it is a step in the right (or left) direction. What problems do office workers experience? The Department of Trade and Industry had no thoughts on the matter. Here are some common complaints:

desk drawers on the wrong side for ease of access on some desks; trying to write on paper which is in a ring binder – the solution entails removing the paper, which is not always possible (one man asked why they couldn't be made in a flip-over style with the rings at the top); writing on the left margin of any thick ledger book or thick-spined book (perhaps the first column could begin at around five centimetres from the spine); function keys of office calculators to the right of 0–9 keys; confusion in filing documents – left-handers file the opposite way round to right-handers.

Business discrimination

In 1940, one woman was refused an office job because all the clerks sat at a long sloping desk in line and the chief clerk said she would cause difficulties using the wrong hand. Another was turned down by a steelworks office as left-handers could not work the punching machine – yet the disgruntled applicant had been the fastest shorthand writer at commercial school and was a good typist. Some years earlier, a woman applied for a job making fishermen's nets but when she revealed that she was left-handed, she was turned down because the spool had to be used in the right hand.

One left-hander caused confusion for years by teaching a civil servant how to fold and mark up reference outturn sheets from deliveries of paper. Although some of the manoeuvres involved seemed unnecessary, the civil servant refrained from querying established procedures. Several years later, he found himself in charge of some employees who had been made redundant from the paper industry and who appeared to be 'departing from traditional procedure'. When he remonstrated with them, they said they had always done things that way and asked if he was left-handed. 'I then recalled that I had been taught by a left-hander who had caused not only me but the entire staff to adopt this unnatural and time-wasting practice. Does that illustrate sinister power or the unthinking nature of civil service hacks?' he asked.

Do other industries turn away left-handers? One woman lost her chance to work for the post office during the war, despite her excellent qualifications, because she could not operate a right-handed board as she was unable to stretch over with her left hand to dial numbers. Another suffered the same fate on leaving school because the hand stamping had to be done with the right hand. One telephonist told me: 'I have never seen a switchboard that takes left-handed people into consideration. They are all designed (even the modern computerised ones) with all the main functions, including the hand receiver, on the left-hand side and the dial and extensions on the right, so a right-handed person merely picks up the receiver and dials or takes a message with the right hand. I always had to pick up the receiver with my left hand and transfer to my right to enable me to take messages ... I never felt I had given a poor service but the equipment made me do tasks the opposite way to which my brain told me to do them.'

David Nuttall, British Telecom operations support manager, says that in twenty years in the business he has never encountered any discrimination against left-handers, although many years ago this may have happened because positions were one foot eleven and a half inches wide with operators working shoulder to shoulder. The card index file was in a 3 x 3 inch holder, which flapped over on a hinge and was normally on the right-hand side, which may have created difficulties for left-handers. Since 1968, the modern cordless positions have about 5 feet of room. The present VDU systems involve some manual indexing but the operator's position is unimportant. New VDU systems dispense altogether with manual indexing.

More complaints

My research produced a barrage of letters from frustrated lefties. The fashion and textile trades gave some a hard time. In dressmaking right-handers and left-handers pin material in opposite directions so working in a factory results in confusion and scratched hands. One school leaver found her employer refused to teach her the tailoring trade unless she used her right hand. A cutter in a knitwear factory was diverted to finishing because the machinery was designed for right-handers. And one machinist gave up her factory job after ten months because she was not allowed to use a sewing machine.

In the catering industry it is difficult when using the left hand to serve customers from the right using silver service and some utensils such as pots with pouring lips on the left side are designed for right-handed use only. While working in a shoelace factory, one woman found one job which no left-hander could do. 'It does not matter how much you try, the labels on the lace always come off the pins the wrong way round and this cannot be accepted, so no left-handed people work at that job,' she said.

The Plessey pin system used by librarians to issue and discharge books is designed for right-handers. As one librarian put it, 'It makes this very basic aspect awkward, back to front, and takes more time to do.' Even a paper girl complained that folding the papers before putting them through the letter box was awkward because the fold which has to be folded first is on the left side.

A seed analyst found some of the handles on the machines had to be changed round (she was the first left-hander to handle the job). A fondant dipper in a toffee factory used to hand dip some ingredients and was forced to sit by herself to avoid clashing trays with the person next to her. When the Swiss chocolatier made continental chocolates, the poor woman had to wash dirty chocolate pans while someone else took over her job, because she was too awkward to be of help to him.

Firearms apart, the armed forces presents other problems for left-handers. Morse code operators have to cross over to hold the keys sideways. Left-right orientation causes confusion for some – one sergeant was expected to give commands as his foot touched the ground but he confused the left and right feet. 'I had to mount guard the first night – I had no time to overcome my disability so I just ignored the rule and gave the order as it chanced. Fortunately, the men were friendly and if necessary corrected my order. If they had not been friendly, an incorrect timing of my word of command could have produced chaos,' he said.

Jack Fincher in his book, *Lefties*, doesn't tell us which European country's soldiers were so stupid that they had to have hay tied to one foot and straw to the other. They marched to the commands: 'hayfoot, strawfoot'. Perhaps they were all left-handed. One man in the catering corps was among those faced with the task of peeling 2,000 lbs of potatoes every morning for three months with a right-handed potato peeler. But during the war, left-handed navvies were in great demand, for as soil was needed on both sides of the trenches, they were paid a few pennies extra because they could throw to the left.

One man, now in the Navy, had intended to become a helicopter navigator. After taking his examinations and going on the simulator, he found that all the instruments and switches were on the right side of the cabin. Consequently, he was unable to complete his course. His mother said, 'The surprising thing was that he was not the only applicant who was left-handed on the course. There were four and none of the instructors were aware of the fact that left-handed people would not be able to operate the controls.'

Photography and cameras

Photographers have their fair share of troubles, common complaints being film-loading facility and shutters on the right. The Exacta appears to be the only camera to cater for left-handers, with the firing button and the wind-on lever on the left. The Disabled Photographers' Society, which receives many enquiries about left-handed use of cameras, took a close look at the situation and came up with some basic solutions. These included turning the camera upside down so that the release button could be operated by the thumb; fitting the camera with a tripod and operating it with a cable release; fitting a pistol-grip into the camera tripod-bush or making ambidextrous a Konica FT1, which has an accessory terminal at the left front that can take a special shutter-release button.

Brian Maddison, a left-handed Tyne Tees Television cameraman, considers his special 'condition' to be a gift, not a handicap. 'Left-handers are the only ones in their right minds,' he said. Musing on fellow sinistrals, he wondered in which direction Michelangelo had begun painting the Sistine Chapel and remarked, 'Anyone who paints a ceiling by the light of a candle, while he is on his back on some scaffolding, has to be admired.'

In TV studios, mainline cameras present no problems. Brian recalled the Varotal 3 camera with manual controls – a left-hand twistgrip focus and a right-hand zoom wheel – which were fine 'as long as you were the sort who could rub your tummy and pat your head at the same time'. Crib-card holders are mounted to the left of the camera body or at the back of the camera. But problems have arisen with hand-held cameras. These are designed for use on the right shoulder and left-handers – and the left-eyed – find it hard to position the viewfinder comfortably. In addition, noise-cancelling cans force the head away from the camera body and the right eye is blocked by the viewfinder support to add to the discomfort.

'Left-eyed cameramen have to shift their eye in and out of the viewfinder more than their right-eyed counterparts. The obvious answer to this is to have a modified viewfinder support system with greater movement of the viewfinder. The price paid for this kind of flexibility is a potential loss of rigidity – and there's nothing worse than a wobbly viewfinder when trying to frame shots.'

One complainant pulled himself up and reminded himself of the thalidomide victim, born with no arms, who is a keen photographer. 'He could get his camera up round his neck on a special harness and operate the shutter release with his chin!! It is true that no matter how badly off you think you are, there is always some poor soul in a worse predicament,' he said.

The medical profession

The nursing profession is fraught with irritation. Left-handed operating theatre nurses have to remember not to lay the instruments from left to right. Even if they are the only person using the trolley, it must be set up the right-handed way. All the instruments open right-handedly. Theatre technicians working from a trolley set up for a right-hander find it confusing. 'If the surgeon is right-handed. I find that my hands get in the way when retracting or that I hand things to him the wrong way round. The most common mistake is sutures mounted for left-handed use on a needle holder for the right-handed surgeon, which can be frustrating for him and me,' said a trainee operating theatre technician. One nurse found difficulty adapting to a dressing technique which was designed for a right-handed person to carry out. One SRN Occupational Health Nursing Adviser said she had never been able to use sharp/blunt scissors unless she bought her own left-handed pair, or put on a bandage the correct way out-inwards – only the orthopaedic way in-outwards.

Similarly, dental students have grappled for years with equipment designed for right-handers. Students at the London Hospital's Dental School are more privileged because their head of department is a leftie and equipment there is designed for left- and right-handed use. Professor Harry Allred had noted that operating on the lower left meant standing in front of the patient, picking up the handpiece behind and sitting in the spittoon. 'The handpiece wouldn't angle itself conveniently for you,' he said. Now he positions the drills and machinery behind the patient's head, which means it is within reach for everyone. The University of Leeds already teaches undergraduates using the Ash Satellite unit, which revolves around the chair.

One left-handed dentist remarked that he preferred a right-handed nurse 'because her right hand easily meets my left hand for passing instruments ... the only problem is, of course, that a right-handed dentist should therefore advertise for left-handed nurses!'

Ruth Barrie, while a fourth-year dental student at the University of Glasgow, carried out an elective study on the problems encountered by left-handed operators in dentistry. She found that 9.2 per cent of fourth-year students and 9.4 per cent of third-year students were left-handed, compared to 30 per cent noted in one year at a Dutch Dental School. Ruth's assessment of qualified dentists was 3.4 per cent, compared to 25 per cent in America, where dentists insist on using left-handed equipment. 'Could the lack of left-handed British dentists be due to the lack of sufficient facilities?' she asks.

Her subsequent enquiries revealed that left-handed dental students felt disadvantaged by having to use equipment and dental units manufactured for the right-hander. Dental companies and manufacturers are making slow progress, mainly because of the minority demand, without considering that an order for left-handed equipment, estimated at from £7,350 for a unit, would surely be worth having. Investigating manufacturers, she was most impressed by one unit which could be used inter-changeably on either side. 'If more companies came up with a similar design, there would be more competition in the left-handed market ... left-handed dentists would have a better range of equipment to choose from. This type of unit would also solve the problem of left- and right-handed dentists sharing a surgery,' she declared.

She puts down the overall lack of suitable equipment to the failure of the dentists themselves to insist on what they need. Her conclusion is that left-handed students in general practice probably would have to work with right-handed equipment, and this might affect their performance. 'Attitudes of the right-handed dental population would have to change dramatically before left-handers are given equal opportunities,' she stated.

Trainee hairdressers it seems also have a hard time following instructions from a right-handed teacher. Lisa Harlock, a trainee with Tony and Guy in London said, 'I would try and copy them and I couldn't do it ... many people see it as a disability in some ways and ask, "Are you sure you can manage that with your left-hand?" '

International art director, Anthony Mascolo, winner of the Hairdresser of the Year Award, 1988, is left-handed and advises, 'Students have to look at the mirror, not the teacher.' Tony's main problem is finding good quality scissors. He finds it easier to reverse his hand and cut upside down. 'Instead of moving just the thumb to keep one blade still, you move your fingers and still keep one blade still but reverse the hand,' he told me.

Tools of the trade

Joiners always find the vice on the wrong end of the bench. One seventeen-year-old apprentice was beleaguered by the 'old hands at the game' to hold the hammer, chisel or saw in his right hand, which he found quite impossible. But left-handers are always useful in left-hand corners which a right-hander cannot reach and most seem to have the ability to use a paintbrush in either hand with ease. (Actor Paul Shane told me that left-handers are indispensible in the coal mines because they can reach the parts that others can't.)

A left-hander in agricultural and general engineering, involving the supply, repair and maintenance of machinery and plant, finds measuring with rulers, tape measures, micrometers and vernier calipers difficult because they are all upside down for him. 'Any hand or small power tool that can be handed is invariably right-handed and sometimes dangerous as a result,' he said. 'Pistol-grip electric hand tools frequently have a trigger lock which the left hand cannot help but apply, causing the tool to continue to run, despite releasing the trigger. The standard small hand drill is a hoot as the crank has to be wound backwards by the left-hander. It always feels quite unnatural.' Most machine tools present no problems, although left-handed ones would be easier to operate.

'Generally speaking, everything is designed for the right-hander – machine tools, combines, tractors, hand tools, car controls, heavy contractors' plant ... the chain saw is positively lethal to a left-hander,' he ended.

Ergonomics and handedness

Most of the relevant organisations I contacted about ergonomics and safety in industry seemed bewildered by my questions. Most had never ever given it any thought. Many did not even reply to my letters. I could trace no statistical data and little official research in this field and what there was mostly originated overseas. One study by the United States Department of Agriculture did look at chain saw safety and noted that the left-hander who tried to control the throttle with the left index finger had a poor grip on the front handle bar and was in a more dangerous position. Various tips were given to counteract such dangers.

The Advanced Manufacturing Technology Research Institute (AMTRI) at Macclesfield, Cheshire, told me: 'So far as the general operation of machine tools is concerned, the Health and Safety at Work etc. Act requires machines to be guarded to prevent the operator from coming into contact with dangerous parts of the machine. The possibility for a left-handed operator to be in greater danger than a right-handed operator therefore should not arise. In any event, most machine tools require the use of both hands, sometimes simultaneously, and for sensitive and precise manipulation. Undoubtedly there will be some machines which a left-handed person may find easier to operate and others which might be preferred by a right-handed operator, generally because of the way the controls are set out.'

They were unable to point me in the direction of any studies on handedness in this field. The Federation of British Hand Tool Manufacturers and the Federation of British Engineers' Tool Manufacturers told me that most tools are easy to use by either right- or left-handed operators, with the exception of plasterers' floats and bricklayers' trowels, which can be obtained left-handed, and that machine tools cause no trouble because controls are simple push button or levers.

Ian Gaylor, Director of The Institute of Consumer Ergonomics at Loughborough University, does not believe that handedness is an issue. 'I am not aware of any health and safety matters that have arisen as a result of people using inappropriate designs. One has a trade-off between convenience and safety and cost. Clearly, if two versions of a product are going to have to be made or a product made so it is capable of adjustment for left or right use, one has to decide whether it is worth doing,' he told me.

'The criteria I would use to judge that is how frequently the product is used and how important it is. If you make an error and the consequences of that error are severe, that would point the way for a need for something that can be used equally efficiently by left- and right-handers. If the consequences are trivial, it is not worth it. One of the problems would be on trying, in the event of error or accident, to prove it was due to a handedness problem.'

He does not feel that handedness is sufficiently immediate to be worth considering in design. And right-handed scissors with left-handed grips were considered to be adequate. Another conversation there, however, revealed that they had worked on the design of a control centre for a large industry, which uses radio operators on a work station. This contained drawbacks for left-handers who could not press the button on the microphone to speak and take notes at the same time because the cable was not long enough to place the 'mike' on the right-hand side. I was assured that this sort of situation cropped up frequently in design.

Design for the user

Vic Wyman, writing in *The Engineer*, highlighted the emphasis in the United States and Japan on design for the user, pointing out that in the UK human factors were rarely taken into consideration. Cost was all-important. Designers trusted to luck and adopted a 'suck-it-and-see' attitude. The Design Council has been trying to encourage ergonomics in industry and the importance of putting the user first for some time. Unlike the British, the Japanese always find out what their custdmrs want, however inconvenient or costly, before going into production so that they can then translate their products into healthy sales.

Professor Peter Doyle specialises in Strategic Management at the University of Warwick's Business School. He labels the sort of companies primarily orientated to market domination and therefore long-term performance, as left-handed companies, of which today's major Japanese companies are typical examples. Right-handed companies are primarily orientated to return on shareholders' funds, in other words, short-term profit, typified by British companies.

He feels that British companies should try and achieve more of a balance and that their marketing strategies should be weighted towards achieving both a left-hand effect on performance and a right-hand effect on profit.

Right-handed marketing

Professor Doyle carried out a survey among the chief executives in *The Times* Top 1,000 British companies to define their objectives and a second survey contrasting top British and Japanese companies, matching those in competition with one another, to compare their objectives.

He found top British managers were pressurised to improve profitability, whereas Japanese managers were expected more to work towards building long-term positions to dominate their particular markets. They were generally less profitable than British and American companies but were valued at higher levels by the financial world because they were basically stronger. In contrast, there is no certainty that today's top British companies will exist in 20 years time.

Where did the right-handed British pressure come from? The British and American financial markets are more short-term orientated than they are in Japan, Switzerland and Germany, where relations with financial institutions are rather different, and British companies have not tried to educate the stock market in the differences between long- and short-term profit.

The point of all this is that left-handed companies are concerned with innovation and satisfying consumers. It is difficult to develop and launch new products onto the market and create new distribution systems because it takes a long time and most British companies find it easier to cut costs and go for quick profits. Consequently, we should not be surprised at the attitude of British ergonomics experts and manufacturers who feel that satisfying left-handed consumers is not in *their* interests financially, because their marketing policy is a right-handed one.

A totter to the left

Professor Doyle's findings tie up with my earlier point that British companies are under pressure to get their goods onto the market as quickly as possible, with the result that the rate of goods returned by consumers is high. But there is a rise in awareness of this failing and some domestic equipment manufacturers are looking closely at left-handers in their current marketing policy. They have begun with the launch of cordless electric kettles with the measuring guage on both sides, a totter that will hopefully develop into bigger strides in the future.

Several domestic appliance manufacturers have produced irons and water jugs with centrally-fixed power leads or leads which can be turned to left or right. Some are producing cordless items, as are some DIY manufacturers. And although some white goods manufacturers are producing fridges with doors which open to left or right, Loughborough assured me this had nothing to do with handedness but was purely so that they would fit into the design of the kitchen, a right-handed approach if ever there was one. Some left-handers have no cause for complaint. Said one: 'As a left-handed person I have found no difficulty, nor felt the need for any special gadgets, tools, etc. I consider being left-handed to be as easy and natural as for someone to be right-handed. As a teacher I would observe that about a tenth of children are left-handed – perhaps slightly more. Their difficulties, if any, in handwriting stem from not having been taught suitable pencil/pen grips. This, however, is true of right-handed children also!'

Government studies

The Hungarian government undertook an eight-year study into handedness in the 1930s which has been impossible to obtain but I did acquire a report on the biggest industrial investigation on the subject, undertaken by the French in 1962. In the House of Commons in May 1969, right-handed Gwilym Roberts, MP for South Bedford, asked for statistics on left-handers in employment and requested an investigation into the increase in productivity which might result if left-handed working arrangements were to be instituted. Barbara Castle, Secretary of State for Employment and Productivity, could see no point in an inquiry, could not supply statistics, placed the percentage of left-handers at 5 and said, 'Most left-handed people satisfactorily adapt themselves to existing machinery and plant layout.'

The French *Médecine de Travail*, on the other hand, launched its enquiry with official backup from the government, the medical profession and many of their largest industrial organisations. Its estimations of their gauche left-handed manual workers amounted to at least a million and a half and its long report discussed laterality in depth and took the different degrees of left-handedness into consideration. A separate enquiry took place among doctors (9 per cent), dentists (13 per cent) and musicians (8 per cent violinists and 10 per cent pianists) and a third covered over a thousand miners (7.5 per cent and 9 per cent trainees) and metal workers. In all, male left-handers constituted 11.2 per cent and females, 9.1 per cent.

After an exhaustive survey in all sections of industry, the resultant report revealed that there were no significant problems for left-handers in safety, hygiene, adaptation or absenteeism and that any special needs they have were looked after in the various industries. If some left-handers had psychological problems it occurred in addition to left-handedness, not because of it. The fashion (3.4 per cent females) and metal-working industries presented problems and dentistry, as we have seen. Contrary to expectations, the report found the left-hander to be an asset in certain industries, particularly where the use of both hands is concerned and right-handers were even urged to cultivate the use of their left hands. The answer to the left-handers' problems was adaptation.

The stress factor

Left-handers do learn to adapt, but is there a price to pay? Does the mental effort and concentration involved in the changeover create more stress for them than for their right-handed colleagues? Not according to the French survey but what do British left-handers feel?

Even preparing for ordination has its drawbacks, since blessings and the distribution of communion wafers must be meted out by the right hand. One trainee in an American seminary complained that he had never liked giving communion with the 'wrong' hand and that he found it stressful.

A print shop worker found collating papers and making stacks had to be done right-handed according to the supervisor's wishes. 'I manage, but not very fast and some things, such as cutting with knives, I refuse to do her way. Yes, this makes for stress.'

Professor Stanley Coren's four-year research into the high rate of accidents among left-handers, revealed that they were 54 per cent more likely to injure themselves with tools, 25 per cent more likely to have accidents at work and 49 per cent more likely to experience serious domestic injury.

Tony Milne, director of counselling at CEPEC, the centre for professional employment counselling in Bromley, Kent, noted that around 60 per cent of his clients were left-handed. All are white-collar males, mostly managers. He feels that, because they are very much in touch with their right brain in terms of intuition, imagination and feelings, they try to fit in with a left-brain environment, which results in stress.

Milne's awareness of left-handers was aroused by a colleague who had noted a proliferation of them among personnel staff. He felt that this might be because they were good at dealing with people if they were more in touch with their feelings. Right-hander Milne became fascinated by the subject and began researching laterality, even issuing questionnaires to his clients. 'There is a pattern of vague discontent among them which they can't quite verbalise. As a counsellor you cannot help them to concretise it ... they are finding it is costly to them in emotional terms to try and fit into a basically right-handed society, and they can do it well but at a personal cost.'

He tends to analyse what he sees as typical characteristics of left-, right-, mixed-brain and integrated processors. Left-brain processors deal with problems logically. They are active, verbal, conformist, like structured assignments and are more likely to come to conclusions based on specific information and develop existing processes rather than invent new ones. Right-brain processors, he sees as intuitive and visual, producing new ideas – unconventional people with their own way of doing things. Mixed processors can use either brain, depending on the particular task, which would be useful in personnel work. Milne finds many left-handers fall into this category. Integrated processors use both brains simultaneously.

Tony Milne's hypothesis is that left-handers may be more right-brain orientated than right-handers and that, because of their tendency to daydream and their non-conformist characteristics, which are rarely understood in the educational process, they may have emerged from the system feeling misfits or failures. Another of his theories is that left-handers may be too aware of pejorative words, like cack-hander (derived from the Greek *kakos*, meaning bad), relating to them, although I feel this is questionable. He also advises personnel officers to learn to read body language for left-handers and to watch out for tactile pursuits on the cv to spot a possible leftie, the inference being that this can extend into the workplace, although tactile jobs tend to be classified as 'manual labour'. The kind of sports listed are windsurfing, sailing, skiing, rock climbing, model-making, DIY and racket games.

As we have already seen, there appears to be a clash between observers and researchers on the subject of sport and left-handedness. As a left-sided person, my own cv would contain no sports whatsoever, tactile or otherwise. If any child could be guaranteed to be hit over the head by someone's tennis racquet sweeping backwards in a magnificent serve, I could. Likewise rounders balls on the wrist, hockey balls on the ankles and netballs in the chest. My limbs were constantly mummified in bandages at the dreaded grammar school and never was anyone's presence on a sports field less desired. Ice skating was my only sport − not very tactile but limited in scope because I could only turn on the left foot.

Milne's antidote for left-handed working stress is to encourage employers to redesign equipment and to try to understand left-handers. Left-handers themselves should try and negotiate a change in their job. One client working in the engineering department of his company was suffering from stress and negotiated a change to the training department in a more people-orientated job where he is now far happier.

Milne believes that left-handers are gifted and that there is a wealth of unused potential among them which employers should use more fully. 'Do you know what you have got in your organisations in terms of left-handed people, what are they doing, are you utilising their potential to the full, are there any simple things that you could do to make them more effective in their work, whatever it may be?' he urges employers.

Do they make it to the top, though? My attempts to reach some of Britain's entrepreneurs failed dismally because of the barriers created by their right-hand women who 'thought' their bosses were right-handed, although they hadn't really noticed either way. One informal survey among 40 top company chairmen found not a single leftie among them, although 7.5 per cent of their secretaries were.

Does this signify that left-handers spend so much time dreaming, visualising and creating 'left-handed' long-term concepts that the logical, verbal right-hander shoots past them on the career ladder? How many brilliant creative people have died impoverished after which 'right-handed' enterprise has boosted them to posthumous financial glory in the interests of a quick profit? Left-handers, take note!

Career choices

Numerous studies have been carried out identifying laterality in specific disciplines, which frequently conflict, particularly on verbal v visuospatial issues. Researchers have produced little consistency in the pattern of differences in percentages between right- and left-handers in the arts and sciences. But are they putting the cart before the horse by identifying left-handed people in specific occupations?

Many people embark on careers for reasons which have nothing to do with suitability or choice. Often this is due to parental pressure or inadequate career guidance, so there may not be great value in analysing the percentage of people studying or working in a particular profession. It makes more sense to look at the percentage of left-handers who would *prefer* to be working in specific professions, whether they are doing so or not. In other words, researchers should be finding out which careers are most suitable to left-handers in view of their hemispherical characteristics.

If tests could be administered early on in the educational process to determine which of Milne's four categories schoolchildren fall into, many of them might be saved from channelling their adult energies into unsuitable professions.

A study in 1983 into the verbal/visuospatial conflict carried out by Joyce Shettel-Neuber and Joseph O'Reilly, considered hand preferences of 109 faculty members in the college of architecture, the art department, the law college and the psychology departments of the University of Arizona, Tucson, and found no differences in handedness between them. They found fewer left-handers and ambidexters in architecture and psychology, with the largest concentration of them in law. They also felt that previous studies had ignored the importance of the corpus callosum and that too much emphasis had been placed on hemispherical dominance, despite the fact that normal individuals have almost instantaneous communication between their hemispheres.

'Reports that individuals utilising one hand instead of the other are more likely to be in certain fields and possibly more suited for particular fields, could facilitate the formation of potentially harmful stereotypes. Research which can affect selection policies or career choice, thus, should be the result of carefully designed methodologies,' concluded Shettel-Neuber and O'Reilly.

Right-brain thinking

Recent research by S. F. Witelson (1985) revealed that the corpus callosum *is* larger in left- and mixed-handers than in right-handers, indicating that the former groups may have better access to the functions of both hemispheres. Surely this should place left-handers at an advantage? So why don't they develop their brainpower more?

What is so striking about the left-handed issue throughout my research into laterality is that the negative aspects appear to have been highlighted at the expense of the positive attributes of being a right-brain individual. Certainly, policies in ergonomics, industry and education *should* be revised to accommodate left-handers instead of simply ignoring them. At least the majority of teachers and parents have stopped viewing sinistrality as a stigma, which represents a quantum leap against discrimination in our time, but the next step for this important minority group *must* be recognition.

Amazingly, left-handers themselves (probably because they have been so put-down in the past) have failed to recognise the potential storehouse of creative energy lying dormant within them. What have they done with their right brains? The answer, sad to report, is not enough and in the vast majority of cases, very little.

We can clearly see a thread running through this book, bringing together all the underlying currents of movement towards right-brain activity being developed in diverse disciplines – and it is being developed by right-handers. Lefties are being left behind and it is their own fault because so few of them have made any conscious attempt to tap the extraordinary source of creative energy and power that is their privilege.

Tony Buzan, as long ago as the 1970s, was among those who saw the potential of the human brain and how it *could* be tapped.

His classic work, *Use Your Head*, has been translated into 15 languages and sold well over a million copies. He has encouraged people to improve their reading abilities and memories and to think more creatively *and* analytically by tapping their inner resources. He recognises that our performance as human beings in no way matches even our minimum potential, mainly because we are taught nothing about our brains, their functions and abilities at school.

We have seen the move by some teachers and heard Kate Sladden's plea to incorporate more creative right-brain activities into school curricula, we have noted Betty Edwards' right-mode techniques in drawing, Tim Gallwey's Self 2 techniques in sport, the Swedish innovation from right to left in golf, and Professor Peter Doyle's call to British industry to incorporate left-handed marketing.

Right-handers are going to overtake us and leave us grumbling in our boots that we're a downtrodden minority into eternity, unless we start realising our potential. Instead of analysing the reasons for our sinistrality with our logical left we should be populating the world with geniuses with our creative right before right-handers start to queer our pitch.

Leonardo got it right! Now it remains for the world's lefties to follow.

* * * *

BIBLIOGRAPHY

Books

Alston, J. Taylor J. *The Handwriting File* and supplement: *Helping Left-Handed Children with Handwriting: Interpreting Research for Teachers and Therapists*, LDA, Cambridge, 1984.

Alston, J. Taylor, J. *Handwriting: Theory Research and Practice*, Croom Helm, 1987

Alston, J. *Writing Left-Handed*, Centre for Left-Handed Studies, Manchester, 1990

Annett, M. *Left, Right Hand and Brain: The Right Shift Theory*, Lawrence Erlbaum, London, 1985

Auerbach, Charlotte, *The Science of Genetics*, Hutchinson, London, 1962

Barsley, Michael, *The Left-Handed Book*, Souvenir Press, London, 1966

Barsley, Michael, *Left-Handed Man in a Right-Handed World*, Pitman, London, 1970

Blakeslee, Thomas R. *The Right Brain*, Macmillan Press Ltd, 1980

Blau, Abram, *The Master Hand*, American Orthopsychiatric Association, New York, 1946

Burt, Sir Cyril, *The Backward Child*, University of London Press, 1957

Buzan, Tony, *Use Your Head*, BBC Books, 1974

Carroll, Lewis, *Through the Looking Glass*, 1872

Charles, Bob, Wallace, Jim, *The Bob Charles Left-Hander's Golf Book*, Angus & Robertson, London, 1985

221

Clark, Kenneth, *Leonardo da Vinci*, Penguin Books, London, 1939

Clark, Kenneth, *Landscape Into Art*, 1949, Penguin, Harmondsworth

Clark, Margaret M. *Left-Handedness – Laterality Characteristics and their Educational Implications* (Scottish Council for Research in Education, No, 39), University of London Press Ltd, London, 1957

Clark, Margeret M. *Teaching Left-Handed Children*, Hodder & Stoughton (with the co-operation of the Scottish Council for Research in Education), London, 1974

Clarke, Nicholas R. *Left-Handed Guitar*, The Bold Strummer Ltd, New York, 1980

Cole, Luella, *Handwriting for Left-Handed Children*, Public School Publishing Company, Illinois, 1955

Corballis, Michael C, Beale, Ivan L. *The Psychology of Left and Right*, Lawrence Erlbaum Associates, New Jersey, 1976

Critchley, Macdonald, *Mirror-Writing*, Kegan Paul, 1928

Edwards, Betty, *Drawing on the Right Side of the Brain*, J. P. Tarcher, Inc, USA, 1979; Souvenir Press Ltd, London, 1981; Fontana Paperbacks, London, 1982, 1989

Fagg, Ruth, *Helping Your Left-Handed Child*, Left-Handed Co, 1988, reprinted from *Where Magazine* (now *Ace Bulletin*), London

Fincher, Jack, *Lefties*, Perigee Books, 1977

Freud, Sigmund, *Leonardo da Vinci, A Memory of His Childhood*, Ark Paperbacks, 1984 (1st published 1957)

Gallwey, W. Timothy, *The Inner Game of Tennis*, Random House, New York, 1974

Gallwey, W. Timothy, Kriegel, Bob, *Inner Skiing*, Random House, New York, 1977

Gardner, Martin, *The Ambidextrous Universe*, Allen Lane, The Penguin Press, London 1967

Gesell, Arnold, *The First Five Years of Life*, Methuen, London, 1954

Gombrich, E. H. *The Story of Art*, 13th edition, Phaidon Press Ltd, London, 1972

Gooch, Stan, *The Double Helix of the Mind*, Wildwood House, London, 1980

Gordon, Neil & McKinlay, Ian (editors), *Helping Clumsy Children*, Chuchill Livingstone, London, 1980

BIBLIOGRAPHY

Hurlburt, R. *Left-Handed Needlepoint*, Van Nostrand Reinhold Co., New York, 1972

Jackson, John, *Ambidextrality*, Kegan Paul, London, 1905

Jaynes, Julian, *The Origin of Consciousness in the Breakdown of the Bicameral Mind*, Houghton Mifflin Co, Boston, 1976

Johnson, Wendell, *Stuttering and What You Can Do About It*, University of Minnesota Press, Minneapolis, 1961

Joseph-Renaud, J. *Traite de'Escrime Moderne*, Rouen, 1928

Merezhkovsky, Dmitri, *The Romance of Leonardo da Vinci*, Modern Library, New York, 1928

Milne, A. A., *The House at Pooh Corner*, Methuen & Co Ltd, London, 1928

Newman, Horatio Hackett, *Multiple Human Births*, Doubleday, New York, 1940

Orton, S. T. *Reading, Writing and Speech Problems in Children*, Chapman and Hall, London, 1937

Parson, B. S. *Left-Handedness – A New Interpretation*, The Macmillan Co, New York, 1924

Paul, Diane, *Left-Handed Helpline*, Dextral Books, 1993

Wile, Dr I. S. *Handedness: Right and Left*, Lothrop Lee & Shepherd, Boston, 1934

Wilson, Colin, *Afterlife*, The Leisure Circle Ltd, 1985

Sassoon, R. *The Practical Guide to Children's Handwriting*, Thames & Hudson, London, 1983

Sassoon, R., Briem, G. S. E. *Teach Yourself Handwriting*, Teach Yourself Books, Hodder & Stoughton, London, 1984

Shepherd, Margaret, *The Left-Handed Calligrapher*, Thorsons Publishing Group, UK, 1989; Prentice Hall Press, New York, 1988

Smith, Anthony, *The Mind*, Hodder & Stoughton, London, 1984

Treffert, Darold A., *Extraordinary People*, Bantam Press, London, 1989

Wile, Dr I. S. *Handedness: Right and Left*, Lothrop Lee & Shepherd, Boston, 1934

Wilson, Colin, *Afterlife*, The Leisure Circle Ltd, 1985

Zangwill, O. *Cerebral Dominance and its Relation to Psychological Function* (The Henderson Trust Lectures, No. 19), Oliver & Boyd, Edinburgh, 1960

Magazine Articles

Agnew, Margaret, Identifying Dyslexia, *Montessori Today*, January, 1989

Agterhorst, Barend, Golfen We Rechts of Links? *Golf Benelux*, August, 1988

Alston, Jean, The Left-Handed Writer, Getting it Right from the Start, *Links*, Summer 1984. Vol. 9, No. 3.

Anderson, Max G. Letter, *Nature*, 14 September, 1989

Benbow, Camilla Persson, Possible Biological Correlates of Precocious Mathematical Reasoning Ability, *Trends In New Sciences*, January, 1987. Vol. 10, No. 1

Brain, Herbert, Are the Best Accountants Left-Handed? *Management Accounting*, April, 1988

Brightwell, Robin, Is your child left-handed? Then you may be bringing up a genius, *The Listener*, 7 February, 1985

Brown, Brenda, & Henderson, Dr Sheila, A Sloping Desk? Should the Wheel Turn Full Circle? *Handwriting Review*, 1989

Cavanaugh, Jack, The One-Armed Wonder, *True Magazine*, November, 1975

Clarke, Nicholas, Left-Handed Guitar, *Music Journal*, July, 1976

Corballis, Michael C. & Beale, Ivan L. On Telling Left From Right, *Scientific American*, March 1971

Deglin, Vadim L. Our Split Brain, *The UNESCO Courier*, January 1976

Fagg, Ruth, Why Can't He Write Properly?, *Good Housekeeping*, July, 1969

Fagg, Ruth, Facial 'dyslexics' suffer their disability in silence, *New Scientist*, 25 November, 1989

Frost, Betty, Dr Leboyer Talks about Non-Violent Childbirth, *Independent Journal*, San Rafael, California, 3 December, 1975

Gallwey, W. Timothy, This Man Can Change Your Skiing, *Ski*, January, 1977

Gooch, Stan, Right Brain, Left Brain, *New Scientist*, 11 September, 1980

Gordon, Neil, Left-handedness – is it a disability? *Handwriting Review*, 1989, 8–11

Groff, Patrick, J. (San Diego State College), Who Are the Better Writers – the Left-Handed or the Right-Handed? *Elementary School Journal*, 1964, Vol. 65, Pt. 2, 92–6

Hall, Gay, Psychological aspects of children with specific learning difficulties, which also manifest in their handwriting, *Handwriting Review*, 1988, 28–9

Halpern, D. F. & Coren, S. Letter in *Nature* (1988), No. 333, 213

Harris, Norman, Left-Handedness: Theory and Practice, *Snooker Scene*, April, 1987

— The upper hand for those who use both, *The Independent*, 23 May, 1989

— Left Hand, Right Hand, *British Medical Journal*, 21 February 1981, Vol. 282, 588

— Left-Handed Employee Gets $136,700 in Suit, *New York Times*, 12 February, 1985

— Left Might be Right, *Golf Monthly*, May 1988

Maddison, Brian, The Odd Breed, *Zerb*, Spring, 1987

Milne, Tony, Left hand, right brain, wrong career?, *Personnel Management*, January, 1989

Ponte, Lowell, What's Right About Being Left-Handed? *Reader's Digest*, December, 1988

Reed, Tony, When is left right? *International Musician and Recording World*, November 1985

Sherman, Vivian, It's Time for a Bigger Umbrella, *California School Boards Journal*, 1981

Sperry, R. W. The Great Cerebral Commissure, *Scientific American*, January 1964

— The Left-Handed Report, *Which*, October, 1979

Tootall, Janet, (Tameside Schools Support Service, Stalybridge, North West Regional Examinations Board) A Review of the Report on the 1986 CSE English Examination – Folio of Writing, *Handwriting Review* (Issue 1), 8–9
— Why do humans and apes cradle babies on their left side?, *New Scientist*, 21 July 1990

Witelson, S. F., The Brain Connection: the corpus callosum is larger in left-handers, *Science*, 1985, 229, 665–68
Wood, E. K. *Nature*, 335, 212, 1988
Wyman, Vic, An Ergonomic Necessity, *The Engineer*, 22 September, 1988.
Numerous newspaper cuttings.

Research Papers

Alston, J. The effects of pencil barrel shape and pupil barrel preference on hold or grip in 8-year-old pupils, *Occupational Therapy* (Feb, 1986), 42–4
Annett, Marian, The distribution of manual asymmetry, *British Journal of Psychology* (1972), 63, 343–58
Annett, Marian, Turner, Ann, Laterality and the growth of intellectual abilities, *British Journal of Psychology* (1974), 37–45
Annett, Marian, Manning, Margaret, The disadvantages of dextrality for intelligence, *British Journal of Psychology* (1989) 80, 213–26
Azemar, G., Ripoli, H., Simonet, P. and Stein, J. F. Étude neuropsychologique du comportement des gauchers en escrime. *Cinesiologie* (1983), 1–18, 22

Bakan, P., Dibb, G. & Reed, P. Handedness and birth stress, *Neuropsychologia* (1973) 11, 363–66
Barnes, F. Temperament, adaptability and left-handers, *New Scientist* (1975), 67, 200–02
Barrie, Ruth, Left Handedness in Dentistry [elective report], *University of Glasgow*, 1988
Benbow, Camilla Persson, Physiological Correlates of Extreme Intellectual Precocity, *Neuropsychologia*, (1986) Vol 24, No 5, 719–25

BIBLIOGRAPHY

Bishop, D.V.M. Handedness, clumsiness and cognitive ability, *Developmental Medicine and Child Neurology* (1968), 22, 569–79
— How sinister is sinistrality? *Journal of the Royal College of Physicians of London* (3 July 1983), 17, 161–72
— Are left-handers out on a limb? National Children's Bureau day seminar, 13 May, 1983
— Does hand proficiency determine hand preference?, *British Journal of Psychology* (1989), 80, 191–99
— On the futility of using familial sinistrality to subclassify handedness groups, *Cortex*, (1989) (in press at time of writing)
— Handedness, clumsiness and developmental language disorders (1989) (unpublished at time of writing)
Blau, Theodore H. Torque and Schizophrenic Vulnerability, As the World Turns, *American Psychologist*, December 1977, 997–1005 (Presidential Address delivered at the meeting of the American Psychological Association, San Francisco, August, 1977.)
Burge, Ivor C. (Director of Physical Education and Head of the Department of Physical Education, University of Queensland), Some aspects of handedness in primary school children, *British Journal of Educational Psychology* (1952), Vol. 22–23, 45–51
Byrne, Brian, Handedness and musical ability, *British Journal of Psychology* (1974), 2, 65, 279–81

Calnan, M. & Richardson, K. Developmental correlates of handedness in a national sample of 11-year-olds (National Children's Bureau, London), *Annals of Human Biology* (1976), Vol. 3, No. 4, 329–42
Chamberlain, H. D. The inheritance of left-handedness, *Journal of Heredity* (1928), Vol. XIX, 557–59
Cole, J. Paw preference in cats related to hand preference in animals and man, *Journal of Comparative & Physiological Psychology* (1955), 48, 137–40
Coryell, Jane F., Michel, George F. How supine postural preferences of infants can contribute toward the development of handedness, *Infant Behaviour and Development* (1978), 1, 245–57

Demarest, Jack, & Demarest, Lorrie. Does the torque test measure cerebral dominance in adults? *Perceptual and Motor Skills* (1980), 50, 155–58

Douglas, J. W. B., Ross, J. M. & Cooper, J. F. The relationship between handedness, attainment and adjustment in a national sample of school children, *Educational Research*, Vol. 9 (November 1966–June 1967), Medical Research Council Unit, London School of Economics, 223–31

Enstrom, E. A. The relative efficiency of the various approaches to writing with the left hand, *The Journal of Educational Research*, Vol. 55, No. 10 (August 1962), 573–7

Franks, J. E. & Davis, T. R. (Department of English Language and Literature, University of Birmingham); Totty, R. N. & Hardcastle, R. A. (Home Office Forensic Science Laboratory, Birmingham); Grove, D. M. (Department of Statistics, University of Birmingham), Variability of stroke direction between left- and right-handed writers, *Forensic Science Society* (1985), 25, 353–70. Paper presented in part at the American Society of Questioned Document Examiners 1983 Meeting, Lake Tahoe, Nevada (11–16 September, 1983)

Fryd, C.S.M. The direction of pen motion and its effects on the written line, *Medicine, Science and the Law* (1975), 15, 167–71

Galaburda, Albert M., MD, Biologic correlates of left-handedness, Seminars in *Neurology*, Vol. 4, No. 2 (June, 1984), 120–25

Gesell, A. & Ames, L. B. The development of handedness, *Journal of Genetic Psychology* (1947), 70, 155–75

Geschwind, N. & Galaburda, A.M. Cerebral lateralization, Biological mechanisms, associations and pathology. I: A hypothesis and program for research, *Archives of Neurology* (1985), 42, 428–59

— Cerebral lateralization, Biological mechanisms, associations and pathology, II: A hypothesis and a program for research, *Archives of Neurology* (1985) 42, 521–52

— Cerebral lateralization, Biological mechanisms, associations and pathology, III: A hypothesis and program for research, (1985) *Archives of Neurology*, 42, 634–54

Gordon, Neil, Left-handedness and learning, *Developmental Medicine and Child Neurology*, (1986), 28, 649–61

Guiard, Y. & Millerat, F. Writing postures in left-handers: inverters are hand-crossers, *Neuropsychyologia*, (1984), Vol. 22, No. 4, 535–38

Gur, R. E., Gur, R. C. & Harris, L. Cerebral activation, as measured by subjects' lateral eye movements, is influenced by experimenter location. *Neuropsychologia* (1975), 13, 35–44

Harvey, T. J. Science and handedness, *British Journal of Educational* (1988) *Psychology*, 58, 201–04
Hecaen, H. & Sauguet, J. Cerebral dominance in left-handed subjects. *Cortex* (March, 1971)

Jarman, Ronald F. & Nelson, J. Gordon (University of British Columbia) Torque and cognitive ability: some contradictions to Blau's proposals, *Journal of Clinical Psychology*, April 1980, Vol. 36, 2, 458–64
Jordan, H.E. Hereditary left-handedness with a note on twinning, *Journal of Genetics* (1914), Vol. 4, 67–81

Kellmer Pringle, M. L. The incidence of some supposedly adverse family conditions and of left-handedness in schools for maladjusted children, *The British Journal of Educational Psychology* (June, 1961), 31, II, 183–93
Kimura, Doreen, Manual activity during speaking – II, Left-handers, *Neuropsychologia*, (1973), Vol. 2, 51–5

Lansky, Leonard M. & Peterson, John M. Some comments on Shettel-Neuber and O'Reilly's 'handedness and career choice; another look at supposed left/right differences' (1983), *Perceptual and Motor Skills* (1985), 60, 141–42
Les Gauchers au Travail, *VIIes Journées de Médecine du Travail de France*, Paris, (17–19 September, 1962)
Levy, Jerre, Possible basis for the evolution of lateral specialization of the human brain, *Nature*, London (1969), 224, 614–15
Liederman, J. & Kinsbourne, M. The mechanism of neonatal rightward turning bias: a sensory or motor assymetry? *Infant Behavioural Development* (1980), 3, 223–38
— Rightward bias in neonates depends upon parental right handedness, *Neuropsychologia* (1980), 18, 579–84
Liederman, J. & Coryell, J. The origin of left-hand preference: pathological and non-pathological influences (1982), *Neuropsychologia*, Vol. 20, 6, 721–25

Miller, Edgar, Handedness and the pattern of human ability, *British Journal of Psychology*, (1971), 1, 62, 111–12

Nottebohm, F. Ontogeny of bird song, *Science* (1970), 167, 950–56
Oldfield, R. C. The assessment and analysis of handedness: The Edinburgh Inventory, *Neuropsychologia*. Vol. 9, (1971), 97–113

Peterson, John M. Left-handedness: differences between student artists and scientists, *Perceptual and Motor Skills* (1979), 48, 961–62 (Paper presented at the American Association for the Advancement of Science Annual Meeting, Houston, Texas, 1979)
Peterson, John M. & Lansky, Leonard M. Left-handedness among architects: some facts and speculation, *Perceptual and Motor Skills*, (1974) Vol. 38, 547–50
— Left-handedness among architects: partial replication and some new data, *Perceptual and Motor Skills* (1977), 45, 1216–18
— Success in architecture: handedness and/or visual thinking, *Perceptual and Motor Skills* (1980), 50, 1139–43
Ramaley, F. Inheritance of left-handedness, *American Naturalist*, (1913), Vol. 47, 730
Riddell, P. M., Stein, J. F. & Fowler, M. S. A comparison of sighting dominance and the reference eye in reading disabled children, *British Orthoptist Journal* (1987), 44, 64–9

Satz, P. Pathological left-handedness: an explanatory model, *Cortex* (1972), 8, 121–35
Sawyer, C. E. & Brown, B. J. Laterality and intelligence in relation to reading ability (Psychology Department, Tennal School, Birmingham), *Educational Review*, (1976), Vol. 29, 81–6
Schwartz, G., Davidson, R. & Maer, F. Right hemisphere lateralization for emotion in the human brain: interactions with cognition, *Science* (1975), 190, 286–8
Shanon, B. Graphological patterns as a function of handedness and culture, *Neuropsychologia* (1979), 17, 457–65
Shettel-Neuber, Joyce & O'Reilly, Joseph, Handedness and career choice: another look at supposed left/right differences, *Perceptual and Motor Skills* (1983), 57, 391–7
Sladden, Kate, Left-handed in a right-handed world – handedness

and associated specific learning difficulties in school and society, BEd Honours Bath College of Higher Education, May 1987

Smart, James L., Jeffery, Carole & Richards, Bernard. A retrospective study of the relationship between birth history and handedness at six years, *Early Human Development* (1980), 4/1, 79–88

Snape, K. W. Determination of ball-point pen motion from the orientation of burr striations in curved penstrokes, *Journal of Forensic Sciences* (1980), 25, 386–9

Stein, J. F. Riddell, P. M. Fowler, S. Disordered vergence control in dyslexic children, *British Journal of Ophthalmology* (1988), 72, 162–6

Van Riper, C. The quantitative measurement of laterality, *Journal of Experimental Psychology*, (1934) Vol. 17, 305–13

Van Riper, C. The quantitative measurement of laterality, *Journal of Experimental Psychology*, (1935) Vol. 18, 372–82

Walters, C. S. Chain saw safety tips, US Department of Agriculture, North Central Regional Extension, No 74

Whittington, Joyce E. & Richards, P. N. The stability of children's laterality prevalencies and their relationship to measures of performance, *British Journal of Educational Psychology* (1987), 45–55, 57

Wood, Charles J. & Aggleton, John P. A re-examination of handedness among architects, (unpublished thesis) University of Durham, 1989

Wood, C. J. & Aggleton, John P. Handedness in 'fast ball' sports: do left-handers have an innate advantage?, *British Journal of Psychology* (1989), 80, 227–40

USEFUL NAMES AND ADDRESSES

Advisory Centre for Education (ACE), 1B Aberdeen Studios, 22 Highbury Square, London N5 2EA (0171 354 8321) 2pm–5:30pm

Andy's Guitar Workshop, 27 Denmark Street, London WC2 (0171 836 0899)

Association for All Speech Impaired Children (AFASIC), 347 Central Markets, Smithfield, London EC1A 9NH (0171 236 3632/6487)

British Association for Left-Handed Golfers, Sec: Tony Kirkland, PO Box 2, Alderley Edge SK9 7XX (01625 585561)

British Dyslexia Association, 98 London Road, Reading RG1 5AU

British Orthoptic Society, Tavistock House North, Tavistock Square, London WC1H 9HX (0171 387 7992)

British Psychological Society, St Andrew's House, 48 Princess Road East, Leicester LE1 7DR (01533 549568)

Centre for Left-Handed Studies (research and bibliography), PO Box 52, South DO, Manchester M20 2PJ (0161 445 0159)

Department of Education and Science, Sanctuary Buildings, Great Smith Street, Westminster, London SW1P 3BT (0171 925 5000)

Dyslexia Institute, 133 Gresham Road, Staines, Middlesex TW18 2AJ (01784 463851)

Frank Dyke & Co Ltd, 1–7 Ernest Avenue, West Norwood, London SE27 0DG (0181 670 2224) (Anschutz left-handed rifles)

Independent Schools Information Service (ISIS), 56 Buckingham Gate, London SW1E 6AG (0171 630 8793/4)

James Purdey & Sons Ltd, 57–58 South Audley Street, London W1Y 6ED (0171 499 1801)

The Left-Handed Company, Dept. LH, PO Box 52, South DO, Manchester M20 2PJ (0161 445 0159), Mon–Fri, 9am–5.30pm

National Association for Gifted Children, Park Campus, Boughton Road, Northampton NN2 7AL (01604 792300)

National Association of Left-Handed Golfers, Sec: Jerry Bradley, Gurrane North, Belcare, Tuam, County Galway, Eire (010 35393 55310)

National Autistic Society, 276 Willesden Lane, London NW2 5RB (0181 451 1114)

National Children's Bureau, 8 Wakeley Street, London EC1V 7QE

Peter Cook's Guitar World, 69 Station Road, Hanwell, London W7 (0181 840 1244)

School Curriculum Assessment Authority, Newcombe House, 45 Notting Hill Gate, London W11 3JB (0171 243 9273)

Swing Target Rifles Ltd, PO Box 17, Tonbridge, Kent (01732 357908)

Twins and Multiple Births Association (TAMBA), 51 Thicknall Drive, Pedmore, Stourbridge, West Midlands DY9 0YH (01384 373642)

INDEX

INDEX

INDEX